I0587489

Joseph Parker

Weaver Stephen:

Odds and Evens in English Religion

Joseph Parker

Weaver Stephen:
Odds and Evens in English Religion

ISBN/EAN: 9783337819149

Printed in Europe, USA, Canada, Australia, Japan

Cover: Foto ©ninafisch / pixelio.de

More available books at **www.hansebooks.com**

DR. PARKER'S NOVEL. PRICE 7s. 6d.

Weaver Stephen:

ODDS AND EVENS IN ENGLISH RELIGION.

BY

JOSEPH PARKER, D.D.,

Minister of the City Temple, Holborn Viaduct.

LONDON:

SWAN SONNENSCHEIN, LOWREY AND CO.,

PATERNOSTER SQUARE.

1886.

Weaver Stephen.

Weaver Stephen:

ODDS AND EVENS IN ENGLISH RELIGION.

BY

JOSEPH PARKER, D.D.,

Minister of the City Temple, Holborn Viaduct.

LONDON:

SWAN SONNENSCHEIN, Le BAS AND LOWREY,
PATERNOSTER SQUARE.
1886.

Printed by Hazell, Watson, & Viney, Limited, London and Aylesbury.

PREFACE.

THE peculiarity of this book—which separates it from all other known works—lies in the interesting fact that it should be perused before it is criticised.

Foreground.

A VISION, gentlemen, and Daniel is not at hand.

The cloud over the town opens and closes so rapidly that I can see nothing quite clearly, and as the wind does not blow in my direction, the sounds I hear are indistinct and contradictory in tone. I see the church steeple, and I hear a clang of bells; now and then, too, I catch a noise as of hurrying feet, and a child's cry seems to separate itself sharply from every other sound. Now the cloud has buried the town, church and all, and now it rends, and a gleam of light strikes the grey old steeple, and a generous ray shows where the conventicle shrinkingly hides its pale red bricks. A brisk man that, in clerical attire, about to spring into a dogcart at the Vicarage door, first laying a plump white hand upon a spaniel's head; the other people, obscurely visible, are marked by some variety expressive of diversified character and vocation. One lounges at his shop door, and comments upon the eventless day with nothing more definite than a yawn ; another grins with worldly satisfaction as the copper-shower drips into the bucket which he calls his till ; another patters nonsense to his listless neighbour, and chaffs him on the want of natural gaiety ; and yonder—now that the cloud lifts a little—may be seen groups of men who ask questions with vivacious curiosity, and now make way to let the drunkard stagger past in silent condemnation ; and further on are women with heads inclined towards one another, but no sound comes from the mute deliberation. The cloud returns, deepens, lingers, breaks, and vanishes. Now the general outline is clearer, but the detail is huddled and blurred, and though the wind has veered a point or two, it only brings subdued uproar to my ear. Suddenly, with the swiftness of a dream, the whole scene has changed, and a sound not only inharmonious, but conflicting, shatters the Sabbatic peace, now a sound grand in solemnity, now a croaking as of discontent, now a cadence soft as the blessing of love, now a staccato as of hardened and impious defiance. This may be battle, but worship it cannot be. Yet it ought to be worship, for all nature seems

to be resting—the winds are hushed; the plough
stands still; the birds seem to be wondering and
half afraid; and the green fields blink and doze
in the warm light. Tell me what means this
controversial worship, this battle whose torn flags
flap on the very altar? Mischief of some kind
there must be; else why are all the rooks in the
church elms so hideously disturbed? This is not
the complacent caw-caw which makes the wood-
land so unlike the tumultuous town. See how the
black figures wheel in the air—now high, now low;
approaching, retreating; crowding, yet dissolving:
and see how they make the grey old steeple a
kind of focus. Is some one below plotting to
throw down the sacred pile, and despoil the holy
stones? Has a fire been lighted by felonious
hands? Have the rooks had tidings in advance
of purposed sacrilege and ruin? They are but
brown sparrows that chaffer on the roof of the
conventicle—birds incapable of religious or even
decorous agitation; news they have had none, or
if they have, they cannot respond to the tragedy
of the tale.

My dream varies, but still no Daniel comes to
read the tormenting riddle.

I see vicars and ministers; Stephen released from
his loom; another man skilled in traps and plots,

but talking long words to disarm suspicion ; women
noted for love and patience and sympathy ; a young
heart full of religious wonder, asking how to pray
so as to bring her nearer God.   And what a
tumult of words I hear !   Men are in high debate,
each religiously angry with the other, and wondering
how Providence can suffer the wretch to live.   It
is holy anger on both sides : on the side of the
complacent ecclesiastic whose glebe-lands grow
golden profits, and on the side of the pulpit-
democrat whose trees grow little but disappoint-
ments, but of these many and large.   This is a
most brotherly—most Cain and Abel—war, which
rages in my troubled dream.   Outsiders cannot
understand religious conflicts.   Each side prays that
God would scatter its enemies.   Each side retains
the Almighty and confides in His loving discrimina-
tion.   Certainly it is so in this dream of mine.
Gray knows he is right ; Whiteman is assured of
his own faultlessness ; Paterson is definitely impec-
cable ; Tomlinson knows that Heaven has taken a
strong fancy to him.   The men who wear many-
coloured coats scorn the irreverence of almost naked
Puritanism.   The legitimate priest hates the illegiti-
mate minister.   Surely it is but a dream !   I am now
writhing in ecclesiastical nightmare, not rejoicing
in daylight facts and summer blessings.   Cursed
nightmare !   It has given me an inverted and dis-

tempered view of things, and has made me think
that men who can love the same Christ can assassi-
nate one another. This nightmare is the hideous
missionary of perdition, and has surely been sent
to avenge some omission of duty or lack of human
charity. I will awake and betake me to the land
where there is no lying nightmare and no deceitful
fiction.

Not yet. I must endure the bondage a little
longer, nor complain of the galling yoke. Comfort
says—"Close eyes and see nothing." Another Spirit
says—"To exclude the evil is not to extinguish it ;
look on, and be wise ! " The horizon is now full of
light, so that I can see far and near, and the wind
is favourable to hearing. What a scene breaks upon
my inner vision ! Godly men in groups marked
alphabetically, each group talking according to a
glossary of its own. In one group northward there
is a gathering of iron-grey heads knowing everything,
favourites of a discerning grace, sure of the number
of the elect, with copyright maps of Heaven and
Eternity done neatly in Indian ink, the Islands and
the Highlands being done with special care, but
with a very modified regard for "the adjacent islands
of Great Britain and Ireland." Southward a band
of men in white linen, in black stripes, in embroi-
dered shoulder-pieces, backs rich with gold, fronts

beaming with symbolic spangles, voices mellowed with self-satisfaction. On the right hand and the left are other groups, debating, voting, denouncing, now hot with anger, now radiant with hope. Yonder are men praying like prophets who have the ear of the King, and farther away are men who find their altar in their work. Yet what a multitude remains outside all the groups,—some debased, wrecked, faces burning with shame, eyes alight with fury ; others cold, sceptical, disinclined to pray, unwilling to believe ! And others ingenious almost to the point of creativeness, inventing creeds, displacing orthodoxies, building great churches in the air, the prophets of Reason and the worshippers of Science. Now the weird dream troubles me. Amid the clamour of controversy I hear the cry of pain. Through persistent demands for the restoration of Augustinian theology, I hear the moan of ·social discontent and the sharp exclamation of menace and defiance. Revelry and Poverty dwell in the same city. The gin-palace and the church shoulder one another in rough pressure. The blatant oath strikes across the timid prayer. Would heaven I could awake and forget the uproar and the shame, but the dream holds me as in a chain I cannot break. Who are those blind men crowding down upon me as if they were in terror ? They are not really in terror, for they chuckle to one another in

mutual felicitation, and bandy lukewarm jests about
Evolution, and Biology, and Type ; they will not
look, or they cannot ; people leave them, and they
call the people infidels,—Science refutes them, and
they call Science—godless !   Not only are the men
blind ; they mumble their speech and swallow their
words ; what I do catch of their utterance is archaic,
official, other-worldish ; they think that "assembles"
is secular, and " assembleth " is religious ; they aver
that to assail a Theology is to assail a Revelation,
and that to doubt the Church is to doubt God.
Now the cruel nightmare is hard upon me, for it
travesties men I have been taught to reverence, and
relegates to oblivion or contempt forces which I
deemed to be sustained by Heaven.   A great cloud
—in similitude as a flying eagle—hovers above old
altars, old parchments, old orthodoxies,—it is an
omen not to be comfortably interpreted ; I would
disown it by closing my eyes, yet I should know
that the dark Image was still there, and my infatua-
tion would but double my distress.

But hark ! What is this better voice ?   No argument is in it, no wrangle of words, no war of
lexicons.   It is Music !   This new voice touches the
soul ; surely I am now under the welcome spell
of some celestial wizardry, for heaven's own singing
band cannot be far off ; nor is the singing impaired
because of harp-sounds, and chiming bells, and boom

of infinite organs, but rather sweetened and ennobled
by the sublime accompaniment.   Now is the morning of the world's Sabbath whitening the east, and
empurpling the hills with a glory brought from afar,
and rude Argument is driven away by tender Song.
" This is the day the Lord hath made ; we will rejoice
and be glad in it."   What strange scene is that on
the hillside, wherein a white-robed procession takes
so prominent a part ?   Is the brown scar so visible
on the green slope a grave ?   It cannot be.   Yet
it must be.   A burden is being borne by the heads-
men of the procession, and their intent must be to
inter it in that gaping tomb.   Yes, I am right !   In
that grave—too good for so hideous a corpse—they
bury grim Controversy, the enemy that sought to
rend the Lord's seamless robe, and that spoiled every
feast of the Church, silencing all music, and driving
sweet children into solitude ; down, down, down, the
weary burden is lowered, down into unmeasured
depths, down into eternal silence.   And now what
is heard but a voice, tempest-loud, crying Hallelujah !
Then the soprano of happy women, and the bass of
men whose might has ever been in prayer, can be
easily distinguished.   Now the white-robed cele-
brants turn away from the unblest sepulchre, assured
that the wilderness shall become a garden and the
desert a fruitful field.   Their common speech has
become tuneful, and words which before were ever

followed by battle are now cleansed of all bitterness
and strife. The glad men would say they forgive
one another did not the very word "forgive" seem
to carry with it assumptions which would profane
the new harmony. They have gone infinitely beyond
forgiveness, for they are already in the heaven of
love. And who stands in the midst of this embodied
Music? He is white and ruddy; His head is as the
most fine gold; His eyes are as the eyes of doves
by the rivers of water, washed with milk, and fitly
set; His cheeks are as a bed of spices, as sweet
flowers; His lips like lilies, dropping sweet-smelling
myrrh. What is His name? None other is like
Him. Under all His grandeur there is a mute tenderness as of sorrow long past. What is His name?
My dreaming soul longs to know, so that every letter
may be kissed, and the whole word hidden in the
sanctuary of the heart. The white-robed host
gathers around Him and kneels in lowly worship, so
verily He must be King and Lord, the very Majesty
of life! His legs are as pillars of marble, set upon
sockets of fine gold; His countenance is as Lebanon,
excellent as the cedars. His mouth is most sweet;
yea, He is altogether lovely. Now the people crown
Him. Now they cry, Hosanna! How large the
crowd is now becoming! The grey-haired men
from the north are there; the prayer they prayed
is enlarged and purified, and their whole spirit

chastened and made holy ; the Vicar, too, and
Stephen, and the blind preacher, and others who
once stood far off and were counted unworthy, the
learned dignitary, the now enlightened and liberated
priest,—they are all in the crowd, and each of them
stands at the head of a great host.   Is the crowned
One speaking to them, or is He speaking to Heaven?
Listen :—

" That they all may be one ; as Thou, Father, art
in me, and I in Thee, that they also may be one in
us."

WEAVER STEPHEN.

CHAPTER I.

"LIFE is too numbersome for me, sir," said Weaver Stephen, "for it hits me all over and just covers me with sore places."

I was Stephen's pastor, and quite in the poor man's confidence; hence he trusted me with this view of life, and with all the meaning of the deep sigh which followed it. Stephen was never meant for a complex state of life, or to keep appointments at odd minutes, such as twenty minutes past twelve or twenty-five minutes to three; tell him to come at ten, or four, or seven, and you might reckon upon him with absolute confidence, but the minutes between muddled him and often took away his appetite. I once showed the sweet old man a watch with a second pointer on the face, also a fine steel thread for the measurement of critical periods of time, and he said—

"They all be a-working, sir, some more and some less as one may say, but now which of them tells the time of day?"

I

"Stephen," said I, "what is the smallest point of time you ever heard of?"

"Why, sir, I don't know as I can say exactly; would I be a long way wrong if I said it were in the neighbourhood of five minutes?"

"But what about five seconds, Stephen?"

"Why, sir, you see, as to that, nobody can make nothing of it, or do nothing in it; why, you couldn't lace a boot in such a speck of time as that. I measures time by the work a man can do in it, so I never really cares to go much below half an hour."

With a desperate recklessness far from customary, and with an incoherence which no apology can excuse, I said, "Stephen, did you ever learn Latin?" The eyes of the sweet old saint gleamed in their wells as he replied, "I rather think, sir, I never did, if it has anything to do with pen and ink; pen and ink, sir, I have not seen in my house for two-and-thirty years, and it would be quite as well, sir, if Mr. Daleham would give up such perfumery, as I may call it, for it is nothing better."

Mr. Daleham was another of my hearers, and a most pen-and-inky man, certainly, always turning the universe round to find new flaws in it, or pointing out the places where he could have improved upon it had he been called into consultation early enough. Mr. Daleham's pew was downstairs, and Weaver Stephen's shilling-a-quarter seat was far back in the deep gallery fronting the pulpit; Mr. Daleham's pew was often empty, Stephen's place was always occupied.

"But why do you think so, Stephen?"

"Law, sir, because through his pen and ink he's like to lose his soul, and what with his long words, and what I may call his worldly way of going on, it seems to me as if he's a tolerably long way from heaven."

"At the same time——" Stephen interrupted me.

"Speak o' the de'il, and he'll appear," said Stephen, and, sure enough, Mr. Daleham suddenly joined us. It was but for a moment. Mr. Daleham was burdened with the last suggestion of science, and had barely time to hint at it in breathless haste.

"There is now," said he, "every reason to believe that each constituent part of a chemical atom must go through an orbit in the millionth part of the twinkling of an eye, in which it successively or simultaneously——"

"My dear sir," said I, "has all that been proved?"

"Certainly. See Herschel. Each of those particles is for ever solving differential equations, which, if written out in full, might belt the earth."

Weaver Stephen sighed. He was conscious of some heavy loss. Mr. Daleham said, "See me to-night, Stephen," and then vanished with his perspiration and polysyllables.

"What ever can Mr. Daleham want to see you for?" said I.

"You may well ask," said Stephen; "he likes me to gape at his nonsense and tell him what a great man he is. He would have me up at his house five nights a week, listening to his pen-and-ink rubbish, and it comes rather hard on me when I do not understand

a word on't, and want to be at home spellin' out a bit
o' Bible."

"Then you can make out the meaning of the Bible,
Stephen ?"

"Beautiful, sir. I know it all, but it knows me
better than I know it, and that's how it comes to
take so much notice of such as me: there's a deal o'
hard names in the Bible, mind you, some chapters are
just like what Master Daleham's now been a-splutterin'
about, but I know they's nothing to do with the Lord's
will, or they wouldn't be so long-winded. The Lord
was not in the wind, you remember."

" But how do you know which is which, Stephen ?"

" By the little words, sir ; I never believes no big words,
sir ; when I see any words a-swaggering and a-swelling,
I knows they cannot mean much, and was never meant
to be food for the soul. I always think that things is
all the wrong way about with Master Daleham, like a
driver who has got into the shafts instead of being on
the box."

Now these were both hearers of mine, and I was
expected to feed their souls and satisfy their spiritual
thirst. My trouble was increased by the fact that in
my congregation there were many mental and moral
shades between the magnificence of Daleham and the
simplicity of Stephen, and as I in an indirect and
official way took money from all of them, in fact made
my living by them, I felt bound to give them something
in return. The type of hearer which often fretted me
most, in the early days of my ministry, was represented by Mr. Nehemiah Battison, always spoken of

as "old Mr. Battison," who in some pious nightmare
had conceived the idea of popular and unsectarian
evangelisation through the open and comparatively
inexpensive medium of street names. He thought
that a society might be founded to carry out that
idea. According to old Mr. Battison's opinion, that
society could not fail to prosper, combining as it did
the use of municipal money with the adaptation of
unobtrusive Christian sentiment. Mr. Battison, I am
bound to say, was always prepared to unfold and explain his peaceful scheme.

"How sweet it is to think," said he, "of Sabbath
Street, Gospel Circus, Disciple Square, and Jerusalem
Arcade. The very names are short discourses, and
the very mention of them does one much good."

"You have thought the matter well over, Mr. Battison?" I would say.

"Oh yes, sir; I have given my best attention to it.
I have also desired often that you might, in the order
of Providence, be led to mention the matter in the
pulpit (without of course in any way alluding to me),
particularly about six weeks ago, when his worship the
Mayor was present at the evening service; I thought,
'Now if our dear pastor would put——'"

Mr. Battison said this, concluding with a sigh and
not a reportable word, in less than five minutes after
I had parted with Weaver Stephen. He said it
humbly—though he would have given fifty pounds if
his name could be mentioned in the pulpit in the hearing of the Mayor of Midtown—in no spirit of boasting,
in no ambitious or unseemly tone, as if he belonged to

the ancient family of Korah, Dathan, and Abiram, persons of abiding but melancholy fame; he was only anxious to indicate that he was in no degree unduly exalted by the revelation which a discriminating Providence had vouchsafed to so unworthy a person.

"In no spirit of boasting, sir," he would say, "for who am I that I should boast, or make myself important, or look down upon even the humblest of my fellow-creatures? I am but of yesterday, and although my life has been very wonderful, I wish to be quiet, yet at the same time I don't hold with believers putting their light under a bushel. Oh, sir," said Mr. Battison, interrupting himself, "here is that most flippant person Mr. Daleham."

True enough. Daleham had done his business, and was returning home. He came up to us, and said hurriedly, "The marriage will take place after all." Mr. Battison looked unexpectedly interested. He had six daughters living at home, Jochebed, Hagar, Martha, Mary, Hannah, and Jemima, one married daughter, Miriam, and an unnamed son who was as one dead. Old Mr. Battison made his daughters as little of a burden as possible by amiably and gratefully referring to them as "the girls." I never saw old Mr. Battison look so complacently upon Mr. Daleham before.

"May I inquire to what particular marriage you allude?" said he.

"The marriage of Hypothesis and Experiment," said Daleham, "and your old heart will be glad to hear that the honeymoon is to be spent in Twelve Apostles' Vale.'

Mr. Battison howled inwardly, and was only held

back from public exclamation by the delicate compliment implied in the name of the Vale.

"Mr. Battison," said Daleham, in a tone not without flippancy, "I understand your agitation. You and I may be better friends some day. Just one word: I know you have a great idea, but you must be calm; you lack self-control; let me tell you that you must put a curb upon your impulses; you must bridle that temper of yours; you must sacrifice your emotions on the altar of the Binomial Theorem."

With a flourish Mr. Daleham departed. Mr. Battison said he always felt himself snubbed by this jackanapes, and as a man of an honestly earned and comfortable competence, he would not stand it. He was only held back by the fact that his daughter Jemima (given to a grim kind of humour) had mysteriously taken an interest in some of the worldly and vainglorious questions with which Mr. Daleham foolishly concerned himself, and had even gone so far as to ask this flighty man, who had no visible means of making a livelihood, to look over an intricate calculation which she had made as to the number of earwigs that would be required to move the *Great Eastern* steamship supposing that each earwig could move the nonillionth part of a quarter of an ounce. Mr. Battison had heard of this from the other "girls," and it had made him extremely uncomfortable, because it seemed to him like flying in the face of Providence and being wise above what was written, particularly when so many poor people were out of work and did not know in what direction to turn for a mouthful of bread. Jemima was

a clever and somewhat eccentric "girl," and was intended to have borne her father's Christian name had
not "Nehemiah" refused, with immemorial obstinacy,
to lend itself to feminine adaptations.   This intention
made the old gentleman tender to Jemima, and Jemima's
inclination towards severe intellectual exercise made her
tolerant towards Mr. Daleham, whom she had so far
fooled as to look with well-feigned favour upon his
counter-suggestion to name public places, not Scrip-
turally, but scientifically, as, for example, Evolution
Lane, Quadratic Tenements, Cosmos Crescent, and
Ellipsis Oval, a course which was severely condemned
by her sister Jochebed as most unfilial, and which she
resented with dignity by calling her spaniel Nebuchadnezzar, adding the insane *non sequitur* that "nobody
knew what he might come to."   When Jochebed spoke
under emotion she often lost the thread of her discourse,
and her intensity made her blind to the precipices over
which her animated incoherence stumbled into sudden
ruin.

My pastoral position may be imagined.   I have, in
one sense, to please all these people, and bind them to
my ministry with some degree of appreciation and confidence.   Most people will only come to chapel so long
as they can in some way be entertained or gratified,
unless they come to keep up good traditions or vary
the monotony of home.   In my congregation there is a
butcher who will never stand up to sing if I announce
a hymn in any but long, short, or common metre ;
there is Peppers the shoemaker, who calls his corner
shop "the hospital for worn-out understandings," who

looks upon my acquirements with disdain because I am
so poor a hand at the interpretation of unfulfilled prophecy; there is Wilson the coal-merchant, who begs me
in the name of pity to avoid all head-splitting subjects,
because he has worry enough in his own business;
there is Errick the schoolmaster, who thinks no sermon
worth listening to that does not bristle with historical
references; there is the busy mother who hates all
argument; and there is Thomson the chemist and
druggist, who thinks of "giving up all religion" because
Ruth the beautiful Moabitess was for reasons totally
inscrutable on the religious side made an exception to
the law which forbade a Moabite to enter the congregation of the Lord to the tenth generation for ever.
Thomson has reasons for thinking, greatly to his wife's
aggravation, that Ruth ought not to have been brought
into the stock of Israel, whereas Mrs. Thomson contemptuously bids him keep to his pestle and mortar
and let beautiful Moabitesses, or "whatever you call
them," mind their own business and keep in their own
country. The case of the chemist and druggist is most
peculiar, and is, indeed, very irritating, because he has
such shooting and darting pains in the head that contradiction might put his valuable life in peril, and
expose his wife and ten children, four of them bald-
headed babies, to destitution. This is what Mrs.
Thomson feels, too, for she has often assured me that if
his head was all right, she would "Ruth" him, which
remark, judging by its tone, I regard as a delicate
threat. I sympathise with Mrs. Thomson, because the
chemist puts me to a humiliating disadvantage when he

looks at me from behind a jar of carbonate of soda, and says, "Come, no dodging, *if* you please,—no parsons' tricks for *me*." My impulse is to "Ruth" him, and pound him in his own mortar, but then think of the family!

It must not be forgotten that all these people of mine have their good points: the butcher sends me kidneys and sweetbread (a double portion when all the tunes are short metre); the coal-merchant insists upon giving me a ten-pound note when I go out for my holiday, and advises me not to wear my mind out with things that nobody cares for, whatever they may say to the contrary; the old schoolmaster has three scholars whose parents cannot pay him a penny; my deacons toil for the Church with devoted industry without fee or reward; all this must be set down on the other side in any just estimate of my public position. It is clearly my duty to take an intensely religious view of the whole case, and to seek the healing of any little frets and bruises not in the code of a club, or in the etiquette of a fashionable society, or in the compensations of a well-paid office, but in the redeeming thought which heals the universe and for ever seeks to bless it and crown it with peace.

CHAPTER II.

MR. WHITEMAN, almost blind through over-study—a man with the nicest wife and family imaginable—is the Baptist minister in Midtown, and as true a brother as ever breathed. Wonder how Whiteman came to be a Baptist? Popular rumour has it that Baptist ministers are five feet six high, square, squat, and careless as to appearances, but Whiteman is out of that running altogether. Think of any rational human being sustaining the reputation of being a great Baptist, or Congregationalist, or anti-tobacconist, or vaccinationist! Yet this is quite in the line of history, for Og was remembered by his bedstead, Goliath by his staff, Samson by his hair, and Iscariot by the bag. Men are tied on to fame by very small loops. This aside. Whiteman has had trouble in his church, and has borne it like a Christian hero. There is no merrier laugh in the town than Whiteman's, yet who can pray with so trembling a reverence, or sympathise with human distress more tenderly? His caressing tone is itself a kind of gospel. I sometimes wish my chemist, Mr. Thomson, belonged to his church, for I think he could almost laugh him out of that ridiculous notion about the Moabitess. But White-

man has been stung by a much inferior person, and has
suffered more from a gnat than he is ever likely to
do from a lion.

Mr. Titus Knockey had a front pew in the gallery of
the Baptist chapel, and accounted himself a person
of some consequence in the town, on various grounds,
but principally from the fact that in addition to being
a newsagent and tobacconist, the post-office of Midtown
was under his charge. Mr. Knockey was constitution-
ally social. Mr. Knockey saw all sorts of people, sold
stamps to all sorts of people, and was never known
to be unwilling to talk to all sorts of people. Mr.
Knockey never had occasion to go out of his own house
to see anybody. The whole world of Midtown passed
through Mr. Knockey's well-situated shop. The Vicar
went to Knockey's for stamps, so did the Curate, so
did the Catholic priest (a man with the sweetest smile
I ever saw), so did the retired Quaker banker; besides
these notable persons in the town, there were other
notable persons from the surrounding district, for Midtown was belted with the loveliest stone-built villages
in all green England, a dozen of them at least being
within walking distance, and some so near to one
another that the church bells blended in the dales and
made Sunday doubly musical. When the genial Vicar
of Midtown called at Knockey's for stamps and
envelopes he occasionally bought, as if for a friend,
and quite in a casual way, a couple of ounces of golden
shag. All this could not but have a subtle effect upon
a man so observant and talkative as Mr. Knockey. He
could truly say that he had *seen* a great many people,

and that his public position brought under his notice a good many things which he was bound to treat with confidence; in this respect, indeed, Mr. Knockey was himself a kind of living post-office, written all over with V.R., and gummed and marked like a registered letter. Mr. Knockey always spoke for quite a crowd of people: his opinions seemed to be attested by a great cloud of witnesses, and to have a parliamentary representativeness and value in his own estimation. Mr. Whiteman was bound to call upon this important member of his baptised flock, or this important member would give up his two sittings, for which he paid four shillings a quarter each, and go at once to the Congregationalists, or the Episcopalians, or even the Catholics, for when his pride was touched, his sectarian preferences went for nothing. Besides all this, one Baptist minister was a poor figure in the great public ever crowding around Mr. Knockey's popular counter: when a man sells shag to a vicar, cigars to a squire, newspapers to a landlord, memorandum books to an auctioneer, and valentines to all the housemaids of a parish, a Baptist minister, in the irregular receipt of eighty pounds a year, cannot expect to be much accounted of. Mr. Knockey saw so many people that they naturally fell into perspective, and finely graduated to a vanishing point.

"You know, sir," said he to Mr. Whiteman, "in my important position I cannot help hearing these things: mine is a sort of public position, in consequence of the office being here. That is just what Mrs. Liddell said" —here a customer bought half an ounce of tobacco,

looked at Mr. Whiteman, and went out—"and I felt
very sorry to hear it; at the same time"—readjusting
a pile of railway timetables, and ordering out a
butcher's dog—"at the same time, there may be some
truth in what she says"—here a customer ordered two
post-cards, and laid down half a sovereign ; Knockey's
daughter Jane was called to get the change out of the
office till, during which time the customer grinned in a
civil way at Mr. Whiteman—"for her part she says
she wants more *exhorting* in your sermons, in particular
of an evening, when the gallery is pretty full" ("Plague
on that dog! Johnny, dear, do banish that prowling
beast"), "and when, as one may say, it might be well
to draw a bow at a venture." Here the postman came
in for the midday mail, and whistled in a suppressed
way close to Mr. Whiteman, for whom he had but
small respect, seeing that he himself was the second
tenor in the parish choir, and looked upon Baptists
with more curiosity than favour. Mr. Whiteman,
patient and gracious soul, a very child-man, yet with
a mind large and keen, could stand this humiliating
process no longer, so he turned away sick at heart,
wounded and discouraged.

Well for Whiteman that on his way home he met
his senior deacon, Mr. Robson, a heaven-made deacon,
always genial, always hopeful.

"Why do you go near the wretch?" said Mr. Robson,
noticing his pastor's dejection.

"Why indeed?" replied Whiteman. "I stood in
that rag shop of his, and saw people coming in for
tobacco and stamps and papers, and in came a great

colley dog from the butcher's, next door, and that great hulking lad that he calls ' Johnny dear ' was called in— and there I stood like a criminal——"

"Never mind," said the best of deacons; "come up to Eastfield and dine with us, and the whole thing will be forgotten."

So it was settled. Eastfield looked well even on that February day, when the wind was blowing steadily from the north-east, and a thin mist was lingering among the branches of the old cedars and winter oaks. Eastfield was a home. There was a fire in every room, but the cheeriest of all the grates was in Mr. Robson's well-stored library, a library in which such Puritans as Kingsley, Thackeray, Dickens, and George Eliot, stood in near relation to such romantic thinkers as Sibbes and Charnock, Charles Simeon and Andrew Fuller. On the tops of the book-cases were busts of eminent statesmen and famous authors, and on the walls here and there, where the pressure of the books allowed, engravings of Shakespeare and Milton, with smaller portraits of George Whitefield and Robert Hall. Mr. Robson was a retired banker, with plenty of money, varied intelligence, and a heart big enough to pity and forgive even Knockey the tobacconist and postmaster. "What bothers me as much as anything," said Whiteman, speaking in the softest of red morocco chairs, " is that when the Vicar—Heaven be good to him, for he is a jolly soul—goes into the shop he says, 'Well, Knockey, how wags the world?' but I have to say, 'Good-morning, Mr. Knockey; how is Mrs. Knockey? how are all your children?'—I want to say ' the little Knockeys,' but dare not, whereas I could hear with equanimity of all the Knockeys being——"

"Well, well," said Mr. Robson, cutting off the sentence lest it should end badly, " what we have to do at this moment is to forget the past and enjoy a long afternoon at Eastfield."

Could Mr. Robson and Mr. Whiteman have heard the conversation which two masons, heightening the stable wall, were holding, they would have heard one of them say—

" You should hear Whiteman, Tom ; he's the sort o' parson to make ye think a bit."

" I am not a parson's man," said Tom ; " shouldn't care a bobbin if they was all in the river."

" Hear Whiteman, Tom, and if he doesn't puzzle that head o' thine, I'll give thee all the steam thee can carry away from any boiler i' the world."

Tom chopped off the end of a brick and fixed it in the wall.

" The last time I was at Whiteman's," continued the first speaker, " I sat not far from old Knockey, the 'bacconist, a rare old hypocrite, and there he was, singing like a sand-boy at the tip-top of his voice."

" Knockey's 'bacco is always wet, and under weight," said Tom, " sing or not sing. I want to punch Knockey's head on the quiet some time, the sooner the better. It's about time for a drop o' beer now, isn't it ? Robson and Whiteman 'll have a good do at the table, no doubt, and abuse the working classes over their hot vittles."

"Not they, Bidwell; not a bit of it, I'll be bound. No finer man in this town than old Mr. Robson; a regular king of a man I call him—I wish there was a thousand of his sort—and as for Whiteman, he wouldn't hurt a kitten. Mind, I'm no Baptist, Tom."

"No *what?*" said Tom, with significant scorn.

"No Baptist. I like Whiteman. I even like him when I don't quite understand him. He is a trifle foggy sometimes."

"Old Knockey," said Tom, with an intelligence that surprised his mate, "is a Baptist, and he's a confounded old hypocrite, a regular canting old dog, just as butter-faced an old swindler as ever gave the beam a tip with his little finger to make it look like weight. I will say that for Knockey, let who will speak agin' him."

"Bidwell, thee's in a bad humour this morning, lad. Thee doesn't seem to ha' much stomach for the Baptists."

"I would chuck 'em neck and crop into a clay-pit, if I had my way."

"Come, Tom, come. I like to hear thee whistle better than argue. Let's have a bit of a tune. Whistling suits thy style o' beauty, Tom."

Bidwell was quiet for a few minutes, conducting rather than enjoying a meditation upon domestic affairs; presently, however, his good-nature asserted itself, and he whistled that frivolous but popular tune known by the title —" How Mary hit the monkey."

2

The four o'clock dinner is over, and pastor and deacon are in the library once more.

"Now take the other view of your position," said Mr. Robson. "Your preaching was never richer, your people never saw the finest shades of your thought so clearly, and never did I hear so many quotations from your sermons as at the present time. The wonder to me is that Knockey cares to listen to such preaching, and, on the other hand, there must be something good about Knockey, or he could not so constantly attend your ministry. Why don't you take that view of the case? Why don't you say— 'Knockey was there again this morning; my subject was full of unusual and even bold suggestion— suggestion which some of the fathers'" (nodding towards Fuller and Hall) "'would certainly have viewed with anxiety—yet there he sat, and when the last hymn was sung, Knockey's was the loudest voice of all'? *That* would be philosophy; you preach philosophy; why don't you practise it?"

Whiteman smiled. "A very good view," said he, "but would you have kept Knockey in your bank one week?"

"Certainly not. But a bank is not a church. If a church is a mere place of business—or at the best a kind of pleasure-garden or recreation ground—that is one thing, and that would justify a kind of narrow reasoning; but if a church is a school, a place of education and discipline, an institution in which the best view is to be taken of men in order to their ultimate rescue from all evil, that is another thing,

and an infinitely larger reasoning is rendered necessary
The more patient you are with Knockey the more is
Christ working in you."

Whiteman always responded to a noble appeal, noble
in reason as well as noble in feeling. At this moment
he longed to see Knockey, and his daughter Jane, and
" Johnny dear," and the butcher's dog, and all the
panorama of papers, stamps, post-cards, whistling postman, and casual customers. How base he had been
in the morning, yes, that very February morning. He
ought to have loved Knockey, to have blessed Knockey,
to have lent money to Knockey, to have ——— ; and
so the endless possibility wound itself around his
imagination, until Knockey became the saint and he
the sinner, and the uppermost thought of his mind was
to make amends to Knockey. Besides, Mr. Robson
had used the name which thrilled the pastor's heart
more and more as the mystery of life disclosed its
vastness and solemnity. Literally, in the case of Mr
Whiteman to live was Christ. That name was in very
deed above every name, and the story of which it is
the eternal centre was the sum and crown of all
wisdom. Without one touch of soft sentimentalism,
he held it to be the manliest of all strength, and
the very sublimity of reason, to respond to its pathos
with the tears and sobs of a child's stricken heart.
No hireling was Whiteman—not even for the tempting sum of eighty pounds a year—but a true shepherd
of the flock of Christ, with one aim, one trust, one
hope.

The February light is dying. A star or two, the

keener in glance because of the sharp north-easter,
may already be seen in the deep blue sky.   Presently
the moon, clear-cut and gleaming in silvery splendour,
appears like a mother amongst the stars.   Mr. Whiteman is coming down the gravel path with Mr.
Robson ; at the gate they can stand but a moment
because of the cold, so with a warm grip of the
hand they say good-night, and separate.   Away out
in the night, Mr. Whiteman enjoys the holy scene.
All the stars speak to him.   The moon speaks of
patience and modesty and sweet content ; the great
arch, so deeply blue, bids him always take the lofty
and noble view ; the stars, in their infinite variety
of size and brightness, tell him that he too has his
place in his Father's house.   A night like this is a
night to walk in.   Why not go up the Acomb road,
cross the Abbey Fields, come down Golden Lane, and
thus, through a two-mile walk, keep up communion
with the consenting stars ?   He would do so.   On
the white stile of the Abbey Fields he even sat
a while that he might look the more steadily into the
eyes of heaven.   How grand !   How solemn !   Aloud
he said, "This is none other than the house of
God !"   There was a rustling, and two figures slowly
passed.   They must have heard the pious exclamation,
but they made no sign.   Were they ashamed ?   Were
they also wonder-struck at heaven's wealth ?   Or
did they turn away from heaven's purity as if afraid
it would burn them ?   Nature is to us what we
are to nature.   When we want to pray nature is
never reluctant to become an altar.   In ten minutes

more the town lamps were visible, and Whiteman was sorry for it. In five more he met a friend.

"What, you, Stephen?"

"Yes, sir; just looking about a bit."

"I have had a glorious walk from Eastfield round by Abbey Fields; you have no idea how grand the stars are until you lose sight of the gas."

"You wouldn't meet many people, sir?"

"No; two people passed me near the stile, but I did not know them."

"I know them," said Stephen—"Mr. Daleham and Miss Jemima Battison."

CHAPTER III.

E have an excellent ministerial club, as Midtown is belted with thriving little towns and villages. Baptists, Congregationalists, and Methodists all belong to it, and consequently the club represents no small variety of talent and disposition. At the last meeting we all seemed to be out of spirits, and, as the host of the day, I asked how it was that we were all so dull and silent, whereupon Williams said—

"Paterson will make himself ridiculous presently; then we shall all thaw. Meanwhile, beloved, I simply light a pipe and wait confidently."

"So would I if I had any tobacco," said Nicholson. Nicholson never had any tobacco. Nicholson dined from home four days a week. Nicholson was no preacher, but in his visiting capacity he was supreme.

"Here's tobacco for you," said Paterson. Paterson was poor but generous. Paterson had no humour. He lived to disestablish and disendow the Church. Paterson was an acting Dissenter; his prayers had a political tone, and his hopes of heaven owed not a little to the certainty that the Act of Uniformity would be done away with.

"But what makes you so dull, Paterson? Not been lecturing lately?" Paterson was a Dissenting lecturer and tract distributor, and parted with much perspiration in his vigorous labours. When Paterson was fairly at work on the subject of Disestablishment it had been noticed, even by friendly observers, that he foamed at ·the mouth. This was the more remarkable because when he was in the pulpit he reasoned temperately, and forbore the dispensation of scalding theology.

"Knockey is accountable for my stupidity," said Paterson.

"What on earth have you to do with Knockey?"

"I went in for an ounce of shag, and on turning round rather suddenly to come out I fell over a great brute of a dog—a monstrous colley—and gave myself such a knock that I have not recovered yet."

"What happened then?" said we all.

"A good deal happened. Old Knockey called his hopeful son and daughter, and they set a dish of cold water behind a pile of waste paper, and after I had cooled my face and recovered my tone a little, he ventured in a carefully Christian manner — the old hypocrite Knockey, I mean—to give me a bit of his mind about you, Whiteman, and your lovely ways, and I went at him so——"

"That was wrong," said Whiteman; "the worse the man, the better the minister, is my motto." Then aside — "Very aggravating, though, whatever Mr. Robson may say."

"Hang it all," said Williams, in the bosom of fraternal confidence, and in the innocent licence of

Monday, "the fact is Congregationalism in every form is a failure."

" Ho! ho!" Paterson responded ; " I thought I was the man who had to make himself ridiculous !"

" Nothing ridiculous about it," Williams continued. " We have about two thousand ministers in Independency, and if the Government called upon me to make· out a schedule, this would be my return : Half of them wish they had never entered it ; eight hundred of them want to make a change of sphere ; and the rest of them are tolerably contented, because of good congregations, good salaries, and opportunities for doing real good. I am not an evil speaker ; don't imagine it. Some of our fellows are as good as gold, many of them in fact ; but democracy in churches is a failure."

Tomlinson agreed. Tomlinson was a short, fat man, wearing spectacles, and looking when seated as if he had swallowed his legs. Tomlinson was not wanted by the churches. He was a heavy preacher, severe upon all successful men, fond of good eating, and proud of having been five years at college. Tomlinson despised the taste of deacons, and sneered at the intellect of the churches. Tomlinson carried about a tremendous grievance.

" I tell you what it is, brethren," said he, " if a place is not found for me soon, I shall do something that will surprise the denomination. I *will*." And then he closed his lips like a resolute man.

Now, the only way in which Tomlinson could have surprised any one who knew him would have been by the display of a little common-sense. Such a display would have positively paralysed his most intimate acquaintances.

"What will you do?" Paterson inquired, lighting his pipe to hide the smile of contempt.

"Do? Why, I will jack up the whole business, and seek ordination in the Church." Here one of the swallowed legs protruded a little, and brought a thick-soled boot into full view. Tomlinson fell back in the chair, fixed his gooseberry eyes upon his brethren, and asked me whether he could be favoured with a drink of water.

"My dear friend," said Paterson, in a well-feigned tone, "hear me—*don't.*"

"But I will, I tell you," Tomlinson replied. "I will, once; I will, twice; I will, thrice. Why do you say, 'Don't'?"

"Because the Church cannot do with even one additional barrow-load of rubbish."

"Thanks for civility," said Tomlinson, with a jerk of the body which brought the other boot into view.

"No incivility, Tomlinson, I assure you——"

"I differ," said the little man hotly.

"Pardon me; no incivility at all. I must say I detest your reasoning: if a place can be found, you will be a Dissenter; if a place cannot be found, you will be a Churchman. Bah! Where's the conscience? Where's the reason? Where's the courage?"

"To change the subject——" said I.

"But I will not change it," said Tomlinson. "I am insulted."

"Come, come," said the brethren, "after all, the

laws of hospitality must be observed.   Our host wishes
to change the subject, and we are bound to comply."

Tomlinson's boots were withdrawn once more by a
sudden jerk of the body, and his face assumed an
expression of vindictive acquiescence.   Even if the
scene had not passed away upon my suggestion, it
would have been ended by the entrance of Professor
Stokoe, the only absent member of the club.   Dr.
Stokoe had long retired from the active service which,
as Professor of Natural Science in a northern college,
he had ably discharged for many years.   The Professor
was universally beloved.   Whilst his talents and acquirements entitled him to the highest position as a teacher,
his modesty, his simplicity, and his grand integrity gave
him a supreme place in the heart of every man who
knew him.   When the Professor had any news to com-
municate he told it all before he took off his hat and
gloves, and told it with a kind of infantile and im-
petuous gurgle, as if at last he was able to do something for his friends.   No matter what the company,
no matter what the subject, the Professor must get the
news off his mind and then settle into a silence the
more remarkable because of the eagerness of speech
which preceded it.   The Professor was the most silent
public man I ever knew unless he had some news to
tell, and having news to tell, he simply put every other
speaker down until he had told it.   Walking behind
. the Professor, his friends could always shrewdly guess
whether he had any news upon his mind.   When he
had charge of news his walk was brisk and urgent, as
if a wager were to be won ; when he had no news he

looked steadily at the clouds and made calculations as
to their density and their velocity, and put in danger
the life of every child and kitten on the road which he
unconsciously passed. It is, indeed, on record that on
one occasion when he was considering how far the vapour
of the Gulf Stream affected the rainfall in various parts
of Great Britain and Ireland, he fell over a tiny barrow,
and suddenly sat down in a gutter. That piece of
news he was just as eager to tell as any other, adding,
" Some little rascal, you know, must have forgotten,
you see, that he had left the barrow there, you perceive." But the barrow would bring back the rain,
and lead the sweet old man to assure his hearers that
" rain is the most irregular of all meteorological pheno-
mena." On the Monday morning in question the
Professor had something to say. Standing just inside
my study door, with one glove partly drawn off, he
said :—

" Have you heard the news ? " .

" What about ? "

" About Jenkinson. The best news you ever listened
to."

I may say that Jenkinson was a minister in a neigh-
bouring town, " a fellow of infinite wit," the best of
companions, but unhappily easily persuaded to take
more wine than was good for him. Not that he was
a drunkard, for he who is a drunkard drinks with his
soul as well as with his lips, and Jenkinson never did
that. A designing old pork butcher who attended his
ministry, a man whose chief pleasure was in boasting how much champagne he had in the cellar, had

apparently made up his mind to ruin Jenkinson through
the medium of wine-drinking. The old pork butcher
would boast that "the parson" sat up till midnight
smoking and drinking, and that he had induced "the
parson" to carry away an unfinished bottle of brown
sherry, and had one night given a lad threepence to see
"the parson safe home." Jenkinson was an old fellow-
student of the Professor, and the Professor entertained
a sincere affection for his gifted friend. The Professor
had affectionately warned Jenkinson, saying, "Surely
in vain is the net spread in the sight of any bird," and
Jenkinson had wept like a child, and asked the Professor to pray with him and for him. They knelt
together in the Professor's study, and the Professor's
tender and most womanly heart pleaded mightily with
God. How far the prayer availed, the Professor must
tell.

"He has told me all about it himself. He has
written it out just as it occurred. Brethren, let us be
glad, and sing praises to a delivering God——"

"Let us hear the story," said Williams, impatiently.

The Professor took out a letter, and read :—

"I called upon the designing man, and acted, so
far as manner is concerned, without any change of
feeling or purpose. 'Now what will you have, Mr.
Jenkinson?' said he; 'all that is in my house is at
your service.' 'Whatever you please,' said I. 'Well,
it's a little too early for champagne; I call that,' said
he, 'an evening drink; but what do you say, my dear
pastor, to a drop of real old brown?' I said, 'All
right; but what do you mean by a drop?' The pork

butcher laughed, and said, ' Ha, ha ! that was a downright mean way of putting it ; you know how welcome
you are to everything you can eat and drink in my
house.' I looked very seriously at the old rascal, and
said, ' Make it a bottle, and I'll show you the end of it.'
' Make it two if you like,' he replied. ' Two be it,'
said I, and two bottles of old brown sherry were produced. I then said that the thing would be incomplete
without a smoke, whereupon he brought a jar contain-
ing most of a pound of shag. 'Enjoy yourself,' said
he, and I replied, ' That's exactly what I mean to do.'
Now came the crisis. I must say, Stokoe, that every
bone in my body trembled, but I was not to be turned
from my purpose, the purpose created by that prayer
of yours, so full of tears. Looking at the wine, I said,
' My happiness would be increased if a third bottle
could be produced.' The pork butcher replied, ' First
make an end of the two.' ' May I do what I like with
this wine ? ' ' Certainly,' he replied. ' Then I will.'
I paused a moment ; how long it seemed ! ' There
goes bottle one,' said I, dashing it into the dim fire,
' and there goes bottle two,' dashing it into the same
place, ' and there goes the shag,' thrusting it into the
grate : ' you meant to ruin me,' said I, ' but God has
delivered me ; your heart was filled with cruelty, but
God's grace has abounded on my behalf, and now
my soul is escaped as a bird from the snare of the
fowler.' That is the happy report, Stokoe; rejoice
with me ; a new day dawns, and a new song makes
me glad."

When the Professor ceased reading there were tears

in his large grey eyes, and there were tears in his voice
as he said—" There is joy in the presence of the angels
of God over one sinner that repenteth." After a
moment's pause he continued—" We ought to give
thanks to God for this ; it is a miracle ; brother Tomlinson, will you lead us ? "

" No, sir, I will not," said Tomlinson. " I mean to
jack up the whole business : I preach no more, pray no
more, write no more, in connection with Congregationalism."

" My dear sir," said the Professor, " my dear brother !
the propriety of your remark I am totally at a loss to
perceive ; what has transpired ? have I said anything
to grieve you ? have I——"

" Not at all," said Tomlinson ; " you are a gentleman
as well as a minister : the two terms may be synony-
mous in theory, but they have no necessary connection
in practice."

Paterson relieved the Professor's perplexity by explaining. Williams accompanied the explanation with
" Paterson's right, too," and I endeavoured to encourage that view, as did Nicholson, as it amounted to a
conversion on the part of a man who had just declared
that Congregationalism is a failure.

" It is true," Paterson said, " that in the heat of the
moment I used an expression which was strong, to say
the least of it ; that expression I wish to withdraw ; at
the same time, do not misunderstand me ; the expression
was rough, but it expressed a sound sentiment ; I am
utterly sick of the way in which some of our men conduct
themselves, it is so wanting in every feature of moral

dignity, and so calculated to bring our principles into contempt. No man must assume a Nonconformist attitude merely as a personal convenience, or as an expression of patronage. Some of our men seem to think that Nonconformity ought to be extremely obliged to them for espousing it; Nonconformity washed them, clothed them, sent them to college at its own expense, and put them into the ministry, and they no sooner put themselves into long coats and soft hats than they strut about as if they ought to have been vicars and deans——"

The Professor cleared his throat as if about to speak, but Paterson rushed on—

" If they don't succeed, they blame the deacons, men who gratuitously devote all they are and have to the cause of Christ ; if they don't feel comfortable, they charge their discomfort upon the deacons, and ask contemptuously what can be expected from butchers and bakers and candlestick-makers, as if Nonconformist ministers themselves did not come from the middle classes of the country."

Nicholson put himself into a speaking attitude in vain, for Paterson was not to be stopped.

" The fact is we had better accept the disagreeable conclusion that half-hearted men must either go from us, or be put away. They must be got rid of. It is better to be strong in quality, than to be showy in number. My distinct conviction is that the churches are a good deal too long-suffering. Tomlinson," Paterson continued with energy, " you had better go ; we do not need such men as you are—if I must either

affront you or conceal my convictions, I deliberately
adopt the former course."

Without saying one word, Tomlinson walked straight
out of the house.

"The position," said the Professor, "is an awkward
one. I came into the meeting late, so I feel myself
placed at some disadvantage. What brother Paterson
has said about Nonconformity entirely commends itself
to my judgment. His remarks are very just. My
father was a barber——"

Here we all applauded, not, of course, meaning to
pay any invidious compliment to barbers, but to mark
our sense of the Professor's dignity in not being ashamed
to own an origin not distinctly aristocratic.

"But an honest man, well informed, and most devoted——"

Here we expressed our admiration in harmonious
murmurs.

"Brother Tomlinson's father may have been——"

"A greengrocer," said Williams. "I know him well,
a little bleary-eyed hunchback that would jaw at you
by the hour if you cared to fool away your time."

The Professor was stunned for a moment, as he
always was by the copious use of inexact terms. His
was not a mind that could suddenly change its point of
vision, or an imagination that could move otherwise
than along a straight line. A habit of his was to follow
up any remarks he had addressed to others by a few
observations mutteringly addressed to himself, and in
this habit he markedly indulged when excited by any
subject. This morning he muttered much. Evidently

the inward tumult was beyond control.   He had re-
joiced over the restoration of one brother, and now he
was unexpectedly mourning the loss of another.   A
mind like the Professor's easily falls into a moralising
strain; he said something, more or less incoherently,
but with genuine emotion, about "ups and downs,"
"chequered scenes," "lights and shadows," yet there
remained the fact that as Jenkinson came in at one
door, Tomlinson went out at the other.

3

CHAPTER IV.

R. DALEHAM and Miss Jemima Battison
had gone for an evening walk in the direction of the Abbey Fields, as they had a
perfect right to do.   In our provincial town
nobody disapproved of such pleasant excursions,
and certainly if any one had disapproved of
them, his opinion would have had no effect upon
the general sentiment of the community.   We were just
population enough to allow us to keep a friendly eye
upon one another, without exposing personal liberty
to undue encroachment.   We seemed to know one
another's movements without prying into them, and to
be thought unneighbourly if we did not know who had
gone, who had come, and when, and how, and for what
purpose.   In this way we showed our public spirit
as citizens and our *esprit de corps* as neighbours and
friends.   Weaver Stephen was no spy when he observed Daleham and Jemima proceeding upon their
evening walk, and if there was anything in his voice
which betokened apprehension, and seemed to involve
him in a kind of collateral guilt, it was to be accounted
for by his dislike of some of Daleham's ways and his
unreasoned rejection of some of Daleham's theories.
Stephen had never to account for his logic, for he

reached his conclusions without any. How white the
February moon became as the two townsfolks slowly
made their way up the Abbey Fields! How she gleamed
upon them almost eagerly as if she were a pure spirit
yearning over lives that might become even purer than
herself! Far away were white clouds, snow faintly
flushed with amber, catching the radiance as if in
crystal vessels, and farther away still were solemn
shadows willing to be foils to so holy a splendour.
Oh, the peace! Under a spell so tender men might
fitly resolve to take a new start in life, and resume
the interrupted prayers of childhood. Such a night is
the sabbath of the day which it concludes. But most
men care as little for this sabbath as for any other;
hence the solitude of night, and the wasted brightness
of the stars. Not that Daleham and Jemima are to be
mistaken for worshippers of the moon and her host, for
probably they did not see the nocturnal glory. Daleham had no sky in his cloudy universe. He was
without God, [and therefore without poetry,] in the
world, and without beauty, and without music; "without God" means infinitely more than without theology.
What, then, was the subject which engaged their
attention? Daleham had heard of Jemima's interest
in curious calculations and mathematical inquiries, so
he was pleasantly calling upon her, with a familiar
and encouraging "Come now," to show her knowledge of the first proposition in Euclid. Surely no
exercise more severely innocent could have been
invented. So shrewd a man as Daleham knew well
the uses and advantages of innocence, and therefore

he kept that white dove in his cage and fed it with
ostentatious care.   But even Euclid can unconsciously
assist in many directions not strictly geometrical.
Arithmetic spoons over " the affections of numbers,"
and geometry lingers with willing explanation and
critical sympathy over " the point of osculation."
When a man says in an open field and in silvery
moonlight, Let A B be the given finite straight line,
he finds himself very much in need of a blackboard,
a necessity which the palest moonshine can do nothing
to relieve.   But Jemima could hold Mr. Daleham's
walking cane between her eyes and the moon and
imaginatively regard it as a given finite straight line,   .
and Daleham could bring Jemima's right hand to the
proper point and Jemima's left hand to the proper
point, and this he could do with a touch most gentle
and more than merely delicate : this he did ; then
he described two circles, and made two other lines
come down to the given finite straight line, and called
upon Jemima to fasten her mind's eye intently upon
an imaginary triangle, which Jemima protested had
no existence and could have no existence, for all she
could really see was a black walking stick, and all
that Daleham had been saying was fudge which he
had made up out of his own head.

    " So you may pretend to think," said he, " but I
believe, excuse me, that you could excel in geometry
if you gave your mind to it, and I would advise
you to make a study of it ; at all events, these are
the subjects in which I now take the greatest interest, and if I may make a confidante of you, I don't

mind saying that I like geometry much better than theology."

Jemima did not see by what curve Daleham had come round to this remark, nor could she divine his intention. She had noticed that for some time his attendance upon my ministry had been extremely irregular, and that even when he was present his attention was but languid at the best. She had noticed, too, that latterly he had been almost constantly at chapel, and that when there some improvement was visible in his manner. Jemima was by no means destitute of good sense, notwithstanding her intricate calculation about the earwigs and the *Great Eastern*, upon which instance of supposed feebleness of mind Master Daleham founded his hope of success in any direction he thought fit to pursue. Jemima was shrewd without any pretence to brilliance, shrewd enough to know the difference between earnestness and insincerity, and shrewd enough to draw the line at the point of self-protection. Yet was not Jemima Battison perfectly human, as she had a right to be? It is happily not my business to account for the constitution of nature, but I have observed in not a few instances that the attention paid to women by masculine monsters is not always resented; in fact, the monsters are apt to have far too much attention paid to the merits created for them by the feminine imagination. The Lord no doubt created the first man, but ever since that instance of divine action, every man, as to his ideal qualities and uses, has been created by the motherly fancy of more or less infatuated woman. Where is the suitor so ugly

that the woman cannot see some point of beauty hidden
to every eye but her own ?   Even Daleham was not so
great an infidel to Jemima as he was to the suspicious
orthodoxy of Weaver Stephen.

" I am glad," said she in reply, " you have come so
regularly to chapel lately.   That is an improvement."

Daleham hardly expected this, yet he relished the
compliment implied in the fact that his actions were
noticed by Jemima.   He complained that there was so
little to be heard at chapel, and what he did hear he
only half believed ; " always," said he, " the same old
humdrum about Adam and Eve, and a lot of people
who never lived."

" Never   lived ! "   Jemima   whisperingly   exclaimed.
" What ever can your meaning be ? "

" Never mind.   I don't care for ancient history even
where it is true, much less where it is doubtful.   Why
don't preachers speak about the things of to-day ? "

" Such as ? "

" Such as the marriage laws, the lunacy laws, and a
hundred other things, and not prate about things
invisible."

" 'Take the marriage laws," said Jemima ; " what could
my minister say about them ? "

" Denounce them, put an end to them ; why should
there be any laws about marriage ?   What is there to
hinder people making their own conditions of union ? "

Jemima was shocked by a novelty which seemed to
be strongly tinctured with profanity.

" Don't misunderstand me," said Daleham, noticing
the effect of his remark ; " it seems to me that marriage

is far too sacred a thing to be determined by human law."

He stopped. The lie must have choked his utterance. How pure was the white moon How stainless .the diamond-stars that jewelled the night ! Yet was there not a low moan made by the wind in the copse which skirts the higher end of the Acomb road ?

"I don't quite understand what you would wish to have done," said Jemima.

"Perfectly clear to my own mind," Daleham answered. "Suppose—merely for the sake of illustration —that two people walking along this road to-night were disposed to take each other for better, for worse" (the wind moaned more bitterly in the copse)—"why should they not say so to one another lovingly and confidingly, and at once enter upon all the happy relations of the marriage state ? What has the magistrate to do with an act so personal and solemn ? To my mind it really seems—pardon me ; I am not a superstitious man —quite a profanation for any third party to be present at a wedding." (Here some old branch fell heavily in the copse, and a sharper tone was heard in the wind.)

"My idea of a wedding," said Jemima, "is not at all like that."

"Of course not," Daleham quickly replied, "of course not. I do not expect to make many converts, at least not suddenly, to such a view. But I may tell you that the last wedding I was at quite shocked me. It was performed—no, that's not the right word—celebrated—or whatever you like to call it—by that blatant and foul-mouthed Dissenter at Mixford—whatever is the fellow's name?—excuse my language—a great stout blacksmith-looking fellow—a most awful Dissenter———"

"Mr. Paterson is the name of the Mixford minister," said Jemima.

"That's the man, an awful Dissenter; a black-guard I call him; he can never let the Church alone. Well, there we all stood around him, and with a dog-like bow-wow he barked out a lot of nonsense, and the little rat of a registrar heard the legal assurances and then popped out, and no doubt had a glass of beer at the corner pub, whilst old Paterson——— "

"Mr. Paterson is not old," said Jemima.

"He was never young," said Daleham, "but young or old, he barked away, and then we signed a book, and went off to breakfast, and had a lot of miserably small speeches, and then came rice and slippers, and—bah!"

Mr. Daleham was altogether too refined to tolerate this debasement of the humanities, and absolutely too spiritual to have anything to do with vulgarity. The utmost limit of the walk had now been reached, and the return journey must be undertaken. As Mr. Daleham looked towards the copse, he thought he saw a rook alight upon one of the highest branches and look down upon the scene like a black spirit, but it was impossible. Impossible, yet again and again he looked; impossible—nonsensical—superstitious—yet Mr. Daleham looked. But the sobbing of the wind was real, so tender, so pathetic, and so reluctant; the sob came as if by necessity and not by consent. The travellers turn round, leaving the moon behind them, and walk briskly into the Abbey Fields. Now they see what they had not seen before, their own shadows stretching away in front of them, now touching, now parting, now turning aside, now lost in the deeper shadows of old trees. Mr. Daleham turned round as if to look for the black bird that he foolishly thought he saw in the copse, but he saw nothing. Presently, just before coming to the white stile, he stood still, and said—

"What a church for a wedding! Now if I could have everything my own way, I would marry at this very spot, the moon and the stars should be bridesmaids and witnesses, this white stile should be the altar, and the bride and bridegroom should exchange the most solemn vows."

A tuft of black cloud concealed the moon for a moment.

"But we cannot have things our own way," said Jemima; "weddings so easily done might be as easily undone."

"I differ," said Daleham; "upon my honour, I do. The parties make oath to one another, and by that oath they are bound. Do not mistake me. I am not the man to make light of nuptial responsibilities. I am speaking merely in the spirit of a public reformer, and as a disciple in the school of rational progress. You asked me what subjects I wish to have discussed in the pulpit, and I mentioned the English marriage laws. You asked me for an illustration of my meaning, and I gave you one. I am not trying to convert you, or to affect your mind in any way, but I hope you will have the courage to study the subject."

"A good old-fashioned wedding for me, if ever I marry," said Jemima.

After a few minutes' silence, Mr. Daleham said— "Now just before we enter the town let me know what you remember about the equilateral triangle. Let A B be the given finite straight line ; then at point A draw the circle——"

"You said you did not believe in ancient history, Mr. Daleham."

"So I did. But the base A B, and the line C D— hallo, here's Weaver Stephen ! Well, old friend, what are you thinking about to-night ? "

"Well, sir, I be a-thinking as how it says in the Bible, 'Though hand join in hand, the wicked shall not go unpunished.'"

"You are a regular old parson, Stephen ; good-night."

CHAPTER V.

ALF-HOLIDAY in Midtown. Knockey's shop was practically closed, though the post office arrangements obliged him to be on the spot and to keep the door open until the evening mail had been despatched. A meeting is being held in Knockey's back parlour, a rather large square room, lighted by a straight pendant with two jets, and furnished with sofa and chairs in black horse-hair stuffing, a long deal table covered with mahogany-coloured oil-cloth, a high old-fashioned kitchen clock, and a large number of strongly-tinted paper pictures which came cheaply to hand through the peculiar business of the shop. The meeting is composed of about twelve of the gallery seat-holders drawn from the Baptist chapel of which my friend Whiteman is minister, and is convened in this dignified manner to discuss chapel affairs in general and pulpit affairs in particular. Baptists, like Independents, have rights which some of them are not disposed to relinquish, and the right of parlour teas and parlour parliaments is one of them.

"Good-evening, Mrs. Lambert; how *are* you, friend?"

"Thank you, Mr. Knockey, pretty well for me; only two fits this week."

"Sit down, Mrs. Lambert, just where you please. I am glad to see you. Ah, my dear friend Mr. Langport; how *are* you, sir? how *are* you?"

"Among the middlings, friend Knockey, only among the middlings. My breathing gives way a deal. Your nice warm room will just suit me. Do you know, friend Knockey, that the worse the air is the better I can breathe it?"

Mr. Langport's breath might well "give way a deal," for he was sixteen stones in weight, fifty-two inches round the body, with limbs like an elephant's. As he dropped himself upon the creaking sofa his "Ah!" nearly blew the gas out.

"And Mrs. Bidwell, ma'am, good-evening; so friendly of you to come, so very sweet and Christian; how *are* you?"

"But so-so, friend; I said to Bidwell as I was coming out that only Mr. Knockey could draw me from the house to-night. I understand we are to talk over things to see what is best to be done, for the gallery at Bethel is in a pretty state; souls we may have none, my soul never hears a word worth listening to, and my peace at home, through Bidwell not being a member, and being, one may say, too fond of his jokes, is no peace, for a word of sympathy I never get, for Bidwell is so fond of whistling that when I complain of the poorness of the preaching he whistles 'Villikins killed the parson,' and some stuff of that kind."

"I hope we have not come to say anything disrespectful of our husbands," said a woman whose hair was alive with roses.

"Far from it," Mrs. Bidwell replied. "Bidwell is a steady old file, but most of you know how fond he is of his jokes, and if Mrs. Wales had to hear him whistling in the morning 'How the cow looks on Sundays,' and in the evening 'What Polly did for the monkey,' and when I speak to him about our troubles in the gallery he cuts a caper on the floor to the tune of 'The Bonny Piper Lad'—if some people had their patience tried in that way, perhaps they would not wear so many roses in their hair, or cut up so mouldy when nobody's speaking to them. At the same time, I hope we have met in a Christian spirit; if Mr. Knockey will tell us—— "

"Yes, friends, we have met for deliberations; we have met in a sort of what the papers call a crissis—— "

"Crisis," Mr. Langport wheezingly interposed.

"We have not met to quarrel about words, or to put one another in the wrong, I do solemnly hope; at the same time, we are Christians and Baptists, and through all sitting in the same gallery—— "

A heavy and mysterious snore here occasioned surprise. "We have come together for a purpose Mr. Riddle will explain." Mr. Riddle was the youngest man in the company and a little inclined to be rhetorical. Mr. Riddle held a handful of notes, and amongst other ways in which he showed his respect for the host and his appreciation of the honour conferred upon him, he wore a stiff black stock which literally propped up a chin which without it would have been nowhere. Mr. Riddle said he had no intention of making a fool of himself; at the same time, he held to the good old saying "Fair's fair," to which he would venture to add even in the presence of the ladies that "fair play is a jewel"; having said this much by way of introduction, and in no spirit of prejudice, he would venture most respectfully to inquire whether he could be accommodated with a drink of water.

"Daughter Jane, bring in a jug, love," said Titus.

"Now, coming to the point, friends, and not to spend idle breath, may I ask you to survey the herculean situation, or, as some would say, the gigantic circumstances, without regard to time and place? I venture, in no spirit of depreciation, to ask this."

Mr. Langport thought it would not compromise them; Mrs. Lambert felt that after so beautiful a speech they were bound to; Mrs. Wales would never answer in a hurry, in particular after what Mrs. Bidwell had said about the roses, which were bought and paid for long before this meeting was thought of, and which would be worn long after this meeting was over, and she did not mind what was done now she had had her say.

"Then be it so," continued Mr. Riddle; "that clears the ground very considerably, and prompts the mind to those onward movements and creates those blessed impulses which, whatever may be the condition of affairs at home or abroad—I say boldly at home *or* abroad— raises the question, How is the gallery to be treated?"

This inquiry was followed by applause. It was felt to be the question before which every other inquiry must literally give way. A thrill of terror made all hearts beat in unison. Marking the effect of his noble appeal, Mr. Riddle invigorated himself by using the jug.

"And now," said he, "we may gratefully exclaim, 'Land ahead,' and give one another the hand of fellowship."

"How lovely!" exclaimed Mrs. Lambert.

"If we had more of that," said an elderly lady in spectacles, "we should in many ways, I humbly think, be more dissimulated and miscellaneous."

"Then," said Mr. Riddle, "the only question before us is, What next?"

"Just so," said all voices.

"Shall we, beloved friends, proceed by way of resolution?"

Mrs. Bidwell ventured to think that course too promiscuous.

"Shall we, then, create and subscribe a bye-law?" Mr. Riddle once more inquired in a spirit "equally removed from retrogression and treachery."

Mr. Knockey could see no harm in a bye-law, "in particular if it was so worded that it could be read either backwards or forwards, and clearly made out that the gallery was not to be put upon." Mrs. Wales did not set much store by bye-laws. The elderly lady in spectacles was favourable provided that jurisprudence did not prevaricate in any way, as she was much opposed to that. Mr. Langport was not opposed, but would reserve his judgment.

"One question," said Mrs. Bidwell, "I wish to ask : are you aware that Cobbler Roberts is not our friend?"

All were sorrowfully aware of that. The view taken of Roberts was that his meanness was unfathomable. He was a snake in the grass. But for him there would be unanimity in the gallery. And that dark-minded man concealed his duplicity under the pretence of quoting the Bible and finding passages that would, as he said, burn every one's particular sins.

"Only the other day," said Mrs. Bidwell, "when I was complaining that Bidwell whistled 'Hoity-toity is the song for me,' Cobbler Roberts said, 'Though thou shouldest bray a fool in a mortar,' and so on ; he tries to imitate that wretched man Weaver Stephen among the Independents. That's his game."

"Mr. Knockey," said Mr. Langport, "we must be fundamental."

"That's the vital point," exclaimed the rhetorical Riddle.

"I am glad to have your able support, Mr. Riddle. Without being fundamental where are we?" (cheers). "Without being fundamental what guarantee have we?" (continued cheers). "Without being fundamental who can calculate results?"

"Now we are getting to the very point I foresaw," said Riddle.

"This looks like the road to business," said Knockey, closing an eye.

"Then," said Langport, "to nail the matter, and clinch the nail, and clear away all doubt from every mind, I boldly ask, Where are we?"

"That's it," exclaimed all voices; "now we see light."

"We are all deeply indebted to Mr. Langport," said Mr. Knockey.

"Not at all, dear friends; far from it. Notwithstanding my weight, I am but a worm, the humblest worm in the hands of Providence. But am I wrong if I say that we ought, one and all, however humble our abilities, to protect our beloved and time-honoured gallery from the intrusion and the contempt of the Robson family?"

This inquiry gave general pleasure. There were too many Robsons in the chapel. One of them had actually been seen looking up the gallery stairs. Mr. Robson, the best of deacons, was held in general contempt in the gallery, without anybody being able to tell the reason why. With so many Robsons swarming all over the place, and showing off their fine clothes, and coming to church in a carriage, and actually sending their coachman to sit in the gallery, it was impossible to hold a confidential interview in any part of the chapel, and of course, where there was such worldliness and such worship of the golden calf, gallery people were not permitted to put so much as their noses inside the vestry: certainly not; the vestry was for people that paid seven-and-sixpence a quarter for a seat, and not for gallery people, whose souls were hardly worth saving. Mrs. Bidwell had once ventured to look into the vestry, and her head was nearly snapped off by that worldly-minded treasurer Mr. Robson, who had a pleasant enough face and a wheedling kind of

4

manner, but who must have always had an eye to the
main chance, or he never could have built so fine a
place as Eastfield and carpeted the very passage and
staircase with flowered velvet. Mrs. Bidwell did not
understand such Christianity. Her husband had been
working at the enlargement of Mr. Robson's stable,
and he saw fine goings-on at Eastfield and fine goings-
on with the minister, who no doubt made himself very
agreeable to the rich just to see what he could pick up,
but Mr. Whiteman ought not to look down upon the
poor, for his own parents may have been people in a
small way of business, as she knew one Baptist minister whose father was a letter-carrier, and did odd jobs
of gardening in the summer, though his son did wear a
white neckcloth, and go about from one tea meeting to
another, and marry a good bit of money by marrying
the only daughter of a lucky auctioneer. Mrs. Bidwell
called upon the gallery people to demand justice and to
venture, come weal come woe, to say that their souls
were their own.

Mr. Langport could not contain himself during
the delivery of these elevated sentiments. He rapped
the table. He pounded the floor with his heavy boots,
and rocked himself from side to side on the sofa. His
opinions, he said, had been most powerfully expressed,
and he desired to thank his fellow-seatholder in the
gallery for her splendid statement, thumping the floor
all the time with his elephantine feet, and suddenly
roaring like a bull. What ever could be the matter?
Was he seized with spasms? Mrs. Lambert went off
in her third fit that week. Mr. Riddle slipped un-

observed out of the room. " Hit him on the back, and
bring him to," said Mrs. Wales. " Try that !" said
the elderly lady in spectacles, throwing most of a jug
of water upon his tortured face. " Pull him off !" roared
Langport, and pointing to the floor, it was found that
the butcher's dog from next door had been sleeping
under the sofa, and being roused by the applause, had
seized Langport by the calf of his leg, and was hanging
on desperately.

" Johnny dear, do remove this beast," said Knockey ;
" he does interfere with our deliberations." But "Johnny
dear " was upstairs shaving. For some time back Johnny
had adopted the unusual practice of shaving in the
evening, being principally influenced in that choice of
time by the fact that it relieved him from attending
chapel twice on Sundays. " Johnny dear " was the
only person who had much effect upon the dog, and
now unfortunately he was out of the way. During
the hubbub a stranger appeared upon the scene, and
made himself active in various ways. Bidwell had
promised to come for his wife, and here he was. Suddenly brought into this confusion, Bidwell's mind was
somewhat upset. Who was who, and what was what,
who was up and who was down, were questions nobody
cared to answer.

" Do make yourself useful, Bidwell," said his excited
wife.

" How? Where? What in ?" said he, quite accidentally toppling Knockey into the fender, and hastily
looking into the brown jug with an anxious expression
of face, and removing a chair just as Mrs. Wales was

going to sit down. "This is the jolliest thing I've
seen," said Bidwell; "you may make me a member,
Knockey, and I'll come reg'lar." Then, swinging round,
he put the gas out, and whistled a tune of his own
composing. Knockey rose slowly from the fender, and,
lighting one jet, he said—

"This will be my ruin if our people" (meaning the
Government) "should get to hear of it. Friends, keep
it quiet. Fellow-members, hush it up in a spirit of love.
Mr. Bidwell, be my friend."

"So I will for a pound of black twist," said Bidwell.

"With pleasure, my friend; take it and stand by me."

"I'll be shot if I will," said Bidwell. "I a'n't a
'member,' but I'll see you powdered into snuff before
I'll take your twist." Then, turning out the gas, he
quite accidentally toppled Knockey into the fender
once more, and led out Mrs. Bidwell to the well-known
and well-whistled tune of " The fiddler's whereabouts
nobody knows."

CHAPTER VI.

THE Vicar has asked me to have a cup of tea with him this afternoon, and as I feel quite drawn to the old gentleman, I will certainly go. Nothing is to be gained on either side by a policy of distrust and isolation, but much solid good may be secured by a frank and even generous exchange of civilities. This morning I went out early to brace myself for a hard day's work at the desk by a walk in the direction of Eastfield, not deterred but rather stimulated by the fact that a considerable fog lay upon the borough of Midtown. Up the Golden Lane and away into the Abbey Fields, and the mist gradually became more and more silvery, lingering amongst the pines and the maples, and wreathing figures above the leafless hawthorn hedges, exciting my fancy and drawing from me all sorts of absurd interpretations. Such a mist is a kind of ghost. Presently a rook cawed. Then a carrier's cart went jogging by, the driver giving me a civil salute on the general ground of humanity rather than on the particular ground of acquaintance. Then I was quite alone. How truly social was that solitude! I can fully adopt the ancient saying, Never less alone than when alone. I seemed

to overhear the meditation of the trees as they antici-
pated the blessedness of another spring, and the joy of
the birds as they twittered in the high branches, and
the sigh of awakening nature as the breeze breathed
rather than blew across the many-coloured fields.
Now I came to a point where many loamy roads met,
and as I looked along the brown paths, without a
visible traveller on all the winding ways, I bethought
me of the meaning of all the foot-prints which had
given the highways a kind of history : the foot-print
of the weary labourer ; the foot-mark made by the little
child doomed to begin life's battle years too soon ; the
blurred place where gossips had smoked and chatted
many an evening hour. Here the plough-horse had left
its broad imprint ; there the riding-horse had struck
fire from the bruised and splintered stones ; and yonder
wheels had rolled to the field, the farmstead, the market-
place, or the still churchyard. Half closing my eyes,
I saw wondrous things in the exquisite anatomy of the
trees, and along all the tinted line of the enlarging
horizon. Birds wheeled and curved in the brightening
air. A hundred yards away lay a little hamlet without
sign of life, a sleeper dreaming on the landscape. On
the other side there was a gleam as of sunlit water in
the distance. This was a place to loiter in, to think in,
to pray in. Standing alone in that soothing quietness,
I made many vows. I would serve the Cross of the
Nazarene as I had never served it before ; my prayers
should tremble with a deeper tenderness ; my appeals
should be enlarged and ennobled by a truer sympathy
with human temptation and sorrow ; my whole life

should be a revelation of the goodness of God. Well for us that we have such times of solitary communion with the Spirit: the tears we then shed are cleansing waters, and the sorrow we then feel prepares us for the fast-coming joy. I never preach so gladly and strongly as after fellowship with nature. Of sharp and eager argument there may be less, but in place of it there is peace, a sense of force not human, a consciousness of ministry and progress covering an infinite space. In the midst of my reverie I heard the footsteps of a horse. A moment more, and the horse was in view. Presently Mr. Daleham rode up.

"What, riding so early as this, Mr. Daleham?"

"Yes, just been having a trot round the copse."

On he passed. "Proputty, proputty, proputty, that's what I heard them say; proputty, proputty, proputty, as they cantered away." The scene was no better for that man's presence. For a moment the sacred glamour was gone, and nature took time to regain her composure. How is it that some men vulgarise whatever they touch? How is it that they scatter the angels? It was always so with Daleham. Come where he might, the atmosphere always instantly changed for the worse. He was a pleasant man, not without intelligence, by no means disagreeable in appearance, and had always plenty to say, yet birds and flowers, parents and children, all felt that he was a shadow, a blight, a living sneer. In a few minutes my mental rest had returned, and I heard further gospel-speech from the gracious sun; but presently a traveller turned the corner, and I was gladly shaking hands with Mr.

Robson, the radiant owner of Eastfield, just starting
on some errand of mercy.

"The very man I wanted to see," said he.

"Of course," I remarked, "some dream must account
for this."

"The fact is," Mr. Robson continued, "Mr.
Whiteman is exhausted; he has had a good deal of
worry lately, and it has told upon him. A few of us
have made up a little purse of fifty pounds, and we
want you and Mr. Whiteman to run down to the coast
for a week and leave your troubles in the sea. Think
of it."

Mr. Robson hastened on, and I was left to think
things over. I could not but wonder what Daleham
wanted at the copse. Though a man of strictly scientific mind, and a severe rationalist, it was surprising
how superstitious he was, how easily shaken, how
prone to run away from shadows and to escape his
own twilight society. Daleham's robust science made
him quite a hero in the middle of the market-place and
in the middle of the day, but it was less potent in the
sunset and in the quietness of his own house. At the
same time, it was a strictly scientific mind. It ranged
itself with great obstinacy against all theological
speculation and supernatural interference with the
affairs of men. The mind of Daleham was of that
severe scientific type that rejected the miracles of the
New Testament and smiled at the feeble arguments
founded upon them. It was an eminently judicial
mind, delighting in comprehensive and philosophical
views, and despising all things narrow in conception

and finite in issue. It was a stupendous mind. No
chapel could hold it. A cathedral must be erected for
its special accommodation. All Midtown knew that
for tearing an argument to pieces and showing up
with contempt, absolutely withering in its severity, all
pulpit sophisms, the mind of Daleham stood alone. It
was undoubtedly very curious that Mr. Daleham was
braver in daylight than in darkness, and that he was
noted for seeing forms and shapes which nobody else
could see, and that no consideration could induce him
to cross the churchyard alone on a moonlight night.
This might be a mere peculiarity of greatness, for it
is certain that Mr. Daleham was so far a devotee of
science, that he borrowed the *Scientific Review* of Mr.
Thomson, the chemist, every month, and never volun-
tarily returned it. I wonder what he was doing at the
copse ? Had the creaking of some branch frightened
him a few nights before ? Had some black ghost
scared him ? Nothing of the kind, perhaps. Why
suspect such a keen debater ? Maybe he had been
putting to the test some novel theory or some much-
involving experiment. Rationalists are bound to be
consistent, and if consistent, they cannot be superstitious.

The day is now closing, and I am on my way to the
Vicarage, which is in many respects the most comfort-
able-looking house in Midtown. Square, stone-built,
grey with years, mullion-windowed, with a large fan of
well-trimmed ivy spreading over one of the gables,
what can look more clerically English, or more domestic-

ally comfortable ?   Dissenter as I am, and therefore
more or less base-minded, I have an instinctive reverence for old churches, old mansions, and old haunts of
all kinds, and this reverence was strongly upon me as
I went up the avenue by which the partially secluded
Vicarage is approached.   The very rooks cawing to
one another were clerical rooks of the most advanced
type.   Not one of them knew that there was a Dissenter in the parish, much less suspected that a
Dissenting minister was actually in the Vicarage grounds.
In such ignorance of contemporaneous history may
even rooks live in ecclesiastical trees.   In a few minutes
I was in the library : nothing with yesterday's freshness
upon it was in that retreat ; fine old chairs on every
hand, fine old books that might have made generations
of vicars wise, fine old pictures that made me feel
shockingly young and immature, and covered with the
stigma of cheapness the one engraving, " Daniel in the
lions' den," which grimly decorated the high-up back-
room which I called my study.   What a dreamy feeling
came over me as I sat in that asylum of ancient history !   Who could enter into the spirit of that literary
sanctuary and not feel ashamed of Dissent and sick of
all ideas democratic ?   The air was fast making me a
Churchman and a Conservative.   I looked round for
something new, but in vain.   Not a single copy of the
Democratic Gorgon could I see, or an odd number of
the *Dissenting Lamp of Glory*, or any sign of that in-
fluential and well-paying weekly newspaper the *Agnostic
Slopbasin*.   No.   The Vicarage library was marked
all over with venerableness, books which Methuselah

thumbed and chairs made out of the oaks of Bashan, nothing new, unless it might be just a little trace of white ashes which might have been made in the act of cleaning out a clay pipe, and that would have been the sole exception to antiquity if I had not caught sight of the clay pipe itself, carefully set up behind a folio volume marked *Codex Theodosianus*, which the Vicar had, no doubt, been anxiously perusing.

Over our cup of tea, served in the library, the Vicar was nearly as cordial as a Dissenter. I was afraid he might have been too learned for me, and that he might have posed me with inquiries about the said *Codex*, or have asked my critical opinion about the *Codex Ecclesiæ Africanæ*, which stood immediately above it, in which case I should have floored him with sundry sharp quotations from the *Converted Watchdog* and the *Christian Passbook*, showing how livings were bought and sold in the Church of England, and how absentee-ism was playing havoc in the land. The point of these remarks may not be evident to my mind at this distance of time, but there was a point, no doubt. There was, however, no attempt to humble me through the medium of the calf-bound folios, but every disposition shown to make me welcome and comfortable.

" Why don't you come over to the Church of England," said the Vicar, "and carry out your plans under proper supervision ? "

" Conscience," I softly said, without attempting to make a sentence.

" Bring your conscience with you, of course. Bring it, and come at once."

"My peculiar views," said I, longing for Paterson to help me out.

"Bring them too," the Vicar hospitably continued. "The Church is national. In a national church all opinions should be represented. Come over, all of you. Plenty of room. Don't delay. Do let us be neighbourly. No good can come of strife."

"The Thirty-nine Articles," I mumbled, with criminal brevity.

"Excellent!" said the Vicar. "I call them thirty-nine starting points, not stopping points. See? You start there, but the Lord knows where you may go to. Look at Colenso."

"But in that way they may be turned into thirty-nine lies, may they not?"

"Too severe, my friend, and you must see it to be so—ridiculously severe. I call the Thirty-nine Articles a kind of wether-bell, don't you see. You have that on your neck, you know, and then you wander where you like, up a hill or down a valley; there you are, and we know where you are, and we can find you if we want to, which in reality we do not, but still the bell announces your whereabouts."

The Vicar looked so intently in the direction of the *Codex Theodosianus*, that I asked him if he wanted the book, but he only wanted the clay pipe which stood behind it. I am bound to say that the way in which the Vicar handled the pipe almost made me regret that I was not a smoker. How delicately he held it between finger and thumb, then cleared out the bowl, applying a long pin to the obstinate ashes which would not be tapped out ; then the filling process was evidently such a mute delight, then came the lighted spill, throwing a soft yellow light upon the jocund face, and finally the curling cloud floating leisurely around the good man's head, expressing the quiet content which filled the good man's heart. To be a dissenter in the matter of smoking made me feel very awkward ; it was like an aggravation of my singularity ; it was most bearish ; altogether this lack of sympathy even in so small a matter as smoking made me feel most uncomfortable. Paterson and Williams, Tomlinson and Whiteman, the dear Professor, too, all smoke, and I alone am a dissenting Pharisee ! I must consider the whole subject.

"Dissent flourishes most in great cities, does it not ?"

"Yes. I suppose so. Probably." This was my halting answer.

"Thought so," said the Vicar ; "question of fresh air largely ; confinement and dyspepsia go together ; small towns and churchmanship ; heated cities and Dissent ; that's how I put it. They tell me that shoemaking places are worst of all, though I don't see why they should be. Now at Mixford there's quite a nest of shoemakers, and there is a flourishing Dissenting chapel there. By the way, that reminds me I have to drive over there soon, and if you will go with me, I shall be glad."

"Thanks. Most willingly. I know the Mixford minister."

"Strange commotion there," continued the Vicar ;

"my friend Sir Hedley Baker lives close to Mixford, and he is on the brink of suicide owing to some rough sort of fellow who has bought a piece of land just outside his property and put up a staring red brick house which the baronet can see from one of the Grange windows. Sir Hedley was here the other day foaming at the mouth. We must not say a word about Dissent to him if we have any wish to save his reason. My brother and he were at Balliol together, so there is quite a family feeling amongst us, and I can go when I like and take anybody I like. From the way he raves about this trespasser you might think he was an arrant cad, but that would be a grand mistake. Between you and me, you know, I fancy the old baronet has been a good deal upset by his daughter, not now so young as she used to be, having got hold of some Dissenting tracts or something of that sort, and there's a fool of a curate has got into a controversy there with the Dissenting minister, a fiery sort of fellow, so that altogether things are not so pleasant at Mixford, as they are at Midtown. I want to be good neighbours all round."

"I am bound to say that I never heard the Vicar spoken against."

"Well; let us be thankful. I positively know next to nothing about Dissent. I don't like the word, you know. It is not a pleasant word. It sounds so very unneighbourly and uncharitable. I wish we could hit upon some better term, something not so porcupiney and prickly. Now, between you and me, do you find much Dissent in the parish?"

"Well, sir," said I, "in the parish we have Congregationalists, Baptists, Wesleyans, and others, and I believe the chapels are fairly well filled."

"Now what on earth," said the Vicar, with a little more spirit, "do all these people find to talk about? It seems to me that they dissent from one another quite as much as they dissent from the Church, else why don't they all meet together and pass under one name? That shows me that there is something wrong somewhere, and that after all the Church may be right. It never struck me before that the Dissenters dissent from one another, but I see it now. Important point that."

"But," said I, "there are many denominations within the Church: Broad Church, Low Church, High Church, and so on."

"Yes, yes, but, don't you see, they are, as you say, within the Church; they don't boil separate kettles on separate fires, or get their meal from different millers; that's the point; they don't attempt to break up the Church or scattter the property: they all love the old mother, and do what they can for her. Heaven knows there's no Puseyite tomfoolery about me. I never made crosses in my spelling book like Newman. I am a Protestant to the backbone——"

"Then you are a Dissenter," I interrupted.

"Dissenter?"

"Yes; to protest is to dissent; you dissent from the Church of Rome."

"Ah! that's a very different thing," said the Vicar, "of course; certainly."

So much for the point of view.   If you dissent from me, you are foolish, but if we both protest against somebody else, we are wise ; not only so, our protest is an expression of conviction and an assertion of the sovereignty of conscience, but another man's dissent from us merely shows that other man's perversity and selfishness, and is deserving of severe reprobation.   It is nothing more nor less than a wicked exaggeration of individualism, and in the soul of it is simply a piece of inexcusable popery.   When another man refuses to adjust his conscience by the meridian of my convictions does he not display the pettiest of little-mindedness and the most contemptible phase of personal vanity ? I merely ask the question.

"An idea occurs to me," said I, "which may be of some use.   You want to know something about Dissent in Midtown, and it so happens that I have been writing a connected history of recent events, which, if you will peruse in strict confidence, I will put into your hands."

The Vicar instantly agreed, and next day I sent him the first five chapters of this book.

As I was close at home I met sweet old Weaver Stephen, who said that all day long he had been looking up to God, saying—" Hold Thou me up, and I shall be safe."

CHAPTER VII.

OLD Mr. Battison was in most respects a negative character, always excepting his audacious thought that street names might be made the medium of evangelising the town. In his opinion it would be impossible for any tradesman to date an invoice from Ephraim Street and to overcharge a customer, and simply inconceivable that any young man could write a letter from Salvation Corner and tell lies in the epistle. The very address, he used to say, would be a silent guarantee of fidelity. But Mr. Battison's idea made no progress, owing to the stupidity of the town authorities and to an unavowed conspiracy amongst worldly-minded men. Nehemiah Battison comforted himself, however, with the thought that perhaps in this instance, as in others, familiarity might breed contempt, particularly as he had noticed, without making any audible remark upon the significant circumstance, that Jochebed, who had so far nailed her colours to the mast as to call her dog Nebuchadnezzar, had lately taken to the detestable practice of calling the brute by the depraved name of Nezzy, for which he could find no sufficient authority in nature or in reason. With all due respect for old Mr. Battison, I sometimes wished that his pro-

5

perty had been a little less, for having enough to live upon comfortably, he was too much at liberty to call upon his minister and fritter away my time. It was with positive terror that I saw his white hat at the other end of the street I lived in, or heard the thud of his walking stick upon my doorstep, for I knew that he had nothing to say, and that he never thought of closing a visit under half an hour. But ministers must not be abrupt, nor must they be engaged when their hearers call upon them, nor must they show the slightest sign of impatience under the harrow of the most insufferable bore. I knew all this, and submitted to it with average restraint. Mr. Battison thought he was doing me a favour when he asked me to take a morning walk with him, and that he was conveying valuable information to me in relating how he began the world with fourpence, then found a horse-shoe which he sold for threepence, and then got a situation at half-a-crown a week, and then advanced in a manner which, if written in a book, would beat any novel he ever heard of. He assured me that sometimes he had been on the point of putting down upon paper an outline of the singular way in which he had been brought forward, and I devoutly wished that he had begun the writing and kept his head steadily over the desk for the remainder of his days. Mr. Battison's deep conviction was that nobody would have believed his story, that, in short, everybody would think he had made it all up, particularly the part of his romantic life when he kept a carrier's cart, and let out a pony chaise by the day or by the week, and how he lost the pony, and consequently had to sell the chaise for what practically amounted to an old song.

"However," said he on one occasion, "not to trouble you with my story any longer, for I am but a poor creature in the hands of Providence, I may tell you that I have made up my mind to compromise matters."

"With your creditors?" said I, confusing "compromise" with "compound."

"No, no, no," said the little man sharply, "oh dear no! thanks be, I have a comfortable thousand a year which cannot be touched——"

"Pardon my blunder," said I; "it was awfully stupid."

But old Mr. Battison was thankful for the opportunity of assuring me that all was right in that matter, and he did not mind telling me that beyond his fixed thousand per annum he had a few nice little sums which would enable him to buy up some people in the Congregational chapel who thought a good deal more of themselves than he thought of them; at the same time, he wished to be allowed to go on quietly and to live in his own obscure way, if anybody wanted to regard it as obscure.

"What I mean by compromising," said he, "is that as it is quite evident the town authorities will not adopt a Christian renaming of the streets, I had better endeavour to persuade private owners to give Christian names to their dwelling-houses, such as Ebenezer Villa, Capernaum Cottage, and the Lily of the Valley. People living in houses with such names must be worthy of

the titles, and in this way they might be gradually
induced to support the ministry."

I was really provoked by the old gentleman, and
hardly restrained from offending him.   His nonsensical
tattle was doubly painful to me in view of his age, and
especially in view of his relation to my ministry.   What
interest could my preaching have for a mind of this
order ?   My aim has always been to interpret human
nature to itself and then to interpret God to human
nature ; to show that the deepest and fullest answers
to every cry of the soul, in all the moods of its emotion
and experience, are to be found in the Bible, and that
inspiration is proved by its influence on the life rather
than by some crafty trick in professional terms.   Yet
here is a man whose narrow mind is cobwebbed with
ridiculous conceits and whose loose tongue wags incessantly in the recital of anecdotes of the most
contemptible order,—what am I to do with him ?   To
offend him is to send away eleven people from my chapel,
yet to look complacently upon him is to be guilty
of a species of hypocrisy.   He thinks he interests me.
He is under the impression that I owe him something
for his acquaintance.   He openly says that he loves to
converse with me.   Converse !   I must enlarge his good
points by my imagination, and make a better man of
him by my charity.   Certainly.   That will be to act a
pastor's part, even at the cost of some self-crucifixion.
For the moment I had put my feelings above my office,
and forgotten the patience of Christ.   Life will be
reduced to misery if we consider our sensibilities, or
our tastes, or our convenience, or our partialities, rather

than accept the humiliations and crucifixions which precede the noblest honours. In this view I think I will ask Mr. Battison to call upon me often. I think so. I feel I ought to do so. My mind wavers a good deal. At all events, I think I may safely say that I will reconsider the whole subject from that point of view.

Old Mr. Battison had occasion recently to see Mr. Daleham in a new light. Hitherto Mr. Battison had strongly disliked Mr. Daleham on the unacknowledged ground that Mr. Daleham always snubbed and humbled him, not in any merely personal way, but by talking upon subjects Mr. Battison had never heard of and using terms which to Mr. Battison's mind had simply no meaning at all.

"I call him a very bouncing man," said Mr. Battison to me.

"He has read a good deal, and he remembers a good deal," I replied.

"I do not remember," Mr. Battison added, "one word he says; it just goes in at one ear and out at the other; I do not care for bouncing people."

But Mr. Battison modified his opinion somewhat after a pleasant evening's intercourse with Mr. Daleham. No doubt Mr. Daleham could on occasion make himself very agreeable, and leave behind an impression of extreme modesty and winning affectionateness. During the evening in question Mr. Daleham offered to interpret character through reading the lines of the hand, an offer which "the girls" eagerly accepted.

"Oh, do you really think there is anything in it?" said Jochebed, ordering Nezzy to lie down and be quiet.

"That remains to be seen," said Mr. Daleham; "I am ready to read." Taking Jochebed's hand in his, Mr. Daleham said : " I tell you plainly that I shall understand many things by what I may term natural magnetism; your hands" (speaking to the whole company) "will thrill mine: if there is any occult masonry——"

"He's off on the bounce again," Mr. Battison whispered to Jemima.

"There will be some sign of it as between the parties —a sign which will have meaning to themselves alone. As Shakespeare says, 'By the pricking of my thumbs, something wicked this way comes,' but all in due time. Now let us look at this particular hand. I never saw a hand easier to read, so if I make any blunders, I must be very stupid. The line of life indicates a most robust constitution; in the absence of accidents, you may live to a patriarchal age. I never saw the line of life so free from intersections, or one that so completely surrounds the mount of the thumb——"

"The what ? " said Jemima.

" The mount of the thumb ; in other words, the mount of Venus. Now let me take the hand of your sister Miriam and look at both your hands together. What a very different hand Miriam's is ! (excuse my familiarity). Yes, indeed, very different. May I ask, Miss Miriam, if you have had any special trouble of the heart ? "

"Oh, why ? " Jochebed exclaimed.

" See where the line of the heart begins at the mount of Jupiter, and how troubled it becomes before it reaches the percussion of the hand. I am not going to ask rude questions, but if this were a painted hand instead of a living one, I should say, 'This person has had very painful experiences; her heart has suffered untold distress; her affections have been tortured.' Now if Miss Hagar will extend her hand, it may develop further contrasts. A very marvellous hand it is—the mount of Mercury is full of industry. Miss Hagar could manage six houses as easily as one, and as for the force indicated by the mount of Jupiter, I positively never saw anything like it. Miss Miriam, may I ask whether your pride did not lead you at one period in your life to repel an advance?"

Miss Miriam silently withdrew from the room, evidently under the influence of strong emotion.

"I thought so," Daleham continued. "What that heart has suffered, Mr. Battison, no tongue can ever tell."

Mr. Battison intimated that he had his own thoughts, which he had determined never to express.

"But now let me see Miss Jemima's hand. Ah, just what I expected. Yes, every line of it. This is what we call the psychic hand, which is the rarest and most expressive of all. Just note the length of the third phalange, and see how wonderfully marked is the magic triple bracelet round the wrist, and pardon me if, as an ardent student of chiromancy, I intimate that I never saw the line of life move so aggressively towards the mount of Jupiter without the owner of the hand having a strong dash of ambition in her nature. Pardon me; it is no fault in any character."

The girls all insisted that Mr. Battison should

consent to have his hand examined, and Mr. Daleham urged him to accede to the general wish.   Mr.
Battison said he would first go and see how Miriam
was, and try to bring her down again.   Whilst
Mr. Battison was out of the room Mr. Daleham
looked once more at Jemima's hand, and remarked
with pleasure that the way in which the line
of the head sloped towards the mount of the moon
indicated that some rare good luck was in store for her,
and then whispered that he could have said a good
deal more about Miriam's hand if—but here Mr.
Battison and Miriam re-entered the room.   Mr. Battison
drew his chair towards Mr. Daleham, and demon-
stratively, to prove his fearlessness, extended his hand.
Mr. Daleham looked at it for some time, and then said,
" I am simply amazed !   This hand is written all over
with wonderful things.   I may say at once, and without
flattery, that it is a splendid type of what we call the
spatulate hand.   The owner of this hand has made his
own way in the world, or I am sadly mistaken.   Why,
Mr. Battison, from the way in which the line of the
heart passes round the forefinger like a ring, and ends
on the inside like a beard of wheat, I do not hesitate
to say that if you had turned your mind to the most
difficult of the sciences, you would have made your mark
in the world."

" Oh, father ! " all the girls exclaimed in chorus.

" These two branches in the line of the wrist point
to a distinguished and honoured old age."   Mr. Daleham here suggested a little change in the evening's
" amusements "—he said he would not use a more serious

term—by endeavouring to read character simply by
feeling the hand, and in order to make the experiment
real, and to divest it of all suspicion, he would put out
the light and take hold of each hand in perfect darkness. The company must stand quite near him, no sign
of identity must be given, and each person must shake
hands with him, just as would be done in ordinary
circumstances. Mr. Daleham thought that all character
revealed itself in one way and another through the hand,
and now, as he had several members of one family
to deal with, he was anxious to put his theory to the
test. He would speak frankly, so let no one be offended.
The advantage would be that no one would know of
which sister he was speaking ; yet afterwards they
might compare notes, and let him know how far he had
been correct. Mr. Battison entered into this proposition
with great spirit, though he was of opinion that his own
character had been so well described already, that the
darkness would not help Mr. Daleham to go much
farther in clearing it. However, he was willing to do
anything to please "the girls," so if they wished it,
Mr. Daleham might make what arrangements he pleased.
Mr. Battison added that if he had known how interesting an evening they were going to have, he would
have asked several neighbours to come in, but perhaps
Mr. Daleham would give them another opportunity,
and he, for his part, would be quite willing to have his
hand read all over again. The light was now extinguished, and the hand-shaking began. Passing over
the details of the criticism, it is only necessary to quote
one illustration of its surprising accuracy. " This

hand," said Mr. Daleham, "is unlike all the others: even by my touch I can feel that the mount of Saturn and the mount of Venus are of extraordinary size; the owner of this hand ought to be possessed of extraordinary beauty, not of a personal or formal kind, but of an intellectual sort; this is unquestionably a chip of the old block; her children will rise up to call her blessed, and her husband will be honoured in the gate of the city; the grasp is soft yet firm, signifying the union of great affectionateness and independence of judgment and will, the touch has about it an artistic refinement, whilst the length of the fingers indicates a distinct faculty for ordinary daily avocations." Mr. Daleham gently pressed the hand, and raised it to his lips.

"Now may I," he asked, when the light was put on, "ask how far my reading has at all touched the facts of the case?"

"Wonderful!" was the general comment.

"Most astonishing!" was old Mr. Battison's particular criticism.

Mr. Daleham was gazed at with admiring eyes, a process which did not at all disturb his equanimity, which was secured by the consciousness that under favourable circumstances he would have been one of the foremost men of the day as certainly as he was the most distinguished man in the poky old village of Midtown. If ever Midtown became famous, it would be through Mr. Daleham, either, as he cautiously put it, directly or indirectly.

"Now there is one thing," said old Mr. Battison,

" which I should really like to know, and that is, which of you has the hand last—— "

" No, no, no," was the general exclamation.

" May I venture to guess ? " the old gentleman inquired. But he was put down by a shout.

Mr. Battison felt so young and fresh after the very pleasant exercises of the evening that he volunteered to walk part of the way home with Mr. Daleham, and Mr. Daleham accepted the offer with evident pleasure. He said he would really enjoy the opportunity of speaking a little further with Mr. Daleham, as he was deeply interested in the subject of hand-reading, which, measuring every subject by his own boundless ignorance, was the most wonderful thing he ever heard of.

" I tell you what," said he to Mr. Daleham, almost as soon as they were out of the house; " I have a suspicion that one of my daughters, or perhaps our respected pastor, must have given you an outline of my eventful career—— "

" Not a soul," said Daleham, " ever gave me the faintest shadow of a hint."

" Then it is most miraculous," said Mr. Battison; " it is supernatural; you never said a truer thing in your life when you said I had made my own way in the world; you hit the nail exactly upon the head, so much so that I fully expected you to enter into particulars—— "

" Are the particulars very remarkable, Mr. Battison ? "

" Just about as remarkable as anything you ever

heard since you came into existence; I was saying only the other day that if my life was written, nobody would believe it."

"No stranger, you mean."

"Yes, of course, no stranger; even my own friends would think I was exaggerating."

"There you wrong yourself, Mr. Battison; your word is as good as gold; no man in Midtown is more deeply respected."

"I am proud to hear you say so, Mr. Daleham, because you have opportunities of knowing. My object throughout life has been to do things on the square, and I am bound to say I have been wonderfully prospered. Of course, as you know, we have only been in Midtown about fifteen years, and the battle was over long before that. It was a battle, too!"

Mr. Daleham was meditating. Perhaps he was purposely giving the old gentleman space for speech, for nobody ever knew exactly what Daleham was doing. People might know that he was spinning a rope, but they could never say for whose neck it was intended. Daleham knew the art of self-concealment. Of that art Mr. Battison knew nothing.

"How my first fourpence was turned into sevenpence was marvellous."

"Indeed?"

"Most marvellous. You would simply laugh at me if I told you."

"Laugh with you, Mr. Battison; not laugh at you."

" Well, the laugh would come in somehow. What do you think of a horse-shoe ? "

"A horse-shoe ? "

" Exactly. You may well wonder. I knew you would. I told you so."

" But really——"

" Yes, just so. I was not always the Battison you now see. I had to eat my brown bread in my youth, and wait for my plum cake."

" This is very confiding on your part, Mr. Battison, and most kind."

" I knew I could surprise you. I have often wished for this opportunity. I am a child of Providence——"

"Sort of foundling," the innocent Daleham suggested.

" Exactly. Here I am. No deception about me. People say to me, 'Where is the proof of your religion ?' and pointing to my breast, I say, ' Here it is, and come on again if you like.' " The old gentleman was becoming excited ; hence the faultiness of his concluding observation, both as to its logic and its sentiment. His meaning was that he himself was an actual proof of his own religion, and that further questions might be put without offence. He was not using pugilistic language consciously.

" Mr. Battison," said Mr. Daleham, in a solemn tone, " you have confided in me ; may I venture to confide in you ? "

" With all my heart ! Whatever you say to me will sink to the bottom of the sea, and not a soul ever hear a word of it."

"Mr. Battison, I ask you to believe me when I say that I am in trouble."

Mr. Daleham turned away his head significantly and pathetically.

"My dear friend," Mr. Battison answered—"do let me call you by that name—let me know all you care to tell me. I have been in trouble myself before to-day, and I know the value of a friend."

Mr. Daleham could not speak for a moment or two. There was a delicateness in his method which was skilfully regulated, and a pause which was meant to tempt the old man's talkativeness. Mr. Battison was always of opinion that consolation depended upon the fluency of the consoler, and he acted upon that judgment with notable fidelity. On this occasion, however, even Mr. Battison's fluency was kept in check by his ignorance, for he had no idea whether Mr. Daleham was in the agony of love, in the bitterness of family affliction, or in the humiliation of poverty. It could not be the last, if appearances were to be trusted.

"Mr. Battison, my trouble will surprise you. To all appearance I am a most prosperous man. I cannot afford to change appearances and create suspicion. I am bound to keep up a good surface, but I tell you, in reply to your confiding affection, that a loan of fifty pounds would take a load off my heart."

Nothing easier. Mr. Battison would consider himself honoured by being allowed to relieve Mr. Daleham's mind, and it should be done to-morrow on the simple security of a note of hand. Certainly. No other answer was possible to a Christian man. So said old Mr. Battison, and in saying it he was conscientious, and not the less so that his vanity was subtly flattered.

"I am overpowered, dear friend," said Daleham. "I really think we might name this corner Providence Angle. The best of good-nights to you."

On returning home, Mr. Battison met Weaver Stephen, who simply said—"There is that is destroyed for want of judgment."

CHAPTER VIII.

IN a very few days the Vicar returned the five chapters which I had lent him, and sent with them a letter from which I must give some extracts. Before giving the extracts, I must express my sorrow that poor White-man is not unlikely to lose his sight. I am deeply grieved. I know that there are men in the Baptist Church who will love him even the more for his infirmity, and on no account listen to any sugges-tion about his resigning the pastorate ; at the same time, what can compensate for life-long darkness, life-long night ? I was quite touched by his pathetic cheerfulness as he referred to the subject, and, of course, I did not venture to dwell upon the deprivations which must follow blindness ; on the contrary, I may have spoken too hopefully about the case, and allowed benevolence to talk rather than conscience. Say what we may in fine abstractions, when we come face to face with deadly sorrows our sympathy often narrowly escapes a kind of falsehood, due to the exaggeration of pity or of love. To tell a man that he is dying may be to bring him good news, but to warn him that he is soon to be a prisoner of darkness, to see no more of sun, or flower, or kindly face, or book lettered with wisdom, may be impossible to some natures. A man can prepare for death; he can hardly prepare for blindness. If ever man was prepared for this, perhaps the heaviest of bodily afflictions, Whiteman is prepared for it. I envy him the stores of his knowledge, and I envy his extraordinary memory of form and colour, enabling him as it does to recall scenery, images, pictures, and faces in a way which to a blank memory like mine is simply astounding. Mr. Robson told me yesterday that as long as Mr. Whiteman could walk up the pulpit stairs he would never be permitted to give up his position. "We should all be blind together," Mr. Robson added, "if we lost so deep a teacher of religious truth." I told him how glad I was to hear this, because in the case of a minister blindness might easily mean poverty; ministers have no claims upon church property; unlike business men, they are not building up a valuable goodwill which has a market price, and amongst Dissenters, if a man cannot preach, he may consider his work and his income at an end. Mr. Robson admitted all this, and admitted the hardship of it, " but," said he, " I should be criminally ungrateful if I did not myself undertake to provide for Mr. Whiteman; his influence over my life has been unspeakably precious; his conversations have been quite equal to his public discourses, and as for his prayers at the family altar, they have brought down heaven to earth." Under the influence of Mr. Robson's noble testimony, I could not but feel that a Nonconformity so inspired may have yet a profoundly useful work to do in the Christian education of England; on the other hand, a Nonconformity

lacking that inspiration, whatever may be its controversial force, cannot lay permanent hold on the best
affections of the best men in the country.   Nonconformity should balance its argument by its beneficence.
The Established Church has a right to judge not only
of the logic, but of the usefulness of Nonconformity, and
to put the point-blank inquiry, " If you remove me, what
do you propose to put in my place ? "   Perhaps I have
written the last few lines under the unconscious influence of the Vicar's notes.   Here they are :—

" I don't know when I have enjoyed myself so much
as in the perusal of your papers, owing principally to
the fact that they refer to persons with whom I am in
a sense so familiar, and of whom in another sense it
appears I have had no knowledge whatever.   I could
not have thought it possible that people whom I have
treated with the most civil offhandedness as ordinary
fellow-townsmen are persons of quite parliamentary
importance in the Dissenting world.   I have looked
upon most of them as decent and orderly townsfolk, but
it never occurred to me that after shop-hours they
could expand into such dignity and influence.   I almost
reproach myself for want of sense in not discovering
their immense, perhaps I ought to say immeasurable,
importance.   But I certainly did not discover it.   Let me
tell you, in the same friendly spirit as that in which
you have referred to myself, that the reading of your
notes makes me thank God more fervently than ever
that I am a Churchman, and a minister of the good old

Church of England. The kind of hubbub you live in would simply drive me mad ; I should be in a delirious fever certainly in a month. If you have given anything like a fair picture of Dissenting life—and I fear you have —I am deeply grateful that I live on the other side of creation. What speechy and spouty people Dissenters must be ! You always seem to be haranguing one another from an invisible platform, and to be expecting somebody to contradict and anger you. Why are you so combative ? I admit that there is a kind of cleverness among you, but if I may speak frankly, it is of a very crude and rasping quality, the sort of cleverness that is always getting into scrapes by cheekiness and getting out of them by impudence. Dissenting cleverness lacks finish, not blacking-brush polish, put on from the outside, but the sort of bloom which expresses an inner healthiness and does credit to a sunny climate. Do you know that your own English would be the better for a run through the Balliol mill ? I do heartily wish you could have a five years' spell of Balliol ! Pray do not regard me as a specimen of Balliol, because when I was there I was more of a sportsman than a student, but give my word the benefit of being an almost independent testimony to the effect that a man can get in Oxford what he can get nowhere else in the world. I cannot describe in adequate words what it is that he gets, but there is no mistaking its quality. We have clergymen in the Church of England who have come from Nonconformist communions, but I assure you that not one of them was ever mistaken for an Oxford man : they are clever enough, especially at a

rough-and-ready kind of public speaking—a thing on
which I set less and less value the older I grow—but
they carry signs which cannot be mistaken, roughnesses
all the rougher that they are mixed up with a kind of
pedantic propriety that is always wondering what
impression it is making.   One can always feel that
they are trying to talk faultless grammar, and that they
are very thankful when they get to the end of a sentence
without violating some rule in syntax " (here I thought
much of Tomlinson), "but, as I have just said, there
is no mistaking them, and the finer their talk the more
distinct is the mark of (pardon me) the Dissenting
beast. Take the man Paterson, whom you so approvingly
describe.   The honesty of that man, though beyond all
question, is of the very coarsest grain, the sort that
would be immensely popular with a mob of uneducated
and half-educated people.   A man like your friend
Paterson (whom I hope to know some day, if you will
introduce me) could not stand his ground for an hour
against such a reasoner as Barnett, of Balliol.   Paterson
would think Barnett a wriggler and a Jesuit, and why ?
Simply because Barnett sees a thousand things bearing
upon an argument which would never occur to a straight-
line mind like Paterson's,—an honest, shop-keeping
mind, I say again and again, but without a touch of
philosophic genius and grasp.   If a foreman carpenter
talked to me in Paterson's style, I should admire the
bluff honesty of the man and pay him his wages without
grudging, but no Balliol man could drive his argument
over such rough pavement.   Barnett will splinter every
word until he gets its clearest meaning, and urge his

way into the deepest metaphysics to lay hold of a starting point, and when he has ceased to cross-examine
you it will be no fault of his if you have kept a secret
from him. Will you join me in trying to bring about a
meeting between Barnett and Paterson, at the Vicarage?
Paterson will find himself in a new world, and for that
matter so will Barnett. Remember, Barnett is not the
man to rush into a conversation; we shall have to inveigle
him by starting a discussion outside of him, so to say,
and leave him to come in just where he pleases. For a
few minutes he may seem to be dead asleep, but he is
never so dangerous as when he appears to be unconscious. By the way, I like Professor Stokoe as you
describe him. In respect of his impetuosity in telling
news he might have been dear old Watson, of Balliol.
The likeness is simply perfect. I remember on one
occasion we had just started a collect in the Morning
Prayer when Watson broke in—'Excuse me,—Jacobson
has been nominated Dean of Beecham. I might forget
if I did not name it now,' and the collect was resumed.
There is one question about Professor Stokoe which I
must ask. You describe him as Professor of Natural
Philosophy; surely you do not mean me to infer that you
have a Dissenting system of Natural Philosophy? Do let
us have a national philosophy if we cannot have a national
religion. What do Dissenters want—I mean Dissenters as such—with the study of Natural Philosophy?
This inquiry puzzles me. We may presently be hearing of Dissenting Greek and Nonconformist mathema-
tics and English grammar authorised to be spoken in
chapel by chapel people. Old Knockey has been quite

too much for me. I have always looked upon him much as Bidwell evidently did, though without so broadly suspecting his honesty, and have always treated him as a man who would like to do a little mischief if he could do it on the sly. What you say about the dog is farcically true ; it is the stupidest animal in the town, and always on hand at the post office. Let me tell you that your friend Whiteman will have no farther trouble with the letter-carrier who used to be second tenor at the parish church, for he has got an appointment as check-taker at the Boalham Colliery, and will probably never return to Midtown. But I am wearying you. Pray be ready about two o'clock to-morrow, and I will drive you to Mixford, as we agreed." This memorandum was signed " Very sincerely yours, Lambert Gray."

Whilst I was perusing the Rev. Lambert Gray's friendly communication, which showed him to be more deeply in earnest on church questions than I had hastily supposed, an interview was taking place in the business part of the town which it may be important to make a note of.

" It is perfectly clear to my mind," said Mr. Thomson, the chemist, "that protoplasm was first formed at the bottom of the sea."

" I agree with you absolutely," said Daleham, " and I go farther. I say, Give me the origin of water, and you give me the history of the universe."

" Possibly;" Thomson slowly added, " When you return the last number but one of the *Scientific Review* I will look that up. I see a glimmering of it now,—given, fiery vapour, continual radiation, the reduction, by cooling, of the fiery vapour to a molten fluid, more radiation and consequently more cooling, and in due time you come to a solid crust; then the steam in the atmosphere would be condensed and fall as rain,—and there you are! But do return the *Review* punctually."

" Rely on that," said Daleham, with cheerful disregard of what he was saying. " Have you given much attention to the physical and chemical properties of carbon? I have a notion, you know, that carbon has something to do with the very secret of life."

The subject might have been more deeply inquired into had not Mr. Thomson exclaimed—" Of all living men, here is Tomlinson." He was right. Tomlinson knew Daleham as a very clever man, able to advise under difficult circumstances, and not unlikely to sympathise with the bold proposition to throw up Dissent and spend some time in looking round for a new religious standpoint. Daleham knew Tomlinson as the pastor of a family he had frequently visited, and at whose table he had often met Tomlinson. Tomlinson was fervent; Daleham was cool.

" I was just about to say when you came in sight," Daleham remarked, " that the carbon now imprisoned in coal mines——"

" Bother it!" said Tomlinson. " I have come to consult you on another subject, so if you can give me half an hour, I will talk matters over with you and take your opinion. Mr. Thomson will excuse you——"

" Before you go, Mr. Tomlinson," said the chemist, who was not sorry to get rid of Daleham—Thomson was eccentric; Daleham was designing—" there is one

question you may be able to answer; I have often
called the attention of my pastor to it——"

"Your *pastor!*" Tomlinson interrupted, with vindictive bitterness.

"If Ruth was the wife of the elder brother
Mahlon——"

"Bother it!" said Tomlinson, reduced to one form
of deprecation. "I have jacked it all up; I don't care
a button whose wife Ruth was."

Away by themselves, Tomlinson said—

"The fact is, Mr. Daleham, I am in a good deal
of trouble, and I want you to show me the way out
of it if you can, and if you can, I know you will."

"Make your mind perfectly certain upon that point,
Mr. Tomlinson. What I can do is as good as already
done. Let us walk."

The two men went rapidly along Golden Lane, and,
having got into the Abbey Fields, they fell into a
leisurely pace.

"I want to leave the Dissenters,and to enter the
Established Church, but there is a serious obstacle in
the road."

"Confidentially, what may that be, Mr. Tomlinson?"

"I will tell you. I began life as a very Paterson of
a Dissenter."

"I remember."

"Very good. That is fact number one. That fact
got me into the good graces of old Miss Beebee, of the
Green Hollows——"

"The richest old lady in the parish."

"One of the richest, certainly, Mr. Daleham, and a most bigoted Nonconformist. The Church of England is her pet aversion. She would never listen to a preacher who wore a pulpit robe, or go to a chapel where there was an organ; in short, she hated the Establishment with a perfectly irrational animosity."

"Well?"

"Miss Beebee taking a fancy to me as a Dissenter' (here Mr. Daleham threw a stone at a robin) "of her own type, and not having a relation in the whole world, has made her will in my favour, and the property amounts to not less than five-and-twenty thousand pounds" (Mr. Daleham put his arm through Mr. Tomlinson's, and said, "Speak softly; we can never tell who's behind the hedges"). "Well, the old lady must never know that I have any leaning towards the Church, or she would change the will in a moment, and cut me off absolutely——"

"Confidentially, Mr. Tomlinson, who has possession of the will?"

"The will is in my own possession, Mr. Daleham, so that in the event of Miss Beebee's decease, I simply go in and administer——"

"And her present health?"

"Her present health is good, but her age is advanced."

"You think, in short, that she may drop off any moment?"

"Exactly. Or she may linger a year or two. Now here is my position. The property is left to me by a

Dissenter, and because I am a Dissenter, and if I cease to be a Dissenter, the property will be forfeited, yet all my leanings are towards the Church ; the vulgarity of deacons I can no longer stand, and, Mr. Daleham, pardon me, the ministers are even vulgarer than the deacons."

" But, Mr. Tomlinson, what can you expect from a gang of converted carpenters ? Can the Ethiopian change his skin ? I put it to you."

"Just so. They are a narrow-minded lot, and I must have done with them."

" The sooner the better," said Daleham, scarcely disguising the *double entendre*.

" Yes ; the sooner the better, no doubt," Tomlinson replied. " I agree with you, but what about the will ? I am bound to be practical."

" So you are, Mr. Tomlinson, so you are. But there is a way through every gate or over it ; mark the alternative, through it or over it." .

Mr. Tomlinson remarked strongly upon the stubbornness of aged ladies who associated the disposal of property with the adoption of principles, and contended that in the very act of denouncing the endowment of religion they did the very thing they denounced. His mind was not particularly clear upon the point, so his language was wanting in variety and colour, yet it was evident that he wished by some process of jugglery to counterbalance his own scruples by an objection to the unreasoning obstinacy of Miss Beebee. Men do sometimes seek to relieve subjective pressure by objective criticism, but the process is full of risk to the claims of integrity. Mr. Daleham proceeded cautiously and advised Mr. Tomlinson to be extremely circumspect, a piece of counsel which greatly enlarged Mr. Tomlinson's faith in Mr. Daleham's judgment. Rashness would have been fatal to Daleham's policy.

"Be extremely circumspect," he said, "extremely so."

" Precisely, Mr. Daleham. You carry me completely along with you. Not a soul knows what Miss Beebee has done for me. I have kept a close mouth. When I have heard Paterson ranting about his principles I have seen how destitute he was of political wisdom, and how blind to the main chance. But what can you expect of a man with a foot as long as a canoe and a hand of the colour of mahogany ? His hands betray his origin."

"Ah! you believe in the character being shown by the hand ? "

"By such a hand as Paterson's, anyhow. That man is essentially vulgar, and his vulgarity is of course the explanation of his rudeness. I hope, however, you do not misunderstand me when I remark on his want of political wisdom, or suppose that I have in any way induced Miss Beebee to think of me in her will. She has acted entirely on her own responsibility—entirely— without suggestion or prejudice."

"Of course," said Mr. Daleham, "that is thoroughly understood. At the same time, Mr. Tomlinson, you and I must thoroughly understand one another if I am to be of any service to you. I may tell you that I see clearly how I can act with effect in the matter ; but I must have your confidence, all the more so that where

so large a sum is in question it may be worth my while
to give up my whole time to it, in short make a
business of it, make a success of it."

Mr. Tomlinson did not answer immediately.　To
make a business of it was of course to make a living
of it.　Mr. Daleham noted the silence, and mentally
accounted for it without making a mistake.

"It is clear," said he, easily resuming the conversation, "that the will was made in your favour on the one
ground of your Nonconformity?"

"That is absolutely certain."

"Very good; as you said before, that is fact number
one.　Your conscience now permits you, I will not say
urges you, to abandon Nonconformity——"

"Yes, simply on the ground that its vulgarity is
intolerable."

"Simply on the ground that its vulgarity is intolerable; just so; that may be called the social aspect; but
you could not use that argument in talking to Miss
Beebee, because it implicates her own refinement,—you
see that, don't you?　Very well; then be careful as to
its use.　You claim the right to change your mind as
light increases——"

"Certainly; a living man may change his mind."

"Yes; and a living woman may change her will, and
drop you."

"The very point," said Tomlinson.

"The very point," echoed Daleham, "and a sharp
point it is."

The two men had now come to the white stile in the
Abbey Fields, and there they stood a moment or two

in silence.   Mr. Tomlinson's legs really did seem short
as he stood there, and his face looked shiny rather than
radiant as he turned his eyes towards the town.   As
the heir to twenty-five thousand pounds, Mr. Tomlinson
was not without a sense of self-importance, a kind of
landlord feeling, a sort of squirely consciousness making
its way through the fading memories of clerical humiliation.

"If you had the money," said Daleham, "you might
build a house just here."

Tomlinson smiled feebly, and admitted the eligibility
of the site.

"But jesting apart," said Daleham, "you will excuse
me, I am sure, Mr. Tomlinson, if on my side I bring a
little conscience to bear upon the matter, for I want to
be fair all round.   I admit your right to change your
mind, and I cannot deny Miss Beebee's right to change
hers : Now can I, as a man of honour, know that you
have altered your ecclesiastical standpoint, and allow
Miss Beebee to keep alive a will she would not have
made but for the conviction that your Nonconformity
is as obstinate as her own ? "

Mr. Tomlinson sharply demanded what he meant by
the inquiry.

"Pardon me," said Daleham, "nothing is to be gained
by excitement.   I speak as a man of honour, or, if you
like, as a man of the world, and I want to act con-
scientiously and justly in a very critical case."

"I don't want you to interfere in it at all," said Tomlinson in a new tone.

"Pardon me," Mr. Daleham replied, "there is an

implied sequence in business affairs—a sort of unex-
pressed logic—if you change a man's knowledge, you
change his responsibilities; half an hour ago I knew
nothing of this case, but now I know that you want my
assistance to bring about an issue which may bring my
honour into question, and therefore I wish to know
what is right and what is wrong. I can quite conceive
that Miss Beebee herself might desire to consult me
upon the whole subject. A rumour may reach her that
your Nonconformity has become modified; I might be
at the Green Hollows at the very time; I might be
asked to give an opinion; and my one anxiety is simply
to act as a man of honour."

It had not occurred to Mr. Tomlinson, great as was
his political wisdom, that Miss Beebee might consult
Mr. Daleham, but now that the idea had been suggested,
Mr. Tomlinson was so overcome that he sat down on
the white stile and drew up his feet entirely out of sight.
Mr. Daleham walked leisurely round the globular figure,
pausing to take in a good view of the back and to
express his emotions by facial signs. Mr. Daleham
simply wished to know his duty.

"Remember," said Mr. Tomlinson, "you are already
pledged to my side."

"Certainly, Mr. Tomlinson, in the matter of sympathy;
of course I am : but you miss my point. In the event
of my being asked to give an opinion upon the other
side, am I to act as if I knew nothing ?"

"You can say that you have already taken up a
position."

"But if I am asked whether it is right to take up a

position without hearing both sides of the question, what answer am I to return ?"

Mr. Tomlinson was silent.

"You see," Mr. Daleham continued, "I am bound to look at questions of this kind as a man of honour and a man of the world. You have been elaborately trained for the pulpit, and of necessity you have had next to no experience in practical matters; in fact, to speak quite candidly, my feeling is that if you had the five-and-twenty thousand to-morrow, you would not know what to do with it; you see, your mind is necessarily under a strong spiritual influence, and is, if I may so say, steeped in theology——"

Mr. Tomlinson threw out his little legs, and turned himself impatiently.

"Whereas I am a man of the world——"

"I always thought you were a man of science," said Tomlinson.

"Incidentally I am," Daleham replied; "but of course a man cannot live upon science. We must eat to live, and to earn bread we must work at something, or plan something, or in some way set the machine going."

Two men were seen coming as from the Acomb road, and until they passed it was desirable to suspend the conversation. Mr. Daleham aimed a stone at another robin, quite in a playful way; and Mr. Tomlinson stretched himself out of his sitting attitude. As the men approached they were recognised.

"Good-morning, Mr. Whiteman," said Daleham; "and, Knockey, good-morning."

"Good-morning; fine morning," was answered, and the men passed.

Mr. Knockey had lent Mr. Whiteman an arm, and was apparently guiding his steps into the levellest part of the path, which led Daleham presently to remark that Whiteman's eyes seemed to be getting worse, and that no doubt somebody paid old Knockey for playing the part of blind man's dog.

"Well, then," said Daleham, as he and Tomlinson walked on, "there is a clear understanding between us. I appreciate your confidence, and promise to respect it ; not a word by way of initiative will pass my lips ; I am as silent as the grave until a question is put to me ; but when a question is put, I must consider what answer I am to make as a man of honour."

This reiteration of the words "a man of honour" quite nettled Mr. Tomlinson. It was a little too much to hear them over and over again, especially as Mr. Tomlinson did not remember ever to have heard any one else apply them to the same person. But he must now hold his tongue as with a bridle, or this man of honour might by some miracle in casuistry transfer his sympathy and confidence to the other side. He so far resembled Barnett of Balliol, as to see more points than one in any subject that came under the attention of his scientific mind. Mr. Tomlinson had allowed himself to be mastered by one idea and to be pushed in one direction, and was now sorely in need of an alternative. It is true that a very severe analysis of his motives might have revealed the active presence of personal vanity ; on the other hand, reproaches will be modified

by the recollection that it must be extremely difficult
to have any intimate relations to so respectable a sum
as five-and-twenty thousand pounds and to go up and
down the world in a spirit of self-oblivion. In estimating
human conduct some allowance must always be made
for circumstances of which we may be ignorant, so we
will not be too hard upon Mr. Tomlinson, even though he
did allow himself to be driven headlong by one despotic
idea.

"A way of escape occurs to me," said Daleham, "a
wide, open way."

"Then why don't you name it?" said Tomlinson,
testily.

"Instead of giving up Nonconformity in general,
give up Congregationalism in particular, and go over
to the Baptists."

"Pshaw! she hates the Baptist crew; she calls
them Dissenting Ritualists."

"For the Baptists myself," said Daleham, "I have
no particular respect. They are a squat lot of people,
about five feet seven high, broad in the back, famous
tea-drinkers, and stupid bigots."

As the two men returned they went over the argument, as in the first instance, without much enlarging it,
the understanding being, however, that strict silence
was to be preserved until they met again. Tomlinson
admitted that he ought to have had something more
definite to put before Daleham for an opinion upon,
and Daleham hoped that Tomlinson would not consider
him unreasonably sensitive in the matter of personal
honour, his one desire being to turn everything into

7

fuel, except his conscience, in the interests of a progressive mind. So the matter was to stand. Tomlinson was much obliged ; Daleham was highly honoured. Tomlinson was sorry to have troubled him ; Daleham considered it no trouble to be consulted in great matters. Once more here is the town. Once more here is Weaver Stephen.

" Well, Stephen, what is the text for the day ? " said Daleham.

And Stephen answered—"The earth also is defiled under the inhabitants thereof, because they have transgressed the laws, changed the ordinance, broken the everlasting covenant."

CHAPTER IX.

COBBLER ROBERTS was an imitator; Weaver Stephen was an original. When Stephen quoted the Scriptures he seemed to do so by right, and to embody their meaning in his voice and eyes. Under the influence of some prophetic passage Stephen was for the moment transfigured and invested with an authority which his social position could not have claimed. Is it not true that great authors lift up their sympathetic readers to their own level, and that inspiration proves itself by inspiring even the poorest men who apprehend its meaning? The apprehension of its meaning is no merely intellectual effort; it is the answer of spirit to spirit; it is the masonry of eternal friendship. In this sense Weaver Stephen was a deep Biblical scholar; "never having learned letters," he yet quoted the Bible as if quoting his native tongue. Hence his wonderful influence in the sick-chamber; hence his welcome to the house of sorrow; hence, too, his disagreeableness to lovers of darkness rather than light. I am not ashamed to say that Weaver Stephen's sudden and unexpected application of many a passage has helped me more in my ministry than many a book that affected to illuminate the Bible; and his simple trust, proved by

simple obedience, has often assisted in the establishment of my confidence.   Hardly in any other instance
have I seen a finer illustration of the solemn words—
"If any man love me, I will manifest myself unto him."
Many a mocker who has affected to jeer at Stephen has
been secretly afraid of him, knowing that he carried a
tremendous sword, and that he was never afraid to
wield it.   Daleham hated Stephen, for Stephen never
prophesied good of him ; and Stephen despised Daleham, for Daleham was a man of tricks and shifts, a
schemer and a charlatan.

When I went to the Vicarage a little before the
appointed time, I found the Vicar occupied by an unexpected engagement, so I elected to look well over the
Abbey Church whilst waiting for him.   It was the kind
of church that had never heard the word "Dissent."   I
have noticed that even Episcopal churches built within
the Dissenting era hardly escape a kind of Dissenting
appearance.   I know they are real "churches," and
really consecrated, and have real priests in their pulpits,
yet the very mortar has an odour of democracy, and
the steeple has a twist in it that must have been made
by Dissenting bricklayers.   Do what we may, churches
have now a chapelly look, and chapels have a churchy
ambition.   The Abbey Church of Midtown knew nothing
of the ecclesiastical small-pox called Dissent.   It was
the gift of Norman times.   Its light and lofty arches,
springing from massive pillars, tall and clustered ; its
almost romantic altar on the north side of the choir ;
its carved oak stalls, so richly canopied ; and its innumerable effigies of illustrious men, combined to

invest the sacred place with deep and tender solemnity. If my study was poor compared with the Vicar's library, how much poorer was my chapel compared with the Abbey Church! The Independent Chapel in Midtown ought to be very religious if it is to exist within sight of so hoary a pile. Pillars it has none, nor arches, nor effigies, though it has one little slab behind its wine-glass pulpit, sacred to the memory of an honoured deacon, and another in the porch in memory of "a sturdy Nonconformist who suffered the spoiling of his goods rather than tamper with his conscience." I own that this slab in the porch touches any heroic vein that may be concealed in my nature, and enables me to stand straight up even in the presence of vicars who were trained at Balliol. The chapel is poor, no doubt, yet it is a comma in the punctuation of a history not wanting in dauntlessness, in sacrifice, or in holy tragedy.

This is the side to look at when we are suddenly faced with the supposed humiliations of Dissent. It is quite true that many of our chapels are poor, but they are our own. It is true, too, that many of them are in out-of-the-way places, but who is to be credited with their obscurity? As I thought of the time when Non-conformity was under some circumstances punishable with death, when hundreds of the most conscientious ministers were silenced, imprisoned, and excommuni-cated; as I thought of them in the swamps of Holland and the wilds of America, and recalled the dismal days when men could only pray together in darkness and whispering, the dismal days of Corporation Acts, Con-venticle Acts, Five Mile Acts, and Toleration Acts;

when I remembered that fine, and imprisonment, and torture, and murder, could not quench the inspiration of Liberty and Faith, I could look the old church in the face and thank God for my forefathers. Only those who are ignorant of English history can be ashamed of the badge of Nonconformity.

"Here we are," said the Vicar, wheeling suddenly up to the transept entrance at the south end. "Jump up beside me, and I will easily do the six miles within the hour." When he had safely cleared the Vicarage gates he continued, "Will you be warm enough with that thin coat on? Let me turn back and get a rough one for you and a pair of driving gloves. Why don't you come over to the Church, and get some warmer clothes to your back?"

I resisted the proposal to turn round, and whispered, "Conscience."

"Conscience?" said the cheery Vicar. "I told you before to bring your conscience with you—steady, mare!—a good conscience has no objection to a good coat—wo, mare, steady—I do think that every honest man has a right to a warm coat."

"But can a Dissenter be an honest man?" I slily inquired.

"Exactly," said the Vicar—"wo, mare—I have admitted too much—come, come, steady—I see;—just so;—now I think of it, I see that my charity has run away with my judgment. By the way, that reminds me, you don't make out old Knockey to be a pattern card—eh?"

"That reminds me," said I, "of what I ought to have

said when I sent you the little manuscript. You are too wise a man to push my sketches into meanings which I never intended them to bear. Do not for a moment suppose that I was laying before you a complete picture of Dissenting life in Midtown, or doing anything more than showing you an etching of one aspect of it. If you have ever attempted anything of the kind yourself——"

The Vicar lay back and laughed at the droll idea.

"You will know how much more tempting is the comical than the commonplace side of life. If we saw a man with two heads on this road, we would say more about him than about a man with one. To give a complete view of Dissenting life even in this little town would require the portrayal of some of the loveliest characters I have ever known, I think I may say some of the loveliest characters I have ever imagined."

"Mostly women, your people, are they not?"

"Nothing of the kind. No finer men can be found in the world."

"Thought they were mostly maidservants."

"The result of ignorance," said I. "Still if we and our people were the poor creatures we are supposed to be, we should hardly fail to remember that not many mighty, not many noble, are called; you know the rest."

"Anyway, Knockey is a man," said the Vicar, giving me a significant nudge.

We laughed. The mare was now nicely outside the town, and the Vicar insisted upon getting down,

opening the box behind, and wrapping my lower
extremities in a thick woollen rug. Whilst we were
standing there who should pass by but Weaver Stephen.

"Well, Stephen, what have you to say?" I inquired.

"What can I have to say, sir, but one thing?"

"And what is that, Stephen?"

"'Behold, how good and pleasant it is for brethren to
dwell together in unity; it is like the precious oint-
ment——'"

"So it is," said the Vicar, as he tucked the rug
round himself; "good-day. Is that one of your
men?" the Vicar inquired after a moment.

"Yes; a born prophet; a weak kind of man everywhere outside the Bible, but a very strong man, and a
very tender man, inside it."

"Now," said the Vicar, "as soon as I pass Eastfield
I always light a cigar, and as it happens you are on
the right side to escape the smoke, I need not ask
permission. I wish you could taste a cigar as I do;
it is the simplest and perhaps the cheapest of all
luxuries—though I am not sure about the cheapness—
and just look at that thin blue cloud. I declare it makes
quite a little sky by itself—wo, mare—I might be a
Dissenter without tobacco, but never with it. Morning!" (to a carrier driving into Midtown). "This is a
busy road now, since the Boalham Colliery was opened.
Now I should think a colliery would be the sort of
place for Dissent; am I at all right?"

"Possibly," said I; "Paterson was telling me——"

"Paterson?" the Vicar interrupted; "I am rather
anxious to see that man."

"He was telling me," I continued, "that some of the Boalham pitmen come over to Mixford Chapel on Sunday evenings."

"Shouldn't wonder," said the Vicar; "he has the bluffness they can admire."

"Paterson is a very fine fellow in his own way," I remarked, "a most self-denying man; his income is not a hundred a year, but no man ever heard him complain, or knew him play the sneak."

"He handled the stout little fellow rather roughly, did he not?"

"You mean Tomlinson, who wants to give up Non-conformity and join you?"

"Yes. Paterson was quite right, though, in implying that we do not want that sort of man in the Church; he seems to think we will welcome him with open arms, and sing a *Te Deum* over his conversion. Nothing of the kind. The Church can do better without him than with him."

We were now within sight of Broxham Grange, and could see something of Mixford, lying a little way beyond. The Vicar understood that I was to go on to Mixford, where I might possibly spend the night, but at all events I would not ride back with him. It was arranged that I was to be introduced to Sir Hedley Baker simply as the Vicar's friend, and that I was to hold my tongue upon all matters which exasperated the baronet. I was to treat him as a man suffering under many vexations, and to humour some of his eccentricities rather than oppose him. The Vicar assured me that Sir Hedley was a man of remarkable

attainments, and that but for local circumstances of an
irritating kind, to which the baronet could not fail to
advert, he was about the gentlest and humanest creature in the whole county. "A very spirited old fellow,
though, mind you, and has seen the day when he
needed no friends but his own fists." I was curious to
make my first acquaintance with a baronet of so long
and good standing, and glad to stand just so much on
one side as to escape the responsibility of leading or
colouring the conversation. The atmosphere would be
new to me, and very likely I should learn something.
I am bound to admit that every man, every public man
especially, is the better for being shaken out of his
nest, and thrown into relations both novel and trying,
and is all the wiser and stronger for hearing other
people express their independent and ruling opinions.
"You should have heard Barnett of Balliol and Sir
Hedley talk, when circumstances were different, if you
wanted an illustration of 'diamond cut diamond,' but
now the baronet is suffering from a sort of monomania.
Wo, mare. Here we are."

A glance showed me that Sir Hedley was no common
man. There was something in his handsome outline
and impressive manner which marked him as a fine
old English gentleman. His voice, too, so round and
complete in every tone, asserted its owner's right to
command as well as advise. The greeting of the
friends was genuinely hearty, and my introduction
was recognised by the kind old baronet with more than
ordinary politeness. No Dissenter had ever received

me with so fine a grace. By a very rapid mental process I compared Sir Hedley and Titus Knockey, and wondered if it was possible that the same Providence was responsible for them both. In a moment more I wondered how I should act with such a man as Sir Hedley as one of my deacons. In another moment I wondered if Sir Hedley suspected my connection with the Dissenting ministry. So the Dissenter always carries his chapel with him, and looks upon creation through a vestry window. Meanwhile the Vicar and the baronet were chatting about personal circumstances of which I knew nothing, and I was ostensibly admiring Broxham Grange and its lovely surroundings. Presently Sir Hedley turned upon me, and shaking his staff at things in general in the southwest, he said in an excited tone—

"That fellow, sir, is an impertinent scoundrel."

"I am a stranger, Sir Hedley," said I ; "who is the person you mean ?"

The baronet could hardly refrain from smiling as he became conscious that he was addressing an absolute stranger, but the smile was of the faintest kind. It was rather the grin of anger.

"Follow the line of my staff," said he, "and tell me what you see ?"

"Do you mean through the opening of the trees, Sir Hedley ?"

"Certainly."

"I see what looks like a new house, and men working on the roof."

"You are right, sir ; that unwieldy, disproportionate,

staring dog-kennel" (I started here, but kept my peace)
" is hateful to me."

" Who is the owner of it ? " I meekly inquired.

" Ask the mud under your feet, ask the mushrooms,
ask the worms, but don't ask me ; don't ask any
descendant of the Franvilles."

I was, perhaps, shamefully unacquainted with the
Franvilles, though I can honestly say that I bore none
of them any ill-will. Though they did not sit under
my ministry, it is quite possible that they may have
been respectably connected, and able to form intelligent
opinions upon general subjects. As the Vicar had
occasion to go to the stables to find a parcel in the
dog-cart (I am not sure as to the exact designation of
the curricle), I was thrown upon the baronet for what
appeared to be quite a considerable number of minutes,
which would have been burdensome to me but for his
ability and willingness to keep up a vigorous mono-
logue.

" Talk of gentlemen ! " said he, though I had neither
thought nor talked of anything of the kind ; " I tell you,
sir, no patent can be taken out for the manufacture of
gentlemen ; you cannot put in rags at one end of a
machine and take them out at the other in the form of
aristocracy ; rattling money in your pocket does not
make you gentlemen : money cannot turn mushrooms
into oaks ; money, sir, is a ladder, not a tree."

As we came upon a full view of the Grange, I
expressed admiration.

" Feast your eyes upon it, and it will do them good
after looking at yonder infernal brick-kiln. I'll give a

thousand pounds to any charity in the county for every red brick you can find in Broxham Grange ; and more than that—now be careful ; your eyes are younger than mine—find me any stucco there, and I'll forfeit ten sovereigns for every square inch." To show that this was a *bonâ fide* offer the worthy baronet waved his staff in the face of heaven.

"But," said I, with most culpable ignorance, and with my usual ill-luck in impromptu speech, "are not bricks as old as stone ? "

The baronet plunged his staff into the spongy sward, and looking over it, he glared at me, but quickly subduing his contempt, he said—"A brick is a manu-facture, and manufactures are insidiously impairing the dignity of the nation. · The difference between a gen-tleman and an upstart is the difference between a rock and a brick. Keep bricks out of sight, use them for inferior purposes, but to put up a brick building yonder, sir, is not only to disfigure the landscape, but to insult the traditions of my family." After this speech I saw in imagination at least five hundred Franvilles turn over in their leaden coffins.

"I asked a very foolish question, I admit, Sir Hedley."

"Never mind," said he, putting his arm through mine in a friendly way ; "my challenge is not done yet : find me anything *but* bricks and stucco in yonder villainous cart-shed, built with money probably made by pawn-broking or bird-stuffing, and I will build a church at my own expense, or a cathedral if you like, or a minster."

Smarting under the recollection of my unfortunate

remark about the antiquity of bricks, I looked steadfastly and admiringly at the Grange.

"Only a fragment of what it was, a mere fragment.
When Rogerus de Franville, the favourite of the first
Henry, lived here, it was at least three times its present
size."

"Indeed!" said I, with a compression which I felt
to be painful, and even this I said with the timidity of
a man who was tempted to speak a foreign tongue.

"Yes, sir, a fine fellow was Beauclerk, scholar as
well as king. The tradition runs that he and Maud
spent part of their honeymoon here."

The Vicar returned just as Sir Hedley said, " Egad,
sir, if anybody had attempted to build a red-brick
house yonder in those days, his neck would have
suffered for it."

"Speaking about the Grange?" said the Vicar.

"I am. Every stone in this building is historical.
I can prove by authentic documents that in the reign of
Henry II.—and you know well enough that Henry II.
did not reign yesterday—this place gave opposition to
William of Scotland ; and in the fourteenth year of
King John, Roger de Franville gave up this very
Grange—Broxham Grange—and his four sons, great
stalwart fellows they were, brought up to digest steel
and powder ; can any pawnbroking, soap-boiling—
pshaw !" and so the hot sentence was left unfinished.

Something within me rose against all this in strong
resentment, and modified my first good impression of
the baronet. I saw that even pedigrees and properties

might become part of as pitiable a cant as was ever
charged upon the peculiarities of Dissent, and that the
main difference between some classes was that the
one talked nonsense downstairs and the other talked
nonsense two storeys higher up, but the quality of the
nonsense was just the same, and the intellectual capaci-
ties of the talkers were about equal. I had no wish to
dim by so much as one pale ray the ancient glory of
this handful of old stones, or to disturb the comfort
accruing to the baronet's mind from the legend that
Henry Beauclerk spent part of his royal honeymoon
at the Grange ; yet, with all my timidity, I was strongly
tempted to charge upon the vain old man after the
fashion of a fearless Roundhead, and shatter his
temporal security by some message from the eternal
spheres. I was certainly beginning to feel much less
uncomfortable as a Dissenter, and to feel also that
Dissent is essential to the balance of power, or the
social equipoise, in any country inhabited by a considerable number of Sir Hedley Bakers. Thus in-
ternally I was a bold hero, but outwardly a humble
visitor.

"Some fine old faces there," said the Vicar to me,
pointing to a long line of grotesque but expressive
portraits; "no signpost-painting."

I admitted the unmistakable antiquity of the whole
series.

"Look at that rich old painting in the corner," said
Sir Hedley ; "be deliberate, if you please ; you cannot
read all that is there in one glance."

"Who is it ? " said I.

"What does that matter?" was the answer. "Does a king need a label round his neck? Say it is Mr. A. B., and instantly you say it is impossible. Your instincts rise against the plebeian suggestion. I want you to fix your mind upon the richness and force of character you see in every feature, and in the countenance as a whole. Why, sir, the blood of many royal generations seems to me to be in that compressed and ardent face. Were I to tell you that it is the portrait of a retired pawnbroker, you would justly accuse me of having lost my head. Were I to say this is the head of a gentleman who sold small wares in a country town, and made money enough to build himself a red-brick barn on the edge of an ancient estate, you would feel at once that the very canvas was giving me the lie. That is not a dough face, sir, put together and scooped out by a talented baker, and you know it. I am never tired of looking at the magnificent lion-like face of a king-maker."

"It is a rugged and noble face," said I, preferring a statement to an inquiry.

"The face of Sir Roger Franville, raised to the earl-dom by King Edward II. immediately after the battle of Borough Bridge; then there is Franville Franville, son of the Earl; and so you come on from soldier to soldier, and from statesman to statesman, until you reach this point," indicating the same with his staff. "Now, sir, look at that face and tell me where you will match it to-day? There's an eye! There's a head! There's a mouth perfect in loveliness! And notice that right hand particularly—take time to it—why, sir, there is more refinement of character in any finger of that hand, than there is in the whole guild of manufacturers. I tell you I am proud when I look at that sweet face."

"May I ask whose face it is, Sir Hedley?" forgetting the danger of interrogation.

"I was just going to tell you. You must pardon the digressiveness of an old man who has been put on his mettle by an adventurer in bricks. At this point the male line of the Franvilles became extinct. This brilliant creature with the celestial face is Alianora Franville, who married Sir Hedley Baker, the tenth baronet, of Broxham, and you may infer the rest."

A period of agreeable silence followed this splutter of ancestral vanity, which gave me time to look meditatively at a few other pictures. The baronet aired himself at the door, with his head, as I thought, a little inclined towards the quarter which gave him all his trouble. I was right in my impression, for on coming towards him the baronet remarked :—

"You observe the position of affairs most distressingly from this point. Just between the parallel of plane trees we shall have a full view of his two stacks of chimneys ; from these chimneys there will of course be smoke—manufacturers' smoke, no doubt—black, suffocating smoke ; when my county friends ask me, as most naturally they will, where that smoke comes from, what answer am I to make?"

"I should just tell the plain truth," said I, with Dissenting bluffness.

"And pray what is the truth, sir? You answer me

8

very curtly, but a moment's reflection will show that
you answer more curtly than wisely. Who can say
what the truth really is in such a case? Who can
tell the painful history of this man's money? Who
knows whether it is his own, or borrowed capital?
And supposing it is his own, who can tell how long it
may be his? These fellows get into fine flare-up
carriages one day, and go through the bankruptcy
court the next; they come from nothing, and go back
to nothing; and in their passage to and fro they
give infinite annoyance to the old families of the
country."

I suggested that perhaps some good influence might
be brought to bear upon the man who was putting
up the building, and that practical men might be able
to abate the nuisance arising from the nearness of
the chimneys. I knew that I had nothing definite
to propose, yet I wanted to move in the direction of
concession and harmony, and to bring Sir Hedley's
better nature into play.

"Now," said I, in a tone not so morally strong as
it ought to have been, "could not some clergyman
mediate in such a case? Could not the Vicar of
Mixford bring you together to some extent?" (then
looking at Mr. Gray) "the clergy have great influence
with all classes, and can often interpose without giving
offence."

"Well, sir," the baronet replied, "under ordinary
circumstances your view would have been correct.
I admit that. If you will not misunderstand me, I
will say that such a view would have occurred to

almost anybody. But the circumstances are pre-
posterously extraordinary. Let me tell you, to your
amazement perhaps, that this retired pawnbroker, if he
ever was anything so respectable, has not an ounce of
religion in body or soul! Now what do you say?"

"That gives a new complexion to the case, I
admit."

"I should think you do admit," said the baronet,
with a slur of scorn; "the fellow is a Dissenter;
now what becomes of your easy plan? The fellow
never enters a church; the fellow has no more fear
of God before his eyes than that painted beagle has;
if ever, which God forbid, you have anything to do
with Dissenters" (the Vicar turned right round to
admire the beagle so suddenly brought into the
conversation) "you will find that a more pig-headed
set of half-washed ignoramuses never attempted to
upset the throne of England. I do not hesitate to
describe them as atheists of the very worst type.
Without wishing to use strong language respecting
them, I may say that if you want to send this country
to the devil, you have only to encourage the spread
of Dissent."

And this raving, bouncing baronet was one of the
"gentlemen" of England! This was the kind of
critic that blended Dissent and atheism, and accounted
them as equivalent terms! This was the furious
assailant of principles avowed by Bunyan and Defoe,
Owen and Howe, Milton and Locke! In my heart I
knew he was a fool, and in my heart I despised alike
his fury and his grandeur.

It will not be wondered at that in every way consistent with courtesy I brought my visit to a close, and hastened to Paterson's house at Mixford to keep an appointment I had made with him. The Vicar accompanied me to the Grange gate, and by his marvellously comical expression of face as he bade me good-bye did more to give me his confidence and make a friend of me than could have been done by eager protestations and studied hospitalities. Surely, after all, it is good for a man to know exactly what other men think of him and his most serious convictions, and good to have another window knocked through the blank wall of his self-enclosure, even with some suddenness and violence, if through the opening he can be made to see something of the real size and colour of things. When I hear that a nice family has taken a pew in my chapel, and that two working men have taken shilling sittings in the gallery, I mentally conclude that Nonconformity is making rapid strides, and that Independency is a chosen instrument in the hands of Providence for working out the regeneration of the land. Six feet more Nonconformist pewing let at five shillings a quarter! The act is full of promise for Dissent and full of hope for the devoted young carpenters who are called to make their living by the ministry. But one visit to Broxham Grange showed me that the habitations of the wicked are full of cruelty—towards what they regard as amateur parsondom and private church theatricals.

CHAPTER X.

N the brick-built town of Mixford there is one long ill-paved street with several small and worse-paved streets branching off it, in one of which inferior streets lived Mr. Paterson, the Independent minister, in a house probably rented at fifteen pounds per annum. A room in front, a room behind, and two rooms to match above, with a tiny kitchen gloomily looking upon a brick-paved yard, about seven feet square, constituted the limited habitation of this devoted champion of Nonconformity, whose vigorous denunciations of the National Church were vehemently applauded by the Dissenters who starved him. My friend, the gentlest of brave creatures, was a widower, under fifty years of age, whose small domestic establishment was ably directed by Janet Snow, as faithful and capable a servant as ever breathed. Janet had been with Mr. Paterson ever since he settled in the ministry; had attended Mrs. Paterson in her last illness; had been all but a mother to the sweet little baby who went to heaven before the life-clock struck three; and, in short, Janet had become part and parcel of the Paterson household. To hear Paterson upon the great question of Dissent, you would suppose that he was the most violent and despotic of men, a red-handed revolutionist, and a very desperado. His controversial epithets were forged in the fire of his personal conscientiousness. He had no idea that he was using strong language when he denounced the clergy as dumb dogs that cannot bark, curates as mumbling puppies not fit to be at large by themselves, patrons as jobbers in the souls of men, and bishops as overfed old women who neither understood the spirit of the age nor grasped the purpose of the kingdom of heaven. All this was quite in harmony with my friend's conception of Christian charity. His murder was all in his words. To do him justice, his exaggeration was not confined to his aversions; it expanded all his partialities, and magnified every kindness that was shown to him into an unparalleled act of generosity. This very spirit, so faulty from a merely literal point of view, enabled him to look gratefully upon his inadequate income, and to wonder how the people could afford to give him so much. Janet did not form the same estimate of the people, and although she might through long association have become affected by her pastor's use of strong language, yet there was a solid basis of truth under all her unfavourable criticism. As I waited several hours for Paterson's return from a great Nonconformist uproar, created under the pleasing form of a demonstration, I had an opportunity of hearing what an honest woman had to say about chapel morals in general. If her style halted here and there, through want of logical connection, there was no break in the consistency of her meaning, nor did her energy suffer in consequence of her grammar.

" And him going about in a coat like a looking-glass, so shiny in the back, and me afeared to brush it, as it might come to pieces in my hand."

" Perhaps, Janet," said I, " the people cannot afford to do any more."

" The people be broiled!" said Janet; " there's that little chubby-faced painter of a deeking who calls himself Mr. Robinson—though what right he has to be mistered I could never tell—has had two topcoats since March was a twelvemonth, and his bouncing wife has had a sealskin jacket and a velvet mantle in the same time, and there they sit as smug as two fat rat-catchers, and a-staring at him, when they might see that his waistcoat buttons have had their heads brushed off. And they call theirselves deekings and officers, and all such fine names."

" The deacons," said I, " are expected to look after the pastor."

" And so they may do," said Janet, " but they take care to let him get out of sight first. Look after him ! my patience ! It would be a bad job for him if nobody looked after him better. There's that pimple-faced cripple, always a-going about swing-swang up and down the aisle a-twisting his gold chain, and a-shaking hands wi' people as can ask him to tea; he says to me, ' Janet, how's our dear pastor to-day ?' and says I to myself, ' He's about the cheapest bit of furniture there is in this dirty brick chapel, and it would be better for you to part wi' that gold chain and buy him a new hat wi' the money, than stand chattering there.' "

"But some of the people are kind, Janet.   I know Mr. Paterson thinks so."

"Aye, aye, that's true.   But who are they?" Janet stood back, and waited.

"Of course I don't know their names."

"But I do," said Janet.   "There's old Betty Black, as brought him two pocket-handkerchiefs of her own hemming, as could ill afford it, I know ; and there's old Billy Freshwood, as killed a pig a week since, and brought three black-puddings and two pounds of spare-rib; and there's old Cobbler Swinburne, and nothing would keep him back from making his minister a present of a pair of thick boots, as I must say he was never measured for them, and if he was a young man, his feet might grow into them, but the cobbler's kind-ness was all the same for that ; and more one may say, for he needn't have put so much leather into them, and they lace up the front, and when they're on they look rather nice with the brass lace-holes."

"Well, then," said I, "there's a bright side to the picture as well as a dark one."

"Aye, aye; had need be.   Only mole rats can always live in the dark.   I don't say there's not a bright side ; but who makes it ?   Not that Robinson, as calls himself Mister, though I see him every day going up and down a ladder wi' a paint-pot in his hand, and a-beckin' and a-bowin' to all the church people as he thinks he can get a bit o' house-paintin' from, and then coming to chapel, and blowin' himself out over a hymn-book as big as a cushion, and lookin' round as if he never saw a paint-pot, and his wife sitting there with gold spectacles on, and fluffing herself up and down like a sack o' feathers. Never a thing do they send to this house. But there's old Neddy Foster, the baker, never puts a spice loaf into the oven without putting in a little one for the minister; and he doesn't want to be mistered and fussed about, and people to think he's a foot higher nor anybody else. As for deekings, I wish they was all broiled in their own pre-spiration, or that they was sent for to the world of glorious immortality they are always a-ravin' about, and as they'll never get into, I do believe; leastways if they does, I don't want to."

"But, Janet," said I, in a pacifying tone, "the deacons may do favours you never hear of."

"Not they," said Janet; "he's not the man to keep good news from me. Lor' bless you, if anybody did him a kindness, he would run in just like a little child and tell me all about it, and say I must not think so hardly of the people, and all sorts of nonsense. But I am glad to say there's a man come to chapel now as is kinder to master nor anybody ever was as ever I knew, and I have known them all; and I do hope they won't make a deeking of him, 'cause the moment they make a deeking of a man he gets as uppy and cheeky as the mayor and corporation, and so bounceable as you can neither hold him nor bind him."

"And who is this wonderful man, Janet?"

"Aye, he is a wonderful man. I don't see why he should not be called a wonderful man. He's building a fine house beside old Dandy Baker's, and rare goings-on they have up there. I expect to hear o' bloodshed

soon, and we may all be burned in our beds for anything I know, and all through building a comfortable
house on land as he's bought and paid for, and a kinder
man I never set eyes upon.   He gave master two
sovereigns for himself the very first time he ever came
to chapel ; and only last night, when Mr. Paterson told
him we was expecting a visitor to-day, which is you
yourself, sir, he sent in as tender-looking a chicken
and as nice a bit of cheek-bacon as ever I had through
my fingers, and the man you saw going away from the
door as you came up the street had just been sent by
that same gentleman with a bushel of potatoes.   We're
in luck."

" Splendid, Janet, splendid.   Mr. Paterson has
another friend living in this very town whose name
you've not mentioned yet."

" Not that I know of," said Janet.

" Shall I name that friend myself, Janet ? "

" Aye, if you can."

" Her name is a short one, a cool one, a pat one; it
is Janet Snow."

Janet laughed a little.   " Aye, aye, sir, maybe; I
won't deny it, and me been wi' him twenty years come
Midsummer, and me nursed her in her last illness and
promised her never to leave him, and kissed her bonny
brow when it was colder than ice, and " (Janet was
stopped by tears) " promised her to take care of the
baby, and held the baby to her to be kissed when she
couldn't move a finger.   O my God ! but it makes my
heart sore to think on't."

And mine was sore, too.   The world is full of heart-

break, and it seems as if some of the heart-break might
have been spared. Why did the young wife die ?
Her baby would have been heaven enough for her for
many a year ; why was she not permitted to enjoy it
in her own sweet and simple fashion ? The great
heaven beyond the stars might have done without her,
for it is full of angels; her little home-world could
ill spare her, and she herself longed to stay. Who
would have been harmed by her staying ? Who
begrudged her room ? Who was the worse for the
mouthful of bread she ate ? But these questions are
naked swords, and we cannot wisely handle them.

"That's where it is, you see, sir," Janet presently
resumed, "as l feel it so much, and as I speak agin'
the deekings ; they might have put up a bit of a head-
stone for the poor young thing, and never missed the
money, and not have left him to pinch himself to pay
off the five pound a bit at a time, and nothing on the
stone but plain letters as a child going to school might
read ; and other stones in the churchyard have draw-
ings on them, and figures and birds, and ours has
nothing." (Janet paused.) "And master used to be
very fond of drawing on paper what he would like to
have cut out on the stone, and he asked me which I
liked best, and we found we could not afford it, and
the deekings never lent a helping hand——   ·

"And then " (resuming) "our little baby was taken
from us—died in my lap—used to call me Ja-Ja and
creep about after me like a little angel. And oh !
the house has never been the same since, nor has the

minister ; and I did think they might have carved just
one little angel on the stone. So we opened the grave
again and laid baby on her heart ; and I do think the
opening of that grave that day and standin' over it
made master ten years older all in a moment like.
Poor soul, he groaned when he looked in, and the tears
rained out of his eyes when he heard the little coffin
touch the big one. And as for me, I was no more use
than a crazy thing——"

Unconscious Janet, how little she knew that she was
ripping open my own heart. I, too, have an eternal
vision. Amid all the whirl and dizziness of life's
tragedy, in which creation seems to be but one great
cloud, I find myself suddenly brought to a sweet baby's
grave. A grey old church, a gurgling stream, a far-
spreading thorn tree on a green hillock, and a grave
on the sunny southerly side. That is it. Thither
I hasten night and day, and in patting the soft grass l·
feel as if conveying some sense of love to the little
sleeper far down. Do not reason with me about it ; let
the wild heart, in sweet delirium of love, have all its
own way. Baby was but two years old when, like a
dewdrop, he went up to the warm sun, yet he left my
heart as I have seen ground left out of which a storm
had torn a great tree. We talk about the influence of
great thinkers, great speakers, and great writers, but
what about the little infant's power ? O child of my
heart ! no poet has been so poetical, no soldier so
victorious, no benefactor so kind, as thy tiny unconscious self. I feel thy soft kiss on my withered lips

just now, and would give all I have for one look of thy dreamy eyes. But I cannot have it. Yet God is love. Not dark doubt, not staggering argument, not subtle sophism, but child-death, especially where there is but one, makes me wonder and makes me cry in pain. Baby! baby! I could begin the world again without a loaf or a friend if I had but thee ; such a beginning, with all its hardship, would be welcome misery. I do not wonder that the grass is green and soft that covers that little grave, and that the summer birds sing their tenderest notes as they sit on the branches of that old hawthorn tree. My God! Father of mine, in the blue heavens, is not this the heaviest cross that can crush the weakness of man ? Yet that green grave, not three feet long, is to me a great estate, making me rich with wealth untold. I can pray there. There I meet the infant-angels ; there I see all the mothers whose spirits are above ; and there my heart says strange things in strange words,—Baby, I am coming, coming soon ! Do you know me ? Do you see me ? Do you look from sunny places down to this cold land of weariness ? O baby, sweet, sweet baby, I will try for your sake to be a better man ; I will be kind to other little babies, and tell them your name, and sometimes let them play with your toys ; but oh, baby, baby, my old heart sobs and breaks !

*   *   *   *   *

Poor Paterson! I never understood that part of his story so clearly before, though he and I have talked his life over again and again. But an outsider is always necessary to fill in the detail. Even Paterson did not know all that Janet knew, nor had he felt the neglect of the deacons as a woman only could feel it. Poverty, indifference, unappreciated labour, bereavement, agony that cannot be spoken, these are the dumb consonants ; we must wait—Lord, how long ?—for the insertion of the music-making vowels.

CHAPTER XI.

SOON posted Paterson upon all the points I wished to bring under his attention, not forgetting to give him the benefit of a few extracts from the Vicar's notes upon my first five chapters, and otherwise priming him in view of meeting the redoubtable Barnett of Balliol. When that meeting would come off nobody could tell; still it was before us with something of the definiteness of a threat, particularly as it conveyed the idea that Dissent would be simply stripped of every pretence to reason or piety. Paterson was quite ready for the fray there and then, having just returned from a "monster demonstration" in favour of free church principles, and left the Establishment without an argumentative leg to stand on. The demonstrators had cheered until they were hoarse, and waved their handkerchiefs for minutes together in the wildest delight. The bishops had been eloquently described as white-robed self-seekers (vehement cheering), the steeple-house had been described as the half-way inn on the road to Rome (tremendous applause), and the sale of livings had been denounced, with some indistinctness of meaning, as the " saturnalia of the pit " (vociferous cheering in round after round,

women waving their open parasols, and men throwing
up their hats in the air). The whole " demonstration "
gave immense encouragement to the Nonconformists,
and led them to think that it might have an important
influence upon " the Government of the day." Paterson
had been a leading speaker at the " demonstration," and
had produced a tremendous effect upon his own throat,
as was proved by a most rasping hoarseness. Paterson's
travelling expenses to the scene of tumult had come to
thirteen-and-sixpence, and after being examined how
he made them amount to so much, the organisers gave
him half a guinea and a vote of thanks. But nothing
could daunt the valiant Paterson. In no fanciful sense
was it true of my ardent friend that he counted not his
life dear unto him that he might magnify and promote
the truth. To himself every argument he used was
true, although to others his reasoning seemed occasionally to be richer in emphasis than in logic.
Paterson's emphasis was undoubtedly forcible.

After all that I had heard I was of course anxious to
see the builder who had made himself so obnoxious to
Sir Hedley, and Paterson was more than willing to
bring about an interview. In the morning we strolled
towards the scene of strife, and as we passed along we
could not but feel ourselves of considerable importance
in the universe, holding as we did the secret of Heaven
as to the true doctrine and polity of churches, and
enjoying a confidence which had been withheld from
the wise and prudent. The Dissenting mind is naturally
energetic, and yet is not wholly destitute of the restful-

ness which accompanies intelligent self-complacency.
We passed through the churchyard, pitying the living
more than the dead, and sighing tenderly over a grave
off whose green covering Paterson plucked the first
daisy of spring. Then we took the open road and
made straight for the building ground. From his
conversation I soon detected a similarity between
Mr. Butterworth and old Mr. Battison, particularly
when he gave me the assurance that if his life was
written exactly as it had happened, not a soul on earth
would believe a word of it. This conceit as to the
power to awaken universal scepticism and to be ad-
judged the very chief and prince of liars, I find to be
rather common amongst men who, having been born
in a kitchen, have gallantly struggled far enough
upstairs to be nothing less than a miracle in the view
of an excited imagination. The case of Mr. Butterworth was quite ordinary, notwithstanding his own
conception of its merits. Mr. Butterworth's notion of
making himself agreeable was to tell all he knew, and
to ask direct and inconvenient questions of other
people. A favourite pastime of his was to find out
whether he and the man he was at any moment
speaking to knew anybody in common, and Mr.
Butterworth had been struck with the number of
instances in which both parties had happened to
know the cousin of a man's aunt who, after lingering
through many diseases, had in a most extraordinary
manner escaped the doctors and proceeded to do
some remarkably stupid thing. Mr. Butterworth was
evidently blessed with a lion's digestion, as he never

9

had a headache in his life, and could not "for the life of him" make out why anybody should ever have a headache.

"I'm blessed, though," said he, "if I didn't very near have one when this crazy old party at the Grange first insulted me."

"Insulted you?"

"Yes. Insulted me within a stone's throw of my own door, but I fancy he won't do it again. I admit I did not spare him when my temper was up."

"How did it all come about?" I inquired.

"In the most innocent way in the world," Mr. Butterworth cheerfully replied, "as my minister here knows well enough, don't you, Mr. Paterson?"

"Yes."

"This bit of land was to be sold—bless my soul! there's less than two acres of it when all's said and done—so I bought it, and I'm building Providence Hermitage upon it, and one day seeing the old gentleman hobbling about, and wishing to act neighbour-like, and thinking it was nothing but what one gentleman ought to do to another, and feeling rather sorry for a man who must find time hanging very heavy on his hands, and who would be very glad, as I thought, to have a neighbour just over the hedge, I lifted my hat and slipped my card into his hand."

"Well?"

"Was there anything in that conduct to rouse a man's bad temper?"

"I cannot see that there was," said I.

"But it did, though. You never saw such a look

on a man's face in your life. If he had seen a ghost,
he could not have been whiter. What do you think
he did, and him calling himself a gentleman?"

"I really don't know."

"No, you don't know, and if you was to guess till
doomsday, you would never hit it. The moment he
caught sight of the card he looked about five-and-
twenty mile down the country, right away, and spoke
no more nor a gatepost."

"You surprise me." A man like Mr. Butterworth
is complimented by surprise.

"I'll surprise you more yet. If it had been a slip
of a visiting card, I would not have minded, because at
his time of life he might not have seen it, and he might
not have had his spectacles with him, but it was the
last new one brought out by my firm—I'm bound to
say a neat, smart thing—and there it was, 'Butterworth & Co., Agents, Factors, and Outlookers, Bank
Chambers, Edlingstone Street, Edlingstone Square,
E.C.' It was not a thing to be ashamed of. It told
its own tale in its own way."

"And how did the affair go on, Mr. Butterworth?"

Mr. Butterworth grimly laughed. "Go on, indeed!"
said he sarcastically; "why, when I saw how it took
him, says I to myself, 'This may end in a fit, perhaps
a fit of apoplexy, and then,' says I, 'who knows how
it may be brought in at the inquest if there is one?' so
says I, raising my hat again, and looking as pleasant
as I knew how, says I, 'Butterworth, of Providence
Hermitage, close,' says I, 'to Broxham Grange.' Could
I have been civiller?"

I was glad to be able to admit the entire absence of incivility.

"Looking full ten mile farther down the country, says he, 'Why do you intrude this upon me?'"

"Well?"

"I didn't like the word 'intrude,' I tell you; it has a sort of bitter taste, that word has, when one gentleman uses it to another even in the open air. 'But,' says I, 'let me give him a fair chance of showing that he is a gentleman,' so says I, 'By way of introduction, Sir Hedley.' I thought I would say 'Sir Hedley' that he might see I had not mistaken my man."

"Well?"

"'And pray,' says he, 'what do you mean by way of introduction?'

"'I mean just what I say, Sir Hedley,' for I felt a trifle nettled: a man who is building a house like this on a freehold site, and putting up a property which when furnished will represent five thousand pounds, may not be a baronet of the United Kingdom, but that's no reason why he should be treated like a dog."

Mr. Paterson and I warmly endorsed this broadly human sentiment. It is pleasant when a windy talker who undertakes to state a disputed case, in the conducting of which he has obviously played the fool, comes boldly down on a generous commonplace which can be adopted without reserve. Mr. Butterworth had done this favour for us, and we were grateful.

"What followed?" said we both, as if our interest had freshened a little.

"Says he, 'Do you suppose I am in want of the services of an agent?' 'Not at all, Sir Hedley,' says I. 'Or of a factor?' says he. 'Certainly not,' says I. 'Or of an outlooker?' says he. 'By no means,' says I; 'nothing at all in the way of business,' says I. Then he roared out, so that the workmen might have heard him—and I believe some of them did—'What do you mean by thrusting this villainous pasteboard into my hand?' Well, if you'll believe me, you might have knocked me over with a feather. I was took so by surprise. It was so unreasonable. It was so uncalled for. I daresay I was as white as a ghost. I seemed to feel myself white all over. But presently the old gentleman rather came to, and says he, 'What happens when the wind is in the south-west?' 'Come,' says I to myself, 'he's been joking all the time, so we'll give and take a little,' so says I, 'Well, I suppose, Sir Hedley, it blows to the north-east;' when I said that I thought the poor old creature would have gone stark mad on the spot, and he did storm away like an old steam engine, I can tell you."

"Can you at all account for this?" I inquired.

"Not for the life of me at first, but I can now. It seems that the last owner wanted to spite the baronet, and would not let him have this bit of land at any price. I don't know how they got to loggerheads, but there they were. I was innocent enough in the business. Not a word was said to me on either side, or I never would have got myself into this hornets' nest."

We walked over the house and admired its commodiousness and the tranquil beauty of the outlook.

Mr. Butterworth was not the less satisfied with the Hermitage that it was built exactly according to his own ideas. In place of ancient paintings; he had a number of modern notions, and where Sir Hedley had a statue in faultless marble, Mr. Butterworth would set up " one of the finest collections of curious walking sticks you ever saw in your life, sir, with carved monkeys, twisted snakes, and dogs' heads cut out of ivory." Mr. Butterworth nodded to us as he said this, intimating that probably he had struck us dumb with amazement. How was it that this man set my teeth on edge, and made me long for an hour with Sir Hedley, or the Vicar, or my own gurgling and sweet-minded Professor ? It is folly to talk about such a man being undervalued or snubbed merely on the ground that he was a tradesman. It was the spirit of the man, not the occupation of the man, that made a chasm between us. He lived in the fussy world of competitions, prices, commercial checkmatings, and barterings, which always gave him the advantage, so that one came to feel that he had made a complete valuation of the clothes we stood in, and had settled how much he would give for the hat if the conversation should end in its being offered for sale. I was wicked enough to wish that this man had been a Churchman, as I have sometimes been wicked enough to wish that some Christian professors had been infidels, as they would have adorned that side much better than the other. But Mr. Butterworth was no Churchman, and the more widely that fact was known the more was Mr. Butterworth gratified.

"You are a thorough Nonconformist, Mr. Butterworth?" said I.

"Bred and born," said he; "christened in an Independent chapel, scholar in an Independent Sunday-school, never went anywhere but to the Independent chapel, so I am a bit of sterling stuff."

"Did you never go to any parish church?"

"Me? Not for the world. Nothing will ever get me into such Popish places. I daresay, though, if I was a Churchman, I could get along better with this poor old creature over the way, but, bless your soul, the church people are the most ignorant set of men in the world; they know nothing about Dissent; they think Dissenters are infidels, and rowdies, and a sort of pickpockets; if they would come to chapel a few times, they would know better, but nothing can move them."

Mr. Butterworth said this with the jaunty confidence of ignorance, and with the air of a free-handed expositor who knew this subject so well as to render critical exactness wholly unnecessary. He represented the advantages of thorough mental independence, and showed the public in general how superior he was to all hide-bound and priest-ridden Churchmen.

"That's one reason why I like Mr. Paterson so much," said he; "he's not a shilly-shally Dissenter, trying to walk on both sides of the street at the same time, or giving you Church milk in a Dissenting jug. I like you best," he continued, nudging Paterson with easy approbation, "when you come down upon the bishops, and show 'em up as a lot of idle impostors." (Paterson turned away from this rough compliment.) "They are an ignorant lot, too, and a mincing lot, going about as if they was afraid of catching the measles by coming near a Dissenter. But we'll stir things up at Mixford, or I'll know the reason why. My missus, too, is just as clear-headed as I am."

As Paterson and I returned we fell into a very serious strain of talk. Paterson was really shocked and disgusted with the representation of his Dissent by the jocund and boisterous Butterworth. In denouncing the bishops himself he knew exactly what he meant, but when he was quoted by Butterworth he felt inclined to apologise to the bishops. Quotation, with an emphasis, is sometimes the most instructive criticism. The sermon is not always the same thing to the speaker and the hearer. Paterson was a genuinely good preacher, yearning over his congregation with real pastoral solicitude, and eagerly looking for the growth of the seed he had sown. We spoke of preaching as we returned. Paterson liked the sacred work more and more, and continually chastened himself by inquest into his spirit and motive. For my own part I liked him much better when he enlarged upon preaching than when he denounced Church establishments. Many a time as Paterson has given me his views of the pulpit I have wished that all aspirants to that eminence could have heard him. I am afraid I can but poorly report some of the things I have heard him utter, but I can never forget the impression they made upon me.

"What does the word 'preach' really mean?" he would say. "Does it mean to read a clever essay upon a text? When I read an essay, do I really trust God? Do I not magnify myself? On the other hand, when I do not read, do I not magnify myself still more? saying in effect, 'Look at me! I want no notes! I need no paper! I do not crawl, I do not walk, I do not even run; behold, I fly!' An awful impertinence it is for a man to preach unless divinely compelled to stand up that God may use him in the sanctuary. I have heard a man of many words and most aggravating fluency speak of firstlies and secondlies until these numerals made quite a jingle in the church. This is not dividing the word of truth; it is clipping it, pounding it, tearing it, and mangling it most cruelly. God does not want our rhetorical fineries. He stains the pride of all glory. The ships of Tyre were built of the fir trees of Senir, and the masts were taken from the cedars of Lebanon, their oars were made of the oaks of Bashan, and their benches of ivory brought out of the isles of Chittim, yet the Lord sank them in the depths of the seas."

"Oh, Paterson," said I, "talk to me in this strain whenever we meet, and let us forget the miserable controversies of the times. Talk to me about things eternal. People think you are always debating and quarrelling, and that you love to fight and to contradict. I wish they knew you better. I wish they could hear you pray."

CHAPTER XII.

I UNDERSTAND better than ever what Weaver Stephen means by life being too "numbersome" for him, for the whole parish seems to be on the alert in a sort of indefinable way; everybody expects everybody else to say or do some unusual thing, and everybody is looking at everybody else with an expression which means, "Well, when is it all coming off? to-day? to-morrow? soon?" What it is that has to come off, nobody knows; but if nothing comes off, everybody will be disappointed. Even old Knockey spoke to me the other day in a sympathetic tone respecting Mr. Whiteman's eyes, and said it was quite touching to see the minister groping his way through the service, and that many a time the whole gallery was in tears when the "dear man" desired the congregation to bear with his infirmity. Old Mr. Battison has, in compliance with the wish of Mr. Daleham, consented to have notes made of his truly wonderful career as a successful man of business, Mr. Daleham himself offering to go to Mr. Battison's house one night every week to take down the particulars of the astounding story. The Vicar has fixed a day for a meeting with Barnett of Balliol. My people are talking of having a congrega-

tional festival in commemoration of the exclusion of the
bishops from the House of Lords in 1642.   Altogether
things are very "numbersome" in Midtown, and history
is being rapidly made.   The most remarkable thing of all
within my own little circle is the change which has
come over Mr. Daleham.   He is not only more regular
in his chapel-going, but much more respectful in bearing,
and undoubtedly more sympathetic with the spirit and
aims of Nonconformity.   He came to me the other day
with a suggestion too novel to admit of being stated in
any terms but his own :—

"I have come to the conclusion," said Mr. Daleham,
"that the whole question of Dissent might be usefully
considered from a scientific point of view.   I am under
the impression that a new argument is possible, and
that by the aid of diagrams, plain and coloured, that
argument might be popularised on the largest scale.
The people cannot follow elaborate processes of abstract
reasoning.   You must engage their senses.   You must
touch their imagination.   In this direction I see no end
to possible usefulness.   For example, make a scientific
classification of the various sects, and get up a telling
diagram for each.   The pitcher plant of China, with its
pitcher full of fluid, might represent the Baptists ; the
pitcher plant of the East Indies, with its pitcher full
of black ants, might stand for the Antinomians ; the
Cryptogamic thallogens might do splendidly for the
Methodists ; whilst a diagram representing the multiple
stars would be the very thing for the Independents,
showing individuality and unity, a revolution round a
common centre of gravity, the lesser ones representing

say branch churches and mission stations, and so on, the details being easily picked up. Here you clearly utilise science, and promote the cause of Dissent."

"But how would you bring the thing to bear?" said I.

"Through a new society," was the reply; "originate a society with a sonorous and elastic name, collect funds, appoint an ornamental committee, make our friend Battison the treasurer, and if I can be of any use as secretary, I am always at command. There you have the thing."

"And the funds?" I remarked.

"No difficulty about funds. I have opened an indirect communication with Miss Beebee, of Green Hollows, and I have reason to hope that if I could lay a prospectus before her showing that the thing was more than a mere idea, she would not take a narrow view of the case."

I objected to the proposed illustrations as too grotesque, and therefore likely to lead to merriment rather than to conviction.

"Then you slightly misunderstand me," Daleham replied, "or I have imperfectly explained myself; the illustrations now proposed are not, of course, to be taken literally; they were intended to suggest to your mind a line of treatment, and not to lay down hard-and-fast lines. Of course 'a little nonsense now and then is relished by the wisest men,' so I do not propose to exclude the grotesque and comical, but to subordinate it to the real and the logical."

"That modifies the proposal, certainly," I admitted.

" By all means. It is due to science to have a serious basis, and, too, care must be taken not to offend religious prejudices ; at the same time, you know, I have an impression that even the Dissenting sects like to have an occasional laugh at each other's expense."

" Possibly," said I.

" Positively," said Daleham. " Take our old friend Battison ; you would not look upon him as a very dazzling luminary, yet even Battison has a quiet chuckle over the Quakers, and thinks the Methodists rather uneducated, and supposes the Baptists are an unusually dirty lot, to begin with, or they would be satisfied with less water. Battison plays the critic, I can assure you, when we are alone. Even Battison is human."

" Then, with regard to the proposed society, Mr. Daleham, what is your idea as to the payment of salaries, say, for example, the salary of the secretary ? "

" None at all," said he ; " the secretaryship must be honorary. At least, it must be honorary so far as the balance-sheet is concerned. That is to say, if any friend of the society wishes to recognise the labours of the secretary, the recognition must be spontaneous and private. The secretary must never condescend to bargain-making : if anything is offered, let him accept it ; if not, he must not degrade himself by grumbling."

" But a good deal of hard work may require to be done," I suggested.

"Certainly ; the more the better. Societies must justify their existence by their labours. But in a case like ours, what is to hinder one or two of Mr. Battison's daughters helping very considerably in the correspond-

ence department ?   They have time on their hands,
and they are fond of chapel."

" Do you think Mr. Battison would like that arrangement ? " I inquired.

" Proud as a peacock," said Daleham.   " Do you
know what I have undertaken to do ? "

" What is that ? "

" I have positively undertaken to take down notes of
old Bat's life ! "

" Does he recognise himself by that name ? " I asked.

" Playful,—playful,—I am prone to abbreviation,—
must avoid it,—yes,—but, seriously, I have undertaken
to act as biographer ! "

I merely remarked, " You must not overwork yourself."

" There's some danger of that, I'll admit," Daleham
replied, " but we get into things one ·after another
without exactly knowing how.   I never thought, however, that one of those things would be to defend my
minister, and that I have had to do lately, I can assure
you."

The innocent man smiles under such assurances, and
calmly awaits explanations.   Innocence is not half so
imaginative as guilt.

" The people cannot make out the meaning of your
riding with the Vicar on the Mixford road.   They
wonder if you are going over to the Church.   Cobbler
Roberts says you'll never catch Mr. Whiteman, his
minister, doing that, though he is turning blind.   Our
own old shoemaker, Peppers, says it all comes through
your not paying attention to unfulfilled prophecy.   As

for Thomson the chemist, his mind is so distracted about Ruth that I don't suppose he cares where you ride to. Our people cannot bear their minister to hob-nob with the Vicar as if their own company was not good enough for him. Old Pratt the baker said you would be getting tired of Dissenting ovens and calling out for Episcopalian bread."

I stopped Mr. Daleham at this point. There is one thing which I always beg my friends not to do for me. I can bear a good deal of criticism, and put up with a fair share of hardship, but when my friends tell me that they always stand up for me " through thick and thin," I cannot altogether keep down my anger. I know their meaning is good enough, but they do not see that such defence implies my need of it, and subtly suggests their own superiority. Besides, a man cannot help feeling that he acquires a kind of lien upon the person whom he is continually defending, and some day he may want to turn that lien to practical account. I have never crucified the pride that deprecates needless defence.

" I sympathise with your general sentiment," said Daleham, " but you must not forget that circumstances are occurring in our own district which go far to justify suspicions which but for them would be simply regarded as insane. I think you will admit that if a church steeple has been blown down, the same wind may have blown off a chapel roof?"

" Your meaning?"

"Tomlinson is my meaning. Tomlinson was once a kind of Beelzebub amongst Dissenters, and now

Tomlinson is making inquiries not remarkable for their Dissenting flavour. Tomlinson has taken my opinion as to the proper course to pursue, but as he did so in confidence, I am bound, as a man of honour, not to say more."

I gave Mr. Daleham to understand that although I was an Independent minister, I had made up my mind not to allow myself to be indecently criticised, and that therefore, come what might, I had resolved not to ignore social opportunities and relations beyond the four corners of the little Independent chapel. I noticed a distinct acerbity in my tone which surprised but did not displease me. One may easily forego certain rights by failing to assert them, and easily come to recognise the right of criticism on the part of persons whose impertinence is equal to their ignorance.

"I wish it to be known, Mr. Daleham, that even Independent ministers may think for themselves on such subjects, and that interference with their liberty of action is not regarded by them as one of the blessings of their lot. If you will regulate your conversation by this standard, I am willing to hear you ; but if not, I will venture to protect myself from your society."

But Mr. Daleham was irrepressible. For some reason he chose to accept my remarks in perfect good humour, as a man might accept with fine temper any remarks addressed to him on his way to the bank to receive an unexpected legacy of fifty thousand pounds. Good fortune is à capital lubricant, and it so far assists Christian culture as to enable its possessor to address many cheering counsels to other people. Good fortune will mollify any theology, although, alas! it may harden some theologians in their wickedness and make them cruel in their judgment of unsuccessful men.

As Mr. Daleham went towards old Mr. Battison's house he was in a decidedly rollicking humour, utterly unlike anything he had ever been to the public eye before, speaking to everybody, and broadly smiling upon the whole town, so much so that many worldly-minded neighbours surmised that Mr. Daleham's "ship must have come."

"I tell you what," said he to Mr. Thomson the chemist, "I feel as if I were on the point of making some great scientific discovery which will bring me fame and fortune. Remember," he continued, "that the good luck of some men may sleep a long time, but sooner or later the sun and air touch the vital ellipsoid, and out comes the harvest,—my dear Thomson, the golden harvest, the harvest that Ruth would have gleaned with pleasure."

"Come," said Thomson, pounding the mortar, "you know nothing about Ruth."

"Don't be jealous, Thomson; I have been inquiring for your sake, not for my own, about the Moabitish. woman, and upon my soul, Thomson, as a man of honour, my opinion is that Naomi was one too many for Boaz. But that's not what I ran across to say. I am just going down to old Bat's to fool him by writing an account of his rise and progress, his wonderful career and tranquil old age, and in a short time I am going to the Green Hollows to see the devoted Ruth of

Nonconformity, and make arrangements for something that will surprise you. Thomson, excuse any apparent incoherence in my speech, and remember, old fellow, that if ever you have offended me by word or deed, I forgive you."

"Stark mad," Thomson muttered to himself, as Daleham left the shop.

"What has he been talking about now?" said Mrs. Thomson, suddenly opening wide the room door that had been standing ajar, and appearing behind the counter with a loose-headed baby in her arms.

"Nothing, nothing."

"It's no use putting me off, Andrew. Daleham and you are always talking about Ruth, and you make out that it is Ruth in the Bible you are talking about, but I want to know what for you bother your head so much about a woman that's dead and gone. I wish some people would look a good deal nearer home." Mrs. Thomson, having said this, withdrew into the parlour and significantly shut the door. You can so shut a door as to give the person on the other side of it matter for rumination. But Mr. Thomson, as an innocent man, kept quietly to the pestle.

When Mr. Daleham arrived at Mr. Battison's house, he was not sorry to find that Nehemiah was not at home. All "the girls" were in, and so was Miriam, the married daughter. Mr. Daleham was received with cordiality, and was introduced to Miriam as "a very dangerous person, for do you know, sister, he can tell all about you by looking at your hand; he can indeed, and he can read your character by taking hold of your hand in the dark." Miriam was not excitable. Miriam was a wife, a mother, a person of experience. She merely looked at Mr. Daleham, and instinctively detested him. Mr. Daleham saw her look, and was shrewd enough to understand its meaning.

"What lovely children!" said Daleham, looking at Miriam's Nehemiah, aged five, and Miriam's Jemima, just turned three. "Won't you come and shake hands with me? Come along."

In response to this invitation, Jemima turned right round and gazed upon an engraving setting forth a church, a churchyard, a few grazing sheep, and a boy lazily watching them. There was mischief in the look of that large-eyed child, a mischief both in quantity and quality quite out of proportion to the tender age of three. As she backed upon Daleham, every line in the little figure expressed aversion and contempt. Nehemiah junior was of a baser type, and began his acquaintance with the stranger by pulling out Mr. Daleham's watch and demanding to have it opened so that he could see the wheels. Mr. Daleham pleasantly complied, and addressed the ladies through the medium of the impertinent little rip whose neck he could have wrung without a twinge of compunction.

"That's right, my little man; now blow, and see how the watch will open; now blow again, and see how it will shut: that's it; you are clever, and so is Jemima, only she is so shy; all the ladies are shy; but what could we do without them, eh? You would not like to do without Jemima, would you? No. No. Of course

you would not. I do wish she would speak to me. I
wish she would love me, for I am sure we could be good
friends. Now blow again, and away goes the watch
case—ha, ha !—that is clever ; now run to Jemima and
ask her to come, and if she won't come, ask if I may
take the watch over to her. Speak nicely and coax her."

"Come away, dear," said Aunt Jemima, but Niece
Jemima paid no heed.

"Me kick her," said Nehemiah, "and make her come."

"Oh, you savage boy ! " said Daleham ; " oh, you cruel
boy ! how dare you say so ? We may perhaps kiss
little girls, but we must not kick them. Oh, you shock-
ing boy ! You are quite a dreadful character ! "

"Me kick you, too," said Nehemiah, totally un-
softened by denunciation.

At this moment Nehemiah's mother happily appeared,
and on being informed of the barbarous spirit of her
son, astonished everybody, not less her sisters than Mr.
Daleham, by saying, "That's right, dear ; go and do it."
The whole company protested. Aunt Jemima stood in
front of Mr. Daleham to protect him from injury. Mr.
Daleham clung to Aunt Jemima to save himself. Meanwhile Nehemiah, nothing daunted, ran to his sister, put
his arms around her, and kissed her.

"That's what he means," said his mother ; " he always
says kick for kiss ; he cannot speak plainly yet, can he,
dear ? Come away, and kick mother," whereupon he
went, and hugged his proud mother with a will.

"Upon my word," said Daleham, "after this I will
pause a long time before I refuse to be kicked. Now,
Jemima, come and kick me as your brother has done ;

come away ; a penny for a kick "—Nehemiah junior
pricked up his ears at the mention of a penny, and ran
affectionately to Mr. Daleham, and jumping on his knee,
said he loved him very much, and wanted to blow the
watch open again—" here's the penny, Jemima ; come
and get it." Mr. Daleham ran after little Jemima, but
Nebuchadnezzar growled and so stopped the pursuit.
Little Jemima was as silent as she was mischievous-
looking, at least she was silent in Mr. Daleham's
presence, and she had the awkward habit of doing
mischief as if by accident and of looking upon the
result with large-eyed surprise. How could she of set
purpose have removed Mr. Daleham's chair just as he
was in the act of sitting down, and caused Mr. Daleham
to fall within an inch of Nebuchadnezzar's nose ? The
thing was impossible as a plan, so it must have occurred
by accident. It led, however, to a good deal of sharp
remark between Jemima senior and Jochebed, Jemima
contending that dogs should be kept outside, and
Jochebed retorting that even outside was too good a
place for dogs with two legs.

"I must say, Jemima, that the more I see of Mr.
Daleham the less I like him."

"That may be exactly what he is saying about you,"
Jemima coldly replied.

"I don't care for any sister of mine to be encouraging such a man," Jochebed pathetically remarked.

"What do you mean by 'such a man'? Explain
yourself."

"Time will show," was the only remark which Jochebed condescended to make.

CHAPTER XIII.

ARNETT of Balliol was, no doubt, a re-markable-looking man, conspicuous for the kind of ugliness which for the moment excludes all other thoughts, yet which mysteriously disappears under the intellectual action of conversation, and replaces itself by the kind of radiance which often silvers the roughest crags and headlands seen on the sea-shore. At seventy the old man was noticeable for bodily as well as mental vigour, and for a keen interest in all the changing aspects of the times, not at all the doubly old man who sighs over his yesterdays, but the venerably young man who believes that the brightest sunshine has all yet to come. The first glance as he came into the Vicarage library showed me that Barnett of Balliol belonged to the Church militant, and that under an undoubtedly pleasant exterior lay a whole armoury of weapons, offensive and defensive. He was withal an English-man to be proud of, because of an inborn dignity and a lofty graciousness which must have made an impres-sion upon the dullest observer. The moment he came into the room I felt I was a Dissenter, and that by no possibility could Barnett of Balliol have been one. No. I never knew any Dissenter of that pattern. I do not know what it was, but something separated him from us, and gave him a right to speak the first word in judgment. We could not have praised him without being conscious of impertinence, yet when he nodded to us we seemed to think that something unusually agreeable had occurred. I was quite touched with Paterson's get-up, the more so that my description of Barnett of Balliol had evidently put him upon his best behaviour. I knew at once that Paterson was a Dissenter. " The dissidence of Dissent" was written upon every seam of his too shiny broadcloth, the deep creases of which showed with what care Janet had been in the habit of folding her pastor's Sunday coat. I did not inquire into the matter too closely, but I believe the Dissenter, in his anxiety not to fall below the occasion, had thoughtfully applied a little pomatum to the stubble which he was pleased to call his hair—a personal attention which implied a subtle compliment to the Church on the one hand and a sense of what was due to Dissent on the other. Paterson's boots I did notice, and I am afraid they caught the wakeful attention of Barnett of Balliol. They were unmistakably Dissenting boots in every dimension known to magnitude, and in the motley character of Janet's blacking, yet with calm audacity, the result of blessed unconsciousness, they were displayed at full length upon the hearth-rug of the Vicarage library. Though Barnett of Balliol saw all this, yet in his smile there was no sneer. The man who had learned Tacitus by heart before he left his father's vicarage, who passed an examination in Juvenal the first day he came up to

Balliol, who read Lysias, Cicero, and Terence, by way
of incidental recreation, and who, from such beginnings,
went forward from honour to honour, until Barnett and
Balliol became almost interchangeable terms, was a
man of the world, a cleric, and "a fine old English
gentleman," much less likely to sneer at the rusticity of
agricultural Dissent than some shopkeepers who have
become too suddenly rich to continue their attendance at
chapel. Barnett of Balliol could shoe a horse or construe
the darkest passages of Euripides; he could light a
poor cotter's fire in the time of sickness, and give the old
man's pillow a shake, and then dispute with Thirlwall
the accuracy of the Bishop's translation of Niebuhr; in
the same summer he had gone holiday-making with all
his poorest parishioners, and filled up odd times by
turning into Greek the "Siege of Corinth," and into Latin
the "Bride of Abydos." What wonder if such a man
understood too well the practical side of life to sneer at
Paterson's boots, and yet knew too much of the philosophy of history to be satisfied with Paterson's Dissent?
Like every man in the class to which he intellectually
belonged, he saw too clearly the intricate relations of
things to be able to talk without punctuation, and on
that account, being unable to reduce the world to an
epigram, he was often characterised, by the ignorance
which is as unjust as it is unrestrained, as a shuffler and a
trimmer. When will the world learn the moral mystery
of distance, the difference between things near and far off,
and the need of telescopes as well as spectacles? Let
us hear the talk of Barnett of Balliol, and measure its
weight as against the assaults of Dissent.

" What I contend for," said Paterson, " is the right of the individual conscience."

Barnett of Balliol leaned slightly forward in the great arm-chair, and said—

" What is the individual conscience ? "

" The conscience of the individual," Paterson concisely replied.

The Vicar assented, and I turned in my chair to intimate that Paterson had scored one. But Barnett of Balliol continued—

" What is an individual ? "

We all murmured more or less distinctly that this was driving things too finely, because surely this was the kind of knowledge that is born with a man. But Barnett of Balliol calmly continued—

" There is no such thing as an individual, that is to say, a personality that is self-contained ; there is a personality *minus* or a personality *plus*, if you like ; but there is no personality of any other kind possible in society."

We took time to consider this, and after a moment's pause Paterson said—

" You will admit, I suppose, that what is mine is my own ? "

" Not at all," said Barnett of Balliol, " simply because it is impossible for anything to be yours. I deny the ownership."

" Barnett, what ever do you mean ? " said the Vicar. " You have not turned revolutionist, I hope ? Isn't my head my own ? "

" In a limited sense," said Barnett calmly, " and in a

much more limited sense than you appear to suppose.
But let me explain——"

"You had better do so," said the Vicar, genially
smiling at Paterson.

"Society has rendered individuality impossible except in a modified degree. As Emerson says, 'Every
man is a quotation of his ancestors,' so we may
add every man is the prophecy of his posterity.
Suppose a world in which there is only one man;
there you have what may be called an individual,
but the moment another man enters the world that
individuality is modified; let a thousand men come,
and the modification is proportionately affected; let
controversy arise amongst them, and some plan of
suppression of individuality must be adopted, or cor-
porate existence will be impossible. In this sense,
society destroys individuality by enlarging it. Society
is a unit."

This was not the turn which Paterson expected the
conversation to take, so he was unprepared to
reply.

"Let me ask Mr. Paterson," said Barnett of Balliol,
"if controversy never arises in an Independent community, say in his own chapel?"

"No doubt of it," said Paterson; "that must be
admitted and deplored; at the same time, you must
look at us ideally and not literally."

"Very good. I am quite willing to do so. But do
you see the consequence?"

"What is it?"

"Why, that if I have to look at chapel ideally, you

must look at church ideally, and that being the case, I
must have the best of the argument."

The Vicar thought this was good. I myself was
about to agree that the demand was equitable, when
the Rev. Edwin Bonas was suddenly announced. The
new-comer was a curate attached to the High Church
party, and had by some means transformed himself
into what appeared to be an automatic coat. I am not
sure that I ever saw so much coat in all my life. We
were respectfully pointed out as two Nonconformist
(Nonconformist is not so offensive as Dissenting) ministers, whereupon Mr. Bonas put a glass into one eye,
looked steadily in our direction, and said, "Rawly!"
Then turning to Barnett of Balliol, he added—"Just
been reading a sweet sermon upon the death of St.
Vincent of Paul—remarkable man—shepherd boy—
foot of the Pyrenees—died at eighty-five." The Vicar
would have said something, but Mr. Bonas turned to
us and continued, first fixing his eye-glass,—"Declined
all dispensations during his sufferings— would not accept
dispensation from the recitation of office—longed for
martyrdom—sorry he was not in Geneva when the
plague was raging—sorry he was not at Barbary when
the pestilence was there——" then suddenly catching
sight of Paterson's boots, he said—"Rawly!"

"Very good man, no doubt," said the Vicar, meaning
politely to change the subject and renew the conversation.

"Oh, very, very indeed," said Mr. Bonas, "so deep;
died in the autumn, early autumn; and here is another
book I wish to read, 'Discourses during the Octave of

Corpus Christi," (then explanatorily to the Dissenters) "the second feast of the Nativity." Barnett of
Balliol was not sorry for this interruption, as it gave
him a little breathing time, nor did Paterson exhibit
any signs of impatience, as he was evidently amused
with a totally new specimen of human nature. The
Vicar, too, rather enjoyed the variation, wondering
much how it would strike the Dissenting mind. Barnett
of Balliol explained the position of affairs, and then
continued—

"See what the Church is when viewed ideally : a
whole nation baptised in the Divine Name ; a whole
nation uniting in common prayer ; a whole nation
connecting itself with the vital currents of Providence
and inspiration,—I own that the ideal argument is one of
the very best for the use of the friends of the Church."

"You see," said Paterson, " our Church——"

Here Mr. Bonas fixed his eye-glass and exclaimed
—" Rawly ! "

" Our Church is built upon the lines of the family."

" Which family ? " the curate anxiously inquired.

" My friend's question is quite fair," said Barnett of
Balliol ; " it is seriously meant, and an answer will help
the argument. Consider a moment. When you say
' family,' what do you mean ? "

" I simply mean ' family,' " said Paterson ; " the word
cannot have two meanings : family means family."

" Pardon me," said Barnett of Balliol ; " I venture to
think you are confusing terms. If you will not think
me troublesome, I will venture to ask you for a precise
definition."

"Find me," said Paterson, "a father and mother, and say five or six children, and you have what I venture to call a family."

"So you have," said Barnett, "and now you have it, what do you make of it?"

"I say," Paterson continued, "that family is in a sense the pattern of an Independent church" (here a voice said—"Rawly!"); "I want no clearer type: the family is self-complete, self-supporting, self-governed; so is an Independent church."

"Every one of which propositions," said Barnett, "I distinctly deny."

"Certainly," said Mr. Bonas.

"But my point," Barnett continued, "is that you have not formed the true conception of a family, or rather, what you say may have some bearing, requiring much modification, upon *a* family, but the higher and nobler idea of *the* family seems not to have occurred to you. I contend that the Church of England can make a stronger use of the term family than any Independent church can, only it must be the true family—the human family."

"But," said Paterson, "the Church is an institution gathered out of the human family."

"Only in a sense," Barnett of Balliol replied; "from my point of view the human family is the material which has to be constituted into a church. But let me point out to you that your use of the term 'family' is argumentatively faulty in being incomplete; it is incomplete because your 'family' must be dissolved by mere time; children outgrow the family lines, and separate, and enter into other relations, but no man outgrows the human family, or can detach himself from the larger relations of society. What say you?"

I believe that at this moment the curate caught sight of the pomatum, for, fixing his eye-glass and looking intently at Paterson's head, he said—"Rawly!"

"But now," said Paterson, evidently feeling that he had never been in so severe a grip before, "instead of talking about the whole human family, let us talk about some particular country, say England, and my contention is that the nation as such has nothing to do with the control of religion."

"What is a 'nation'?" said Barnett.

"A nation is a country; England is a nation——"

"Pardon me," said Barnett of Balliol, seeing Paterson's weakness in definition; "let me ask you one question, Who made the nation?"

"I hardly understand you," Paterson replied.

"I will explain. It appears to me that we are in danger of supposing that nations made themselves, that God did not recognise nations as such; now I protest against such atheism; if there is one truth more vividly realised than another in the historical parts of the Bible, it is the unity of nations and their consequent organic responsibility. We must not create a fancy Providence that favourably regards certain freeholds, and leaves the rest of the earth unblessed or unredeemed. God is the God of families, the God of nations, the God of the whole earth, the God of all flesh. It seems to me, Mr. Paterson, that all your definitions need enlargement."

"All that is true," said I, rashly joining in the conversation, "but as the nation does not attempt to interfere with liberty of political opinion, why should it set up a form of religion? Your reasoning would seem to require consolidated politics as well as consolidated theology,—a hierarchy in the State as well as a hierarchy in the Church." I was amazed at my temerity; yet even in the presence of Socrates, I felt that I had scored a point. My comfort was rudely disturbed by an inquiry made in the most courteous tone by Barnett of Balliol.

"Do you not," said he, "see the sophism of such reasoning?"

I wished he had himself pointed out the sophism instead of asking me to name it. There is cruelty, surely, in asking a man to show exactly where and how he has made a fool of himself.

"I don't see it," said Paterson.

"Nor do I; but if you will call my attention to it, I shall be glad."

"Don't you see it, Gray?" Barnett of Balliol inquired of the Vicar.

The genial Vicar took his pipe from behind the Codex, tapped out the ashes, and admitted that he did not see anything sophistical anywhere.

"The sophism," said Barnett, with Socratic tranquillity and mischievousness, "lies in the fact that the terms are not equal. On the one hand is the term 'religion,' and on the other hand is the term 'politics,' and between the terms there is positively not the shadow of any argumentative relation. Now if instead of 'politics' you will say 'patriotism,' you will equalise the

terms and give the argument absolutely into my hands.
We have a national patriotism ; we recognise it ; we are
inspired by it ; we punish its corruption ;—we allow a
thousand opinions in politics, but we do not allow any
tampering with patriotism·: we hang the traitor ; so it
should be in things ecclesiastical ; difference of opinion
is consistent with unity of religion : a national church
should express all shades of religious opinion if it
would be a national church and not a national
cemetery."

"Look at Colenso," said the Vicar once more.

"But how can Bishop Colenso and Mr. Barnett be
members of the same Church ?" I inquired, with some
confidence that I had put a poser.

"We are members of the same human family," said
Barnett of Balliol.

"But how can you be members and ministers of the
same Church ?"

"Easily. Not only easily, but properly. We could
not both belong to a sect, or a Dissenting communion,
because every Dissenting communion would seem to be
founded upon one or two vital points, wholly exclusive
of the idea of national life and unity, whereas the
Church of England is the Church of the nation, at least,
as I have just said, ideally and as to purpose ; being
thus founded upon national lines, it must of necessity
represent variety and even contradiction of thought, and
in doing so it exactly reproduces the case of patriotism,
—the Conservative and the Radical may represent
nationally what the High Church and the Low Church
represent theologically."

" But," said I, beginning to regret that I had spoken at all, "in the case of religion the subject is one and indivisible; in the case of politics many opinions may be honestly held."

" Pardon me," Barnett of Balliol courteously replied; " you do not preserve the equality and balance of the terms; the question is not between religion and politics, but between religion and patriotism. Variety of opinion is just as allowable in the Church as in the State, and my contention is that opinion may widely differ without affecting the love of truth; more, the very love of truth may provoke or develop variety of opinion."

At this point I subsided in favour of Paterson, the curate looking at me as he might have looked at an ass that had been trying to fly, and the Vicar soothing himself vigorously with Knockey's golden shag.

"I am certainly amazed at one thing," said Paterson, " and that is that you do not see that you dissent from us as much as we dissent from you, and therefore I do not see that the stigma of dissent should lie on one side. The simple fact is that we dissent from one another."

The curate said—" Rawly!"

" Not at all," was Barnett's reply. " We must have regard to historical sequence. The term dissenter may imply an order of succession without involving a stigma. When the Vicar asks me to dinner it is proper for me to say that I dined with him, and not that he dined with me. There is a right way of marking relations, and in that way the use of the description 'dissenter' must be limited."

"How do you Dissenters propose to get hold of the nation ?" said the Vicar.

"A very proper inquiry," Barnett immediately added.

"Man by man," said Paterson.

The curate fixed his eye-glass, and made his usual comment.

"But that is not the Divine plan; with reverence be it spoken," said Barnett of Balliol. "Our Lord did not die for man by man, or man after man; He died for the whole world, and then offered the general blessing to the individual sinner. The analogy is evident."

The courtesy of the speaker's tone produced quite as much effect upon Paterson as did the arguments, and the arguments themselves were not a little increased in force by their adaptation to broader uses. It will be observed that Barnett of Balliol did not dispute the contentions of Dissent merely for the sake of achieving a victory in words. He admitted their force, but enlarged their scope, and simply asked Paterson to be faithful to his own logic. The paternal sweetness of the great ecclesiastic made a great impression upon me, even to the extent of convincing me that if the Church of England were disestablished, he could never find equality or restful brotherhood amongst the general mass of Dissenting ministers. A fine blood warmed his veins, and a broad culture chastened the emphasis whose exaggeration is often mistaken for conviction,

and by so much separated him from men who, though
naturally not inferior, belonged socially and educa-
tionally to a different stratum. Perhaps he might not
show to so much advantage now, inasmuch as at the time
of this narrative Oxford and Cambridge were literally
the seats of English learning, and any culture outside
them almost necessarily partook more or less of the
roughness and pedantry of self-education. Circumstances have wholly changed. An enlarged intellectual
training has done a good deal towards levelling up the
literary strata of the nation; yet even in view of such
progress, it is only fair to say that Barnett of Balliol
would in all times and places vindicate his right to
rank with the noblest minds and illustrate the most
perfect manners.

Up to this time I had been perhaps injuriously
affected by Paterson's controversial violence, in the
sense that it had made me studiously reticent in order,
if possible, to dissipate the impression that all Nonconformists are equally hostile to the State Church.
As a matter of fact, I made myself a kind of foil to
Paterson. But after hearing Barnett the fire burned,
and self-respect called upon me to speak out more
distinctly than I had ever done before. Barnett's
reasoning was so specious as to be at first sight con-
clusive, yet I felt that it overlooked some facts which
utterly destroyed its cogency. If the interview had
terminated at this point, the moral victory could have
hardly been claimed for Dissent.

" With regard to the strong point you made of the ideality of the Church of England," said I, " it occurs to me that some important considerations have been omitted."

" Will you name one of them ? " Barnett inquired with expressive graciousness.

" Yes. The ideal nation is itself a fiction. If the nation were one in sentiment and one in worship, the picture would be really pleasing. Or if we had to invent a nation, we could invent it according to your suggestion. But what is the fact ? A theory ought to have some relation to facts, but yours has none ; on the contrary, it is in direct opposition to them. More than one half of the English people do not attend the State Church. Where, then, is the ideality ? They do not abstain because of spiritual indifference—for then your ideal would not be affected—they abstain because of distinct spiritual conviction and intense religious earnestness, and by so much they are daily destroying the practicability of your ideal, and are steadily and necessarily growing in the direction of another and to my mind better type. I speak respectfully in saying that the growing intelligence of the nation is against you."

Barnett's countenance changed. He had been secretly hoping that his gracious manner and careful reasoning had impressed Paterson in a degree amounting to the first stage of conversion, but now that the quieter man had turned upon him, his hope, if not extinguished, was heavily beclouded.

" Do you make that statement seriously ? " he

inquired, with the Socratic caution which never forsook him.

" Certainly. My belief is that what I may call the independent and energetic intelligence of the country is against your ideal Church."

" I hardly understand the qualifying terms."

" I mean popular intelligence, the intelligence which men have acquired for themselves, the intelligence which is not afraid of tradition or superstition, the democratic intelligence."

"Well now," said Barnett, " to circumscribe a little—the Vicar, my friend Gray, will not be offended, I am sure—would you say that the intelligence of this parish, the parish of Midtown, is for or against the National Church ? "

I felt this to be a home-thrust, and that my answer might involve a good deal in the way of neighbourly feeling and confidence. But I could not silence the inward voice without violating both courage and justice.

" The question is a delicate one," I replied, " and the answer must, of course, be limited by my personal knowledge. If I knew more, I could say more, either on one side or the other, but, with this understanding, which I mean to protect me from rudeness, I do not hesitate to say that the intelligence of Midtown is against your reasoning."

Paterson exclaimed—" Hear, hear."

Bonas put up his eye-glass and exclaimed— " Rawly ! "

The good-natured Vicar smiled, and relighted his ever-friendly pipe.

"Then you give no credit for intelligence on our side?" Barnett interrogatively remarked.

I protested. This was not fair to me. To deny intelligence to the other side was more and worse than simply absurd.

"Let me explain myself," I continued. "I am speaking of the people. I am taking the inhabitants of this particular parish man by man, and judging them as fairly and generously as I can ; my distinct belief is that the preponderance of such intelligence as is open to cross-examination—that is, such intelligence as can give account of itself and vindicate itself—is on the side of Nonconformity."

"I thought," said Barnett, "that, as Nonconformists, you did not set much store by intelligence——"

Paterson stood bolt upright, but I restrained him.

"Quite a mistake," said I. "Our hope is in intelligence ; we are afraid of ignorance, and ashamed of it : our people are hard readers, so much so that if you will make books the test, I engage to find more books and better books in the houses of commercial Dissenters than you can find in the houses of commercial Churchmen."

"But now," said the honest and genial Vicar, "I must put in a word for the parish, you know. What you say about books may possibly be true. I will not argue that point. But you will not dispute that the *gentlemen* of the town are to a man on our side?"

"Excuse me smiling," said I, "but that statement I will meet with a flat denial. I may surprise you by saying that I hardly know an earnest, that is, a self-convinced, conscientious Dissenter, who is not a gentleman. I am able to bear testimony upon this point, and I am glad of this opportunity of bearing it."

Paterson closed the interview with an honest Dissenting speech. Paterson was stronger in lecturing than in conversation, as Barnett was probably stronger in conversation than in lecturing. Some men speak best whilst sitting. Even Douglas Jerrold was a dull man when he stood up. Paterson spoke of the spirituality of Christ's kingdom, of the necessity of the new birth, of the sublime and heavenly purpose of the Christian Church, and in terms which were made strong by true emotion, repudiated all patronage that was merely political and official. I had no reason to be ashamed of Paterson's testimony, and I am bound to add that Barnett of Balliol listened to it with earnest attention. The whole impression produced upon my mind was to the effect that this controversy can never be settled by words. Much can be said upon both sides, upon both sides are genuinely honest and able men, and both sides must proceed along their respective lines, finding practical reconciliation in works of Christian charity. Beneficence is a powerful solvent.

As we left the Vicarage library Mr. Bonas betook himself to a distant corner of the room, and so avoided the formality of shaking hands. I could not but feel that his eye-glass was fixed upon us. A sensation in the back told me that we were being looked at, and I

was confirmed in the assurance when, as we stepped
into the hall, I heard a voice behind us saying—"Rawly !"
As we passed out of the Vicarage gates we met Weaver
Stephen on his way to the prayer-meeting, and on
asking him what text had lately been occupying his
attention, he told us that he had been puzzling himself
over the question, "What communion hath Christ with
Belial ? " and by giving the *e* in the first syllable the
sound of *a*, he suddenly gave our thoughts a new
direction, and probably confirmed· Paterson's Dissent.

CHAPTER XIV.

A VERY pleasant little lady was Miss Beebee, of the Green Hollows, able, like many other of the sincerest of mankind, to hide an incredible degree of obstinacy under an external amiability which seemed to be created for the express purpose of being imposed upon. Her voice, too, was remarkably tender, never meant to say No even to requests not altogether reasonable, yet often used in the utterance of a will best represented by wrought iron. Miss Beebee was quite the head-centre of Dissent for miles around, every noted minister having been her guest on the occasion of anniversaries or other important Nonconformist celebrations, and every Nonconformist institution looking to her, and seldom in vain, for substantial assistance. Of all her clerical visitors Professor Stokoe stood first and foremost on every ground, not the least on the ground of his genial recitals of all the news which he innocently picked up in the course of his ministerial visiting. Miss Beebee liked to hear about ministers, not, indeed, in any merely gossiping sense, but as revelations of a species of character involving a fine mixture of mystery and sanctity. To Miss Beebee

every minister was "a dear man," and every want of
the "dear man" was regarded as a prayer addressed
to her most solemn attention.   In a word, Miss Beebee
was to all appearance predestinated to be the friend
and helper of all Nonconformist ministers.

"Do you know, dear madam," gurgled the Professor,
"I have heard that Mr. Tomlinson is not—what
shall I say?—is not—may I say—without doing him
injustice?—is not as strong in his Nonconformist
convictions as I believe he was at one time."

Miss Beebee suddenly became pale, and startled the
Professor by saying—"Then I am afraid it is true."

"What, madam?"

"What you tell me, Professor Stokoe.   Mr. Daleham has been here, and has told me various stories, but
I suspected their truthfulness.   I do not know much
about that man.   Have you any better authority?"

"My dear madam, my authority is Mr. Tomlinson
himself.   He used a very singular expression, the
propriety of which I failed somewhat to discern; he
said, to the best of my recollection, that he would 'jack
it up,' from which I infer that he contemplates resignation in some form, I may say in some novel form."

"As you know so much, Professor, I may tell you
more.   Mr. Daleham has suggested that it might be
well to set on foot a society for the scientific exposition
of Independency, as he thinks our young people need
instruction and confirmation in our principles, and he
assures me that if I will furnish him with a thousand
pounds, he can commence operations almost immediately.   What do you think?"

The Professor was angry, and gurgled most incoherently.

" I must say, Professor," continued Miss Beebee, " that I was very much annoyed at one thing Mr. Daleham did. I am quite sure some of his words admitted of meanings which I strongly dislike."

The Professor's mind did not move easily from one subject to another. He was still angry, and still unintelligible. Could the whole innermost truth of things be known—those things which have not only never been put into words, but never explicitly admitted by the mind in its own secret communings—it might be found that the only man towards whom Miss Beebee had looked with significant partiality was the learned and gurgling Professor. Even this is almost too much to say, and therefore it must be regarded without prejudice to Miss Beebee ; still the film is necessary to the absolute completeness of things.

" Madam," said the Professor, " how large must a looking-glass be to allow of the whole stature of the observer to be seen at once ? "

Just like the Professor this. Ordinary topics had to be introduced between outbursts of scientific information, and being thus introduced, were in danger of being forgotten or only imperfectly understood. Even love itself had to be set aside in favour of some new example in Natural Philosophy. Miss Beebee thought that the looking-glass must be as tall as the observer, but a serious fixture of the professorial eye showed that the guesses of ignorance cannot impose upon the watchfulness of learning.

"Have you seen Mr. Tomlinson upon this matter, madam?"

"No, Professor, no, no. From Mr. Tomlinson I know nothing. To me he is the same as ever, a firm Nonconformist and a very earnest preacher. Mr. Tomlinson, you know, is very playful in his manner at times, and he may have been teasing Mr. Daleham merely for amusement——"

"Of course," said the Professor, "you must understand that the position of the eye has a good deal to do with the height of the mirror——"

"Yes, sir, but what has it to do with Mr. Tomlinson?"

"Just so," the Professor replied. "I was wandering for the moment. Let me see. What did he say? Oh yes. He said he would 'jack it up'; a singular expression. I never met with it before. I was just going to add that if the eye could be taken out of its socket and placed say on the end of the finger——"

"Oh, my dear Professor Stokoe!"

"Just so," the Professor hastened to say; "a mere supposition, of course; nothing more. Do not be alarmed; we need not pursue the subject."

Nor could they have pursued it if they wished, for at this moment Mr. Daleham himself was announced. He affected to be extremely delighted, that Professor Stokoe was at the Green Hollows, and if the Professor had been equally delighted the joy would have been intolerable. But the Professor was not delighted: the Professor was disgusted; nothing could detain him, but before going, he said to Miss Beebee, whose willing hand he held with professorial negligence, that the eye being where it was, and not on the end of the finger, it was not necessary in order to bring in the whole stature for the glass to be more than half the height of the observer. This was consolatory as well as scientific, though the statement did not wholly satisfy the lay-mind of his admiring hostess. Mr. Daleham was sorry the Professor had gone. He said the Professor's mind always awoke the ambition of his own, and the Professor's modesty always showed him the comeliest aspect of genius.

"On the whole, however," he continued, "it may be as well that the old Professor had not remained ——"

"I have never looked upon him as old," Miss Beebee remarked.

"A term of affection," Daleham quickly answered. "In point of years the dear Professor is anything, but old, but his learning, his humility, his unselfishness, combine to draw out a kind of filial feeling,—in wisdom he is centuries old; in years he is quite one of ourselves."

The last part of the sentence was meant to be impressive, but where the wax is unmelted the stamp takes no effect. Mr. Daleham thought that his influence, so magnetic and delicate, operating by half-expressed hints, rather than by direct appeal, melted all womanly hearts; but even Mr. Daleham was sometimes mistaken, although it must be allowed that now and then a woman had given him the impression that she was innocently blind to his wily ways at the very moment that she was amusing herself with a new phase of hypocrisy.

"Pardon me, Miss Beebee," said he, "but to put the matter delicately, it is only right that you should be made aware of the fact that Tomlinson gibbers——"

"What ever do you mean, Mr. Daleham?"

"I mean, madam, that Tomlinson is little better than a gibbering maniac."

"Oh! how I wish the Professor were here."

"Pardon me, Miss Beebee; I must not be taken too literally. The man is sane enough in one aspect, but when a man trifles with his principles, professes to be a Nonconformist, yet is always pining for the Established Church, I feel that from a moral point of view he is not unjustly described when he is spoken of as a gibbering maniac. The older I grow the more determined am I to uphold the cause of civil and religious liberty all over the world."

"The Professor could help me better than any one," Miss Beebee said as if to herself. "I am walking upon uncertain ground."

"It would be presumptuous in me to offer my services," said Daleham, "nor would I venture even to hint at such a thing had not this idea of reducing the whole idea of Dissent to a scientific form, I may say even a scientific law, taken such possession of me. I do feel that we must get hold of the higher order of mind,—the very highest order, in fact; this is the day of science; everything must be scientific; even morals must be regulated by science. If I had even so comparatively small a sum as one thous——"

"Here comes the dear Professor," exclaimed Miss Beebee, as she saw the venerable figure ambling up the solid gravel walk, appearing and disappearing amongst the thick fresh laurels. " Now I shall have the comfort of his counsel."

"The dear man!" said Daleham. " Good-bye, madam. The Professor's purpose and mine are absolutely identical. We are anxious about the success of Dissent. We would give our all to help the noble cause. Our fathers bled for it. But what can poor men do? Talents they may have, and devotion, but where money is essential——"

The Professor's gurgle broke off Daleham's sentence, and Daleham himself withdrew.

" My dear madam, I have been to see my brother Tomlinson, and should have been here earlier had not my attention been drawn to the remarkable group of tadpoles in a pool a little to the left of your beautiful grounds——"

" And how did you find Mr. Tomlinson ? "

" One moment. I am not prepared to deny that a tadpole begins life as a fish, and then becomes a tailed amphibian——"

" Did you get any information about him, Professor ?"

" Well, I am coming to believe that the lamprey and the tadpole are descended——"

" I meant Mr. Tomlinson."

"Oh, certainly. Yes. I have been to see him, but he was not at home. I saw his partner in life, a person, I must say, whose conversation is a little enigmatical and perplexing."

Mrs. Tomlinson was not exactly enigmatical in the Professor's sense of the term ; she was a very fluent and multifarious speaker, and no doubt bewildered Professor Stokoe by her swift and unreasoning flight from one subject to another.   In ten minutes she went at least twice round the little creation in which she passed her simple life, and did her best to destroy the illusion that the ministry is a celestial profession. Mrs. Tomlinson made no secret of her likes and dislikes, and was notably and even ferociously consistent in her denunciation of "the deacons"; she wished she was "behind them"; she quite longed to "give them a good poking up"; in all her life she "never saw such a sleepy lot"; and "as for that Miss Beebee, she might be, and no doubt was, very rich, but if she was going to do anything for Mr. Tomlinson, she had better do it at once, and not put off until there was a funeral and a will read in public."   Mrs. Tomlinson wanted everything done at once, and in her impatience she had on one occasion distantly hinted something which did not raise her in Miss Beebee's esteem.   Mrs. Tomlinson, it may be added without malice, considered that on account of her having been a sound Churchwoman before marrying an Independent minister, she not only conferred distinction upon Dissent, but acquired the right to abuse it.   Perhaps there was a kind of rough logic in Mrs. Tomlinson's reasoning, for who can doubt that an Independent minister marrying into a church family apes the manners of a higher grade and sacrifices his consistency to his ambition ?

Suddenly catching sight of a faint rainbow when

there was no appearance of rain, the Professor said—
" I remember that something similar was once noticed
at Hurrachandarghur, but—yes—for the moment I
had overlooked the fact—yes—that young man is
waiting for me—his name is Battison—been abroad
—not perhaps wholly exemplary in his conduct—
the rainbow ray is, in fact, the asymptote——"

" Better ask the young man to come in, Professor."

" No, madam; I will accompany him; I have an
imperfect recollection of having heard something of his
career—it is not desirable that he should come into
your house—every ray emerging between two given
points——"

Here young Battison flattened his face against the
window-pane, and the shocked Professor instantly
departed from the Green Hollows.

" You are in luck, mate, knowing such a sweet
creature. Sweet name, too, eh? The dapper little
chit of a coachman told me her name is Baby, and I
reckon it was once."

The Professor turned an anxious eye towards the
pond where the tadpoles sported.

" Most of the Batrachia are oviparous——"

" What are you mumbling about, sir cove?" said
Battison. " Have you and Baby had a tipple? Or is
there something buzzing in your head? I've had
nothing to drink since I had my last mug o' beer. I
borrowed a chew of that little swell of a coachman,
though; he was not going to give it to me until I seized
him by the neck, all in fun like."

I 2

The Professor was profoundly serious, and in truth
he was profoundly uneasy. He knew something of
Mr. Battison and the daughters, and he had an indistinct impression of having heard of the prodigal boy;
but everything was so mixed up in the mind of the
Professor with scientific intelligence and speculation
that he never reached the point of certainty in the
matter of social facts. At some points it would have
been impossible for the Professor to have sworn
whether he was the prodigal and Battison was the
Professor, or whether Battison was the prodigal and
himself the Professor; such were the lengths to which
Mr. Stokoe had carried the processes of mental culti-
vation. In a word, the Professor was the victim of
absent-mindedness.

"The vascular and respiratory systems of these
animals——"

"I tell you what it is, old blinkers, I'm getting rather
frightened of this mumbling; but if you want to fight,
why don't you say so and shake hands? That's what
we do in the colony. We soon square up and settle
down there. So if you would like a turn, there's no
time like the present."

Battison tucked back his coat-sleeves and lubricated
his palms. The Professor was absolutely unconscious
of the purport of the remarks, and gave no sign of
really recognising the presence of Battison until Battison snatched off the Professor's hat and showed the
learned man how to shoot a penny through the crown.
The Professor stared, gurgled innocently, and put out
his hands in a helpless kind of manner.

" Here's your hat, not a penn'orth the worse," said
Battison ; "but mind, let's have no more mumbling.
Now, how *is* Nehemiah ? "

" Your father ? "

"My *father!* bless him, yes, that very same old
duffer."

The Professor was once more mentally at the pond.
It was well that the time of separation had come.
Battison turned off towards Midford, and the Professor
turned towards his own home.   Too much must not be
made of the conduct of young Battison, seeing that he
was under the influence of drink, and all his better
qualities were for the moment thrust into the back-
ground.   When he arrived at the paternal residence,
Daleham was just leaving the house, and Nezzy was
on the doorstep. Stooping down, he caught that petted
brute by the neck and flung it to the other side of the
road, and in reply to Daleham's amusement he said,
with colonial civility—" For one chew I would throw
you after him." So much for the drink upon which
men .rely for stimulus and exhilaration. Was it by
mere chance that Daleham met Weaver Stephen on his
way home, or by mere chance that Stephen quoted a
particular line of Scripture ? It would seem as if
Stephen was always able to give a Biblical turn to the
events which were uppermost in men's minds, and as
if no other book could supply language so fitting and
sublime in view of all possible and actual occurrences,
Even Daleham thought so as Stephen walked by his
side and said—" Who hath woe ? who hath sorrow ?
who hath contentions ? who hath babbling ? who hath

wounds without cause ? who hath redness of eyes ? They that tarry long at the wine, they that go to seek mixed wine."

" I know that to be true, Stephen ; it is awfully, frightfully true."

" All the Bible is true, sir."

" Well, Stephen, I don't mind telling you that I am coming to think so more and more. It is a wonderful book. It positively has everything in it. Life without the Bible is a lock without the key."

CHAPTER XV.

A MONTH has elapsed.

I have seen a wonderful sight to-day. Mr. Whiteman's son George called upon me with a message from his father, and in the course of a brief conversation I saw that amazing sight. George is about sixteen years old. He is a genuine Christian boy, remarkably healthy in mind, and of most responsive feeling. He told me that his father had become totally blind, and that his mother was nearly overpowered by distress.

"George, my boy," said I with unfeigned sympathy, "this throws a new responsibility upon you, and you are very young."

"Seventeen next birthday, sir."

"Quite a child, George, in some respects, yet I have faith in you in view of any difficulties that may arise."

George turned his great dark eyes upon me and looked at me as I had never been looked at before. I steadily returned the solemn gaze, and as I watched all the emotions that expressed themselves in that fine face I saw the boy become a man! The transition was perfectly palpable. Such a spectacle had never come under my attention before, nor can I wish to see it again. Its interest amounted to agony. It seemed as

if the sweet boy must have undergone the severest
suffering in passing into the higher estate, yet no moan
of pain accompanied the acceptance of the heavier life.

"My father says he never knew his people until
now."

"So kind are they, George?"

"More than kind, sir. He says they must think
about him night and day, and spend their lives in
inventing pleasant surprises for him. Mr. Robson and
the deacons are as noble as they can be, but the remarkable thing is that Knockey and all the people of
that class are just as good as they can be. Father says
he would have thought such a change impossible, and
that it helps him to bear his affliction."

"Grand!" I exclaimed.

"Yes," George replied, "and I can say that I never
knew my own father until now. You should hear his
prayers! And never a word of murmuring. Never!
He says he never saw the stars until this darkness
came upon him. As for his preaching, it is beyond
everything you can imagine, and all the people say so.
A solemn thing it is to see a blind man preaching."

"The appearance must be very weird," I said.

"Looks as if some one from another world," George
continued, "was talking to you. I think the very voice
is changed. At home he takes as much interest in
things as he ever did, and seems to have quite a new
talent in asking questions. You must not be surprised
if he puts you through your catechism."

"Tell him, George, that I will be up this afternoon
and take tea with you."

" He will be delighted, I am sure."

George had hardly left when Mr. Daleham called. I was exceedingly annoyed when his name was announced, and there may have been some trace of vexation upon my· face judging from the manner in which he addressed me. Ministers are bound to be civil, although, no doubt, their civility is sometimes hardly less than a sacrifice. It is no trifling matter to surrender a plan of reading for a course of pointless conversation, yet that has often to be done, and the pulpit has to suffer in consequence. I was, however, hasty in the judgment of Mr. Daleham in this particular instance.

"I have come upon business of importance to myself," said he, "and I hope you will not refuse me your sympathy."

"May I ask you to be brief, Mr. Daleham ?"

"Certainly. Stop me when you please. Your convenience shall be mine. I want to say frankly that I have been pursuing a totally mistaken and false course of life, and I want you to help me to get out of it, and abandon it for ever."

"Then the conditions are wholly changed," said I. "You may command me. Go on." I said all this the more willingly owing to the influence of George Whiteman's conversation. George had opened heaven to me. Perhaps I might see Daleham also pass into manhood !

"I hardly know where to begin. My whole life has been set in a false key. Somehow or other I got the notion that the success of life is an affair of good luck, and that adventure is better than industry. ˙Once let that doctrine get hold of a man, and a serpent gets possession of his heart, and then comes a hideous succession of tricks, schemes, devices, traps, and all the machinery of deception. I feel as if my life had been one long clumsy lie, and all the clumsier for its supposed cleverness. Bah! there is no real genius in dishonesty."

I was momentarily puzzled by this novel talk on the part of so wily a dramatist as Daleham, and had some difficulty in withholding an expression of my incredulity. Yet the tone carried with it a subtle evidence of sincerity.

"Remember, Mr. Daleham," said I, "as Protestants we know nothing of the detestable custom of priestly confession. I cannot receive your statement in any official capacity. I must exercise my judgment as to the degree of confidence in which I hold your communications; at the same time, if I can do you any good, I will most gladly advise you."

"Thanks. I feel that I cannot begin the right way until I have got completely rid of the wrong way. I feel that evil cannot be absorbed; it must be dragged out and almost publicly thrown into the fire. I tell you I got the notion into my head that scheming was better than working, and ever since I accepted that tempting sophism I have been a liar and a charlatan. I know these are strong words, and must appear to be even violent to a man of your disposition, but they are not a whit too strong."

"Then let us begin there," said I.

"'Then how am I to get back again? I mean to go to every one to whom I have presented myself in a false light, and tell the plain truth, and ask to be forgiven. I mean to tell Miss Beebee——"

"Perhaps," said I, "it will be better not to mention any names; it is enough for immediate purposes to agree upon general principles, and gradually proceed to their application."

"But there is one case I must [mention, and that is your own."

"Very good; there we are free."

"I have used you badly. I have endeavoured to poison other people against you. When I have been listening to you I have been secretly mocking you, and giving signs to those sitting near me of my frivolity and ill-nature. I thought it funny. I meant to get up a reputation for cleverness and to draw away young people after me. I was wrong, utterly and basely wrong, the dupe of my own vanity, and now I am the prey of an awakened and avenging conscience."

"So far as I am concerned, Mr. Daleham," said I, "your statement is accepted. Here is my hand. Whatever I have to forgive is forgiven."

"Thanks be to God. I feel as if I had got a foothold to begin with."

"How did this new line of feeling start?" I inquired.

"It was through Weaver Stephen, poor fellow, though he knows nothing about it. I never knew such a man for quoting the Bible. Meet him when you will, he seems to know the exact passage you need, and it takes all the more effect upon you because of his absolute ignorance of your circumstances. I have always been rather superstitious, and I confess that now and then it seemed as if God Himself was rebuking me through the quotations made by Stephen. And those deep eyes of his! Positively I have been alarmed by their penetration. That is the only account I can give of this happier feeling, and I am not ashamed of it. A book that meets your life so completely is not a human book."

"A beginning like that," said I, "is likely to have a good ending."

"So I think," Mr. Daleham added. "Now, may I tell you one thing more?"

"I leave everything to your discretion," I replied.

"Well, you know young Battison. He is an awful character when under the influence of drink, but when he is sober he is really a sensible and good-natured fellow. I have had long talks with him about colonial life, and the upshot is that I have arranged to go to Australia, and I sail almost immediately. Possibly he may go with me. In Australia I can begin life over again. My testimony to you before going away is that the way of transgressors is hard, and that he that trusteth in his own heart is a fool. I have your forgiveness. Good-bye."

Daleham's manner pleased me by its simplicity. I had seen him, too, become a man! Cavil as men may about theology, there is a transforming energy in Christianity which cannot be honestly gainsaid.

It turns mean men into kings. By this token it shall live for ever. Did it make only pedants and sectaries, it would soon be as one of the extinct mythologies; but it ennobles the whole character, it makes the heart glow with the spirit of benevolence, it gives new value and dignity to life, and thus by miracles of the sublimest kind it proves how surely it came from heaven. Men may trifle with argument; they are bound to respect character.

I found Mr. Whiteman in the happiest mood, the happiest soul in the circle indeed, the very centre and spring of household joy. Everybody seemed to see the better because of Mr. Whiteman's blindness. Every one was on the outlook to anticipate a want, or read the expression of his radiant face, or tell such news as would give him joy. There was a burden of darkness to be divided, a night to fill with stars, a void to be charmed by music. And how gladly the whole family worked! Mrs. Whiteman, indeed, born to be a minister's wife, sometimes almost suggested that it was a comfort to be blind, and said that for an hour together she closed her eyes and quite enjoyed her release from watching the motion and colour which so much try the vision. Nellie, the youngest daughter, used to count the pulse-beats in her wrist to see how long it would take her father to detect the presence of a sprig of mignonette in the room, and she declared that in from ten to fifteen beats, he would not only find out the flower, but would point to the exact spot where it lay. Then Nellie would kiss the blind man, and tell him that

he was a dear old hypocrite, who was imposing on the
good-nature of his family.   Then Whiteman would put
forth his pale hands to find this sweet tormentor and
draw her to his heart.   And then Nellie's bright face
would darken as she saw the sightless eyes, and felt in
very deed that the dearest of fathers was blind.   The
looks caught, as it were, stealthily were the most
pathetic.   When Whiteman was sitting silently, Nellie
would steadfastly observe him, and her young heart
would ache as he turned his eyes as if in search of
some loved object, and looked up as if he saw blest spirits
visible only to the blind.   It was Nellie's chief joy to
watch her father's new ways.   Many a time, when he
knew nothing of it, Nellie was reading all the meaning
of his face.   His sigh went cruelly to her heart; it
meant so much; it was not a murmur, yet it was a
desire which could never be fulfilled : it expressed
resignation in an undertone that might have been born
of despair.   If father would not sigh !   But how could
he help it ?   Under such a load, who would not sigh ?
Any other man would sigh ten times more.   Yet Nellie
wondered if there was no help in heaven, and if God
would be deaf to her prayer.   She thought of the sight-
giving Christ, and wondered where He was !   Was He
clean gone for ever ?   Had He no more pity for human
infirmity and sorrow ?   " Lord," said she, " he whom
Thou lovest is blind ; he is saying to Thee, ' Lord, that
I might receive my sight '; come to him as to blind
Bartimæus, and make him see."   But no miracle was
wrought.   Yet who may say so ?   What of resignation,
and patience, and chastening of heart, and obedience

purged of reluctance? No greater miracles may be wrought in this direction. What, too, of spiritual vision, the astronomic sight which destroys distance and dwells in sacred trance upon the very face of God? These questions ought to be answered before the miracle is denied.

"It will surprise you," said he to me, "to know what object I miss most."

We were unwilling to make any suggestion, for fear of making a mistake.

"I mean," he continued, "what natural object. I am not referring to friends."

"Well," said I, "as my answer is so obvious, I suppose it must be wrong. I should say that as a matter of course you will miss the sun most."

"I thought you would say so. No. I miss the night more than the day. Nobody can tell what night has been to me. You would think me romantic if I attempted to tell you all. I had come to think that the day is a very poor affair, after all is said and done; the sun won't let you look at him; you really have nothing to look at but the earth, beautiful enough, no doubt, but so small—one little bed of flowers with a stream running through it; but night! Then we can look up without rebuke! Then we look for the earth and cannot find it! Then the garden of stars is in full bloom!"

Nellie looked very wistfully, and mourned that this inheritance had been taken away.

"But the moon I can never forget! I become quite

rhapsodical when I think of the beautiful moon. I see
all her gentle ways amongst the clouds, and learn
many a lesson from her methods. Now behind a thick
and blinding veil ; then peeping over it in quiet but
assured triumph ; then sailing away in white glory over
an infinite sea ; now a yellow line ; now a quarter
trimmed with geometric perfectness ; now fully orbed
and rich with softened light. How I miss it all ! "

Nellie came quite closely up and took the blind man's
hand.

"Talking of the moon," said he, "until little Nellie
is quite jealous ! Ha, ha ! You purring kitten ! " A
great fatherly hug told all the rest.

"Thank God," said I, " there are some compensations even for blindness."

"Quite true," said Whiteman. " I do not want to
exceed the truth, but I can say that at times I could
hardly wish to recover my sight."

" But blind men always wanted to see," said Nellie ;
"look at the New Testament."

" Quite so, little one," Whiteman replied. " I know
that. I speak very guardedly. Yes, yes. I do want
to see mother, and George, and Harry, and—oh yes—I
do. And——"

" And everybody but Nellie," said she, " and Nellie's
nobody."

I see Whiteman's hand as it was put forth towards
Nellie. It was an eloquent hand ! Nor was there any
error of movement.

" I am told," said I, " that your people are very
sympathetic."

"Every one. Yes. Even Knockey is a treasure. Even Knockey! Despair of no man, is my pastoral motto. Stout old Langport comes wheezing up to me whenever he can, to say how much he enjoyed the service. But Knockey is the miracle."

"The Dissenters are not inhuman, take them for all in all," said I.

"What every man wants is patience," Whiteman said with great seriousness. "The people are no more perfect than ministers are. We worry far too much when things do not go fast enough, or when we are not praised enough, or when the attendance slackens, or the income dwindles. Without wishing to be harsh——"

Nellie came nearer to her father in mute deprecation of the idea.

"I must say I am ashamed of some of our men. They are bargain-makers, hirelings, mere wool-gatherers, and they ought to be disappointed."

"They are not all Patersons, eh?" said I, proud as I was of the Philistine.

"Paterson is a true soul," Whiteman added. "You know what he means. I think he rides the Dis-establishment idea to death, and that he is unable to grasp the whole history and genius of the Church of England, but he is sound at the core, without one atom of guile or selfishness, and with a devotional power I have seldom known to be equalled."

"A little different from Tomlinson!"

"Infinitely different! By the way, do you know anything of his plans?"

"Nothing. I suppose he is trading upon what he calls his political wisdom. It is impossible to esteem such a man. He will catch it yet."

"Yes," said Whiteman, "and he will catch it most of all in the Church of England. The bishops don't want such men, and the inferior clergy always look upon them as interlopers. I am quite sure they never can become good Churchmen. What a defect it is to have a divided mind!"

The door was opened in perfect silence, and George entered the room without so much as a creak being heard, but in a moment Mr. Whiteman exclaimed— "Roses!" He was right. George then explained that he had met the Vicar, who desired his best compliments and offered Mr. Whiteman two of the finest roses of the season. Nellie, though a Baptist, instantly described the Vicar as "a dear old thing," and Whiteman himself admitted the justice of the remark, adding—

"After all, there is a kind of fatherly-motherly feeling about the English Church which goes straight to the heart, and as for our Vicar——"

"The sweet old thing!" Nellie interpolated.

"It would be hard to go against him by getting up a liberation meeting."

"That is true," said I. "There is no difficulty in liberationising when the parish priest is hostile and lordly. No doubt the personal element often determines local feeling and action. I know principle is principle, but I also know that personality may be larger and stronger than abstract logic. Of course I know that you Baptists are as far wrong as you can be; still who

can help loving Nellie? are you a very, very great
Baptist, Nellie ? "

George replied—"She would be a Quaker on
Monday and a Swedenborgian on Tuesday if father
went that way. I wouldn't give a button for Nellie's
principles."

" Brothers never have anything good to say of sisters,"
Nellie curtly replied. The curtness was not bitter, for
Nellie knew that George loved her, and the more so
that George never planned anything for father's
surprise without taking her into immediate confidence.
They were filial conspirators, bent upon disappointing
blindness of its prey.

As I left Whiteman's I felt that I must have one
word with Knockey, a really cordial word in recognition
of the change which had taken place in his spirit, and
an encouraging word in view of the future. On the
other side of the road I thought I saw young Battison
somewhat the worse for drink, but my observation may
have been in fault, as the evening was advanced. I
certainly met the Vicar coming away from a sick visit
which he had been suddenly called to pay. I told him
I had just enjoyed the fragrance of two of his roses,
and he told me he had left a third with the poor sick
woman in the garret, and he really felt as if he had
left a light in that dreary chamber. The poor woman,
he added, quite clutched at the rose, as if seizing the
hand of a long-lost friend, and then kissed it as if it
had been a living thing, a kind of angel-visitor. " The
rose is more mine than ever," said the genial Vicar,
"now that it is so much to her." When I got to

Knockey's I was a little disappointed to find him in
some agitation and for the moment indisposed to
comfortable talk.

"Excuse me," said he, "but it is really very annoying, and an end must be put to it. Mr. Daleham
called to say good-bye, and just as he put up his
handkerchief to dry away a tear, he stepped backward
and fell over that horrid butcher's dog, that will hang
about the office so much" (Mr. Knockey seldom said
shop), "and it is all the worse because we are just
going to have a meeting of gallery seat-holders here to
consider in what way we can show our gratitude to
Mr. Whiteman in the form of a nice little testimonial,
all amongst ourselves, you know. Stephen do say, sir,
as she'll come round."

I thought the last words referred mysteriously to
the testimonial.

CHAPTER XVI.

WEAVER STEPHEN soon enlightened me as to Mr. Knockey's meaning.

"Things are getting very numbersome now, sir,—oncommon I call it."

"It must be a fortnight since I saw you, Stephen, perhaps more——"

"Exactly nineteen days, sir."

"So I thought. Time enough to go half round the world. Now, let me hear the news."

"News I don't quite call it, sir, though I'm bound to say it is numbersome enough to be about as bad to make out as a newspaper. I must say she got peace, poor creature, and the Word was very comforting to her, and Miss Jemima was oncommon ; yes, I say Miss Jemima was about as much of an angel as ever my poor old eyes looked upon."

"But I don't know what it is all about, Stephen ; you confuse me."

"I call it oncommon, sir, I do. And she so young and about as pretty a little bird as I ever see, and just as patient—well—she *were* patient."

"Stephen," said I, "this is absurd. Who are you talking about ? "

"All about her, sir, and the Word, and the last few

moments, and even Miss Jochebed were as nimble as a kitten, and they want to make out as she's not far short of forty ; at the same time, when she speaks to any one who is ill, she do speak right pretty, I call it, and so soft-like that it cut me to the quick, and when she saw it would not do to bring the dog with her, she fastened him up at the stair foot——"

"Stephen," said I, "you bewilder me.   Do begin at the beginning——"

"That's just where it is, sir; you cannot say as it had a beginning, because it just happened like, and there it was, you know, and when it was there, it seemed as if it had never been anywhere else ; at the same time, the sovereign that Master Daleham gave me to spend for her was about the best money I've seen, and says he, 'Stephen,' says he, 'Miss Jemima will give you another when that's done——' "

I was helpless.   I saw that the only thing I could do was to listen carefully.

"But that reading business, and messing on with the Word, won't do ; still I will say that the Vicar is a kind man, and it was all through kindness they would not send for you ; they did not much care about you knowing, and the way she spoke about him—a good-for-nothing wastrel I call him—was so charitable like and oncommon.   She was very young when he got hold of her.   That Australia is a oncommon numbersome sort of place.   And she come on the ship as a kind of servant a-waiting on the ladies, and the ladies might feel proud to be waited on by such a beauty, and her dead face was like an angel carved in the snow, and the rose in her hand was like a lamp she might be holding, and the pretty hair—oh, it was a shame to bury it. There was no death in that bonny, bonny hair. But the Word comforted her, and she quite broke me down when she said one night—'Dear Stephen,' says she, 'tell me more and more about that.' Ay, sir, them's the very words, and they are sweeter to me than honey and the honey-comb. There's the Bible again, you see."

"Go on, Stephen; just pour out your heart in your own way."

"And when she moaned in her sleep about her mother, it was oncommon, and about the white cottage where they lived, and the dog-roses making an arch above the door, and says she when her mind was not quite steady—'It is just like Sunday-school at home hearing dear old Stephen talk, and father and mother went to meeting,' says she, 'and Nehemiah is not always bad,' says she, 'and but for the drink he would be good'; and says she, putting her young hand into my old one—'When I am gone give him my love, and say I left a blessing for him'; and says she— 'When all his wanderings are done, perhaps we may meet in heaven.' La! sir, when she got a-talking like that it weren't no use trying to stand agin it any longer, so says I, quite tender like—'Child,' says I, 'what's your name?' And when she said her name was Mary I just gave way. Mary! Mary!"

For some moments Stephen indulged his sorrow, and then said—

"It will not be me as will speak to the young vaga-

bond Battison.   He's a burden to the ground that
carries him.   Oh, Mary, it did me good to be with thee.
Gone!   Gone!   It is well with the child."

It was quite clear that I must leave Stephen to take
his own course, and that I must put two and two together as well as I could.

"And Daleham never used one pen-and-ink word
when he talked to Mary, not one; he quite surprised
me ; and it was wonderful how he liked to be with her,
and how he said Amen when I was done a-praying, and
'Stephen,' says he, 'when you pray, and I am gone, be
sure you always put in a word for me.'   I do believe,
sir, as the Word has got hold of that vain heart and
broke it all to pieces.   No hammering of ours could do
it, but the Lord's hammer was in the Lord's hand, and
the rock was broken."

I was silent, partly in hope that I might hear
more about Mr. Daleham, upon whose sincerity no
suspicion had yet been thrown, yet whose conversion was so sudden as to bring with it a measure of
disquietness.

"They spent a good deal o' time together," Stephen
continued, "and a-praying, too.   She told me what
hopes she had on him, and how she asked him to pray,
and he broke down and cried like a child : lor', it was
oncommon ; her eyes were so large and bright when
she told me that he had made her a promise, and she
knew he meant it, and that I would see him a new
man ; 'and, Stephen,' says she, 'you will see more
than that,' and then she stopped, and presently she
asked me to pray with her, but, lor', sir, I were so

knocked over that I couldn't no way make the words come, so we took hold of hands and just looked up."

" I wonder, Stephen," said I at length, " that all this could be going on without my hearing of it. I have felt that something was going on, but I had no idea of this."

" It was all meant in kindness, sir," Stephen replied. " They did not want things talked about. But she wanted for nothing. Mind that. Miss Jemima, sir, is the one, though I will say that her sister who has the dog offered to let the dog stop with Mary if Mary thought she would like to have something to make a pet of and something to amuse her now and then. I call their kindness oncommon. Our people at the chapel have had a deal to say agin the Battisons, and the old gentleman's watch seal has been remarked upon by a-many as would ha' worn it themselves if they could ; but, says I, the proof of the pudding is the eating of it, and I will say, watch seal or no watch seal, that Mr. Battison and his darters are as kind as kind can be. And Mr. Battison loves the Word, and wants it painted up everywhere, and brought many cards to put up where Mary could see them, and Master Daleham, he nailed them up, and always put the pretty ones right afore her, and then she smiled, and Daleham dried his eyes, and we all felt it."

Stephen, as will be seen, was not an orderly speaker, yet there was no difficulty in putting his points together and making a story of them. But now that the story was tolerably clear, what was I to do with it ? It was plain that the Battisons desired to keep it as private as

possible, and that they wished even those who knew
the particulars to abstain from comment. The story
accounted in some measure for the obvious change in
Daleham's tone, and explained one or two things in the
recent conduct of the Battisons which looked unusual.
I had been wondering whether the Battisons had kept
out of my way to avoid conversation about the prodigal
member of the family, or whether Daleham had been
doing mischief, or whether their zeal was cooling; and
now the mystery was made clear. I do not blame the
Battisons for not coming to me, for who likes to lay
bare all the wounds of the heart? Who does not find
a degree of comfort in the secret nursing of sorrow?
If Mr. Battison had seen me, he would certainly have
told me, so he discreetly kept out of the way. When I
next met the Vicar I referred to the case.

"Yes," said he, "a nice young woman, but I fancy
her disease was quite as much mental as physical.
There was unmistakable grief in the face."

"Did she not explain?"

"Not a word. By the way, what a quaint character
that Weaver Stephen is!"

"Anything new?"

"No. After I had read the Sick Visitation Office, the
young woman said—'Now, sir, will you pray with me?'
I said—'That is what I have been doing.' But she said
she did not mean in that way. 'Then,' I said, 'in what
way do you mean?' And she said—'I want you to
pray like Stephen,' and when I told her I had never
heard Stephen pray, she said it would do me good if
I did, and then, to my infinite surprise, she asked me

if I would have any objection to hear her pray! And
I told her that if she thought she could pray in the
presence of a regularly ordained priest of the Church
of England—if she *could* do such a thing—I would
kneel beside her; and, to my inexpressible astonishment,
she said she would try! And I tell you I never listened
to anything like it on earth! Never! She must have
been in a kind of trance. The words flowed with such
marvellous ease, and were such beautiful words, do
you know, I think she must have been delirious. I
cannot account for it any other way."

"Stephen prays in the same way," I replied; "and
he is of sound mind."

"Bless my soul!" said the Vicar. "Do you know, I
think she really was in a trance."

"Not at all," said I.

"And the way in which she prayed for Stephen was
absolutely sublime. If all men could at all times pray
as she prayed, it would settle the question of extempore
prayer. Really, she might have actually seen God face
to face."

In a moment or two the Vicar continued—

"I wanted to tell you about something else. Everything is very well settled at Broxham Grange. Sir
Hedley has bought off his neighbour—Butterworth is
the name—and levelled the new buildings, so all is quiet.
By far the best thing. I believe your friend Paterson
had something to do in bringing about the settlement.
Do you know, I believe Sir Hedley half suspected you
were a Dissenter. Birds always know when there's a
hawk in the air. He said nothing, but he was excited

and irritable, but of course he had confidence enough in me to know that I hate all Dissent."

The Vicar's genial laugh had hardly died away, when by a sudden turn in the street I came immediately upon Mr. Battison. An impalpable something like a shadow separated us, notwithstanding our cordial greeting. My impulse was to dash into the new subject, but something kept me back. What was the matter with my chatty old friend? Surely he had been long unable to sleep, or there was a cruel pain in his heart, or he saw some mocking spirit in the air. It was not natural for Nehemiah Battison to be so quiet. And where was the white hat? And had not the whole figure shrunk, and turned him into quite an old man? Yet I dare not ask, for asking questions would be like putting sharp knives into red wounds. My heart went out to him in a totally new way, seeing that he so much needed sympathy, and that if he had needed it less, he would have openly asked for it. I gave his hand a grip that he ought to have understood, and spoke with very cordial interest about the weather, as if grateful to him in some mysterious way for having made the sky so cloudless and warm. But Nehemiah's mind was preoccupied, the dapper manner was subdued, the soul so prone to flutter was dejected and afflicted heavily, and the voice was choked. When we shook hands and said good-bye my spirits quite broke down, and, obeying a sudden impulse, I literally ran after my friend, yearning over him with tender solicitude, for was not his heart sore, and did not grief shut out all the light?

"Mr. Battison," I said, "pardon me. I think I know all your trouble——"

"Not all of it," he sadly interposed.

I took his arm and walked with him. "Perhaps not all," I continued, "but enough to ask you to receive my sympathy. I am at your service." As Mr. Battison remained silent, I proceeded—"You must take comfort from the fact that you did not bring the trouble upon yourself. This is not your doing. Nor can we tell what good may come out of such discipline, and may I venture to say that it is under circumstances like yours that Christianity best shows what it can do. It is easy to believe at mid-day; it is hard to do so at midnight."

"That is where I break down," Mr. Battison replied in a subdued voice.

"Then that is where we must strengthen you," I answered.

"I do not see God's meaning. That is my trouble. I think it hard. I am afraid I shall loose my hold upon God and become a disbeliever. The only thing that seems to hinder me from giving up altogether is thinking about her—about Mary—what faith she had—I never saw anything like it; instead of adding to my trouble, she has taken most of it away: that is very strange." Mr. Battison continued in a livelier tone— "To have known her has been a real blessing to me, and a real blessing to all my daughters, and now that she is gone, it feels as if winter had suddenly set in. Mary has been a blessing to many. Weaver Stephen has been quite a father to her, and I shall thank him

for it to my dying day." As Mr. Battison said all this
he warmed into his old self, and continued—" My feet
were well nigh gone; it did seem hard at my time of
life. I began to wonder whether the worldly man was
not really better off than the Christian, and I felt such an
awful temptation to deny the very existence of God; but
just at the very darkest moment Mary seemed to look
at me and bid me hold fast and try again and live more
than ever on my knees. I think even now Mary will
win."

We presently came upon the neighbourhood of
Weaver Stephen's house, and, to our pleasant surprise,
Stephen himself was standing in the doorway. He had
that moment appeared. That something agreeable had
occurred was evident from the serene brightness of his
ever-placid face. Coming towards us, he said—

"I have got him in the house, sir, and I call it
oncommon. He wanted to hear all about it, and he
kep' on asking if there was nothing more I could tell
him, and he would have me say over and over again
what message she sent him, and I have given him the
Word, and really he seems to get hold of it. Now,
come in."

We went in and sat down in silence. Weaver
Stephen walked up and down, as if by that act he
broke the formality of the occasion, and gave us a sense
of ease. I felt as if I were present at a funeral.
Cheerfulness would have been untimely, and might have
set the conversation in a false key; over-solemnity
would not have expressed the hopefulness inspired by
Stephen's report. Whilst we were thus in a state of

uncertainty young Nehemiah found a way out of the difficulty.

"Father!" he began.

"My boy!" said the old man.

Then there was silence. Some speeches break off suddenly at the first word. I saw that Mr. Battison was deeply moved, and that his silence was caused by his emotion. The young man stood up, and the father also rose. Whilst they looked at one another I heard Weaver Stephen say—"He was dead and is alive again," and at the sound of that Christly music the father and son fell on each other's neck.

CHAPTER XVII.

OVED by curiosity to hear a blind man preach, Lily Gray, the Vicar's daughter, has actually been to the Baptist chapel, an offence against usage which was aggravated by the fact of her having been accompanied by Mr. Runch, the highly-esteemed senior churchwarden, who up to this time had stood next to the church steeple in reputation for steadfastness. The plea that Miss Gray had gone "merely out of curiosity" went for nothing in the judgment of many angry parishioners. The leading clothier in the town, so prosperous that he could afford either to give two years' credit or allow fifteen per cent. discount for cash, said that the days of Guy Fawkes were returning, and that the sun of England was setting amid omens which he was afraid to contemplate and unwilling to interpret. Mr. Edwards, the rubicund brewer, bluffly said,—"Omens or no omens"—a phrase expressive of boundless ignorance and independence—"he would be hanged if he would stand it," but as many slender causes had hitherto kept Mr. Edwards from the gallows, his threat was not looked upon as alarming. "I'm blest," said the junior churchwarden, "if I know what's coming

upon us ; they will want the church bells now they've
got the churchwarden.   For some time I have thought
Miss Gray was not with us heart and soul."   " Heart
and soul ! " echoed Edwards, without adding a word, for
what can a man say when he is blue with fury ?   At
such moments words are but idle breath.   The clothier
advised the brewer to control himself, but the brewer
received the suggestion with scorn.

Miss Gray could not imagine what a Dissenting
chapel was like, nor what the people did when they
were in it.   " Do let us go early," said she to Mr.
Runch, " and then we shall see them all as they come
in.   It will be so droll ! Oh dear, Mr. Runch, do you
think, after all, it will be quite safe to go ? Perhaps a
judgment will fall on us.   But, oh dear ! I should so
much like to go."   Mr. Runch paused a moment, and
then slowly gave it as his opinion that the adoption of
proper precautions would render danger almost impossible.   Miss Gray besought Mr. Runch to adopt
anything he liked to save them both from anything like
a judgment, or catching anything either undesirable or
infectious.   " Camphor, Mr. Runch, they do say, is an
excellent thing."   In due time Miss Gray and Mr.
Runch were courteously accommodated with a seat which
commanded a clear view of most of the chapel.   The
young lady's eyes glittered as she looked round with
almost wild expectancy, as if she did not know, yet
could not help wondering at what impossible place the
wild beasts might suddenly burst forth.   Her whispered
annotations were explicit and sincere, though narrowly
escaping cynicism and even rudeness.   "'What a fright

of a bonnet! Oh, Mr. Runch, is that a real Baptist
bonnet, that one with the cockatoo feather? Look."
"And there's that horrid old post-office man in the very
front of the gallery." "Do look at that queer woman
in the corner just under the gas-bracket, with all the
colours of the rainbow in her bonnet." "What rickety
old men! what odd figures! what droll expressions!
I never knew there were such people in the town.
Are they all Baptists? Isn't it well for the minister
that he is blind?" These running comments might
have gone much farther, but were stopped by the
sitting down immediately in front of Miss Gray of a
well-known pastrycook in the town, whose gold eye-
glass and supernatural solemnity signalised him as a
high dignitary in the Baptist chapel, bearing many responsibilities and literally aching with solicitude. But
innocent Miss Gray was unaware, like many other
fluent critics, that she herself and the senior churchwarden were being commented upon by Baptist observers. "Come to take a rise out of us," said Mrs.
Bidwell. "Now that I see Runch with his hat off,"
said Mr. Langport, as he ponderously turned round to
Mr. Knockey, "he is not at all intellectual-looking;
going about with his hat on, he's rather smart-looking,
but he little knows what he owes to his hat." "She
does not know how to behave herself in the sanctuary,"
said Mrs. Lambert, hardly recovered from a fit which
she had had in the afternoon; "I can see, even from
the gallery, how she is trying to keep the laugh down."
"In the last days perilous times shall come," said the
rhetorical Riddle to "Johnny dear," who for some

time had abandoned the practice of shaving on Sunday evenings, and resumed his attendance at chapel. " It is wonderful," Langport continued to whisper, "what a difference a hat does make : now there's our esteemed deacon ; when he puts his hat on he becomes a pastry-cook at once, but when he comes out of the vestry with his hat off he is every inch a deacon." The opening of the minister's door put an end to all this whispering. Once his foot was squarely on the first step, Mr. Whiteman ascended the pulpit as if he saw every step before him. Mr. Whiteman was quite himself, so well prepared for the service as to be quiet, simple, and joyously solemn. His subject lay before him like an open landscape, every turn of the sunny road familiar and inviting. He prayed as if he saw heaven opened and the Son of man standing on the right hand of God, and when he preached he seemed to be delivering the answer to his own prayer. Mr. Whiteman's great ministry had many remarkable aspects and qualities even in its ordinary course, but at times, as on this evening, he looked and spoke like a man possessed of the Holy Ghost and standing between the living and the dead like a prophet of the Lord. On these trans-figuration days it was of small consequence to Mr. Whiteman who was present, or on what pretence.

The effect upon Miss Gray was entirely unlooked for, and probably less looked for by herself than by any one else. The effect was as though an unknown kinship had suddenly disclosed itself, and adduced credentials which it was impossible to dispute.

"Papa," said she, in a tone the Vicar had never

14

heard before, "what is faith? What is the Spirit of
God? What is the spiritual world? Mr. Whiteman
spoke about them as if he knew all about them, and it
was so grand, so solemn, papa, so——"

"Don't distress yourself about these things, my
child," said the Vicar; "read the articles and the
homilies you know, and I will order the trap for a run
over to Broxham; an afternoon with Sir Hedley, you
know; yes, yes, calm yourself, my Lily."

"Papa, the place seemed to be full of spirits, and
although Mr. Whiteman is blind, he seemed to see them,
and he was not the least morsel afraid. I thought him
an angel."

"Just so, dear, just so. I understand it all. The
trap will be round at two."

"Papa, dear, do you think I am an invalid?"

"Not at all, Lily, not for a moment. Better see
Mr. Bonas."

"Oh no, papa; his words have no music in them, no
soul, no fire——"

"Perhaps not, dear, but Mr. Bonas has quite a
wonderful knowledge of the middle ages."

"And what have we to do with the middle
ages?"

"Nothing in the world, my dear, nothing. That's
just where it is. Now settle down."

"Papa, what are spirits? What is the spirit-world?
Oh, papa, what is God?"

"Exactly, love, exactly. It was rather thoughtless
of Mr. Runch to take you. I must see Runch. Yes.
I will see Runch almost immediately. Exactly."

"What do you want to see Mr. Runch about, papa?"

"To get the particulars, dear; merely that; when I get the particulars, you know——"

"What particulars, papa?"

"Everything about it, you know, my dear; now calm yourself," then aside—"Her mother was very excitable; once thought she was an angel; never would calm herself properly; used to call me flippant," then to Lily—"You'll soon be better, dear. I ought to have opposed your going——"

"Going where, papa?"

"Going to the Dissenters, dear; you have not been used to excitement——"

"But, papa, that is where you make a mistake; there was not the very least excitement——"

"Just so, Lily; you don't quite understand. No man can be a Dissenter without being excited; it may be well kept down, but it is still there; if it was not there, the man could not be a Dissenter."

"If Mr. Whiteman is a Dissenter, I should like to be one, papa."

"Oh, my dear! Of course I know what you mean. I will see Mr. Runch, and we must calmly await events."

Mr. Runch received the Vicar almost silently, and put on all the churchwardenship he could carry.

"I am afraid, Mr. Runch, the chapel has not done my daughter any good."

Mr. Runch eyed the Vicar. Although a churchwarden, Mr. Runch—to his honour be it said—was still a man.

"Speak freely to me, Mr. Runch, and let me have the particulars."

"Sir," said Runch, "we have entered upon an upsetting course, deny it who can."

"Your meaning is not overclear, Mr. Runch."

"If you had been here one short hour ago, my meaning would have been but too clear."

"Did something happen then?"

"Something happened then, Mr. Gray; a good deal happened then; my head is in a whiz."

"In a whiz, Mr. Runch?" Then aside—"Excitement is spreading,—lunacy has set in."

"In a whiz. It has not been in such a whiz since I married. The parish church of Midford, deny it who can, is spinning madly round like a teetotum." Mr. Gray sighed. As a man he was tolerably square on his feet, but as a vicar he swooned, and sank into the silence of despair. Speak he could not.

"Little did I think," continued Mr. Runch, "that the insult would have been offered in my own back parlour.'

"Insult?"

"Insult. I deliberately say insult. The base design was poorly masked."

"My dear Runch, do calm yourself, and oblige me with the full particulars. Be calm and explicit."

"Sir, the man Knockey called here an hour ago, and, saying that he wanted to see me on private matters, I invited him, with natural reluctance, into my back parlour, and there the villain——"

"Oh, my dear Runch!"

"The villain I call him; I speak advisedly, and with the responsibility of a parish official——"

"Senior churchwarden," said the Vicar.

"Senior churchwarden; yes; that sinister and deeply designing person asked me, in view of my having been to his chapel, whether I would subscribe to a testimonial to the minister!"

"Testimonial?"

"Testimonial; yes; testimonial was the word he used,—the unblushing renegade!"

Mr. Runch did not know the meaning of the term "renegade," but ignorance does not interfere with fluency.

"You stupefy me, Mr. Runch."

"Knockey," Runch continued, "had scarcely been gone ten minutes, when a most elephantine person of the name, I will not say the nature, of Langport called upon me, a huge man who ought to travel by luggage train, quite a load of grossness, and he asked me if I wished to take a seat at the chapel, because if so, there were some good ones in the gallery, and he added——"

"Oh, Mr. Runch," said the Vicar, "what did he add?"

"He added that the seats in the gallery were not so expensive as those downstairs."

"Most insulting," the Vicar rapidly interposed.

"That was nothing, sir."

"Nothing? Why, my dear Runch, what a memorable morning you have passed through!"

"Langport was just going away, when in came a most curious and revolting woman named Bidwell, who asked

me in the boldest manner if I was in ' a state of grace,'
and she hoped, as I had begun to attend chapel, I would
keep it up, and never return to the mother of harlots."

When the Vicar returned home he found that the
"particulars" furnished by Mr. Runch did not assist
him to deal with the case of his daughter, but he did
find that an old lady called Mrs. Lambert had inquired
at the Vicarage how Miss Gray was after her visit to
the Baptist chapel, and had offered to explain Baptist
principles to that young lady whenever called upon to
do so, and had left a small handbill announcing a course
of afternoon addresses by the Baptised Chimney-sweep,
Mr. Robert Morby, entitled "The Glory Gate : how I
found it, opened it, and shut it again," each address to
be followed by a collection for the conversion of other
sweeps of limited means and corrupt dispositions. Morby
himself had left the profession in favour of younger men.

" Papa, what is the Glory Gate, do you suppose ? "

" It is confounded stupidity and nonsense, Lily, and
I will allow the matter to proceed no farther. I have
got full particulars from Runch, and I am disgusted.
I have made a mistake, Lily, in being too friendly with
the Dissenters. What do people want ? They can be
baptised, confirmed, churched, married, and buried, and
all in a lawful and becoming manner. What more can
they possibly desire ? Is not everything written down ?
I ought to have thought of that, and I ought to have been
very much against your going to the Baptist chapel."

Miss Gray had seldom seen her genial father in this
mood, but in this case the little touch of temper was

perhaps useful in calling up her reserve of strength and courage, and by so much proving that the Vicar was quite in error in supposing that his daughter was either an invalid or a lunatic.

"Papa, you were really not in error at all, so you have no occasion to be excited. You have asked me to control myself, and if I ask you to do the same thing, it is only that I may ask you what all the fuss is about? I have seen and heard something new; I have asked a question or two as to the meaning of things; I believe that Mr. Whiteman knows more than a good many other people know; and I wish to inquire, and consider, and come to right conclusions. What harm is there?"

"Lily," said the Vicar, "you are right. Pardon my natural anxiety. You take a most sensible view. I was altogether wrong in my foolish fears. So you really liked Mr. Whiteman?"

"Oh yes, papa. It was so touching to see his pretty ways, and when he came to preach you cannot imagine what beautiful words he used, or how glorious his face was in the middle of the prayer. I quite longed to ask him all about the sermon and to find out what he meant. As for Mr. Runch, I seriously believe he did not care for what was said; indeed, I know he did not, for when we came out he said such a place as that would kill him in a month, and he thanked God that none of his ancestors were either Baptists or anything like it."

The Vicar secretly sided with Mr. Runch, but wisely said nothing. "You are quite yourself again now," he aggravatingly remarked; "still I will have the trap round, and we can run over to Broxham for an hour. Everything will presently blow over. All these poor cripples will soon see that their game is not a paying one, and in a day or two, a week at the most, everything will be as if nothing had happened."

CHAPTER XVIII.

TOMLINSON "jacked it all up," yet the stars quietly shone upon the earth as if nothing had happened. What the stars felt inwardly no man can tell, but outwardly there was no sign of emotion. I am proud enough of the Church of England to say that priestly illegitimacy cannot impose upon her. The serene old mother knows her own children, but when she looks upon converted Dissenters, there is an undoubted expression of suspicion in her motherly eyes. Such Dissenters, exceptions being granted, generally want to borrow something which they cannot repay; it may be only a character, or a patent of respectability, or so worldly a boon as a "living"; but the want is always on their side rather than on the side of the Church. Tomlinson wanted a good deal, and got nothing. When I last saw him he was chaplain of a cemetery, and in bitter controversy with the "scurvy Dissenter" who had official charge of the unconsecrated ground. To that lucrative office, yielding a little over a pound a week, Tomlinson had been promoted, so perhaps it is hardly exact to say that he got nothing by the change. He thought that as a preacher he would take the benighted Establishment by storm, but so boisterous was his manner that when he first preached in a parish pulpit he drove two of the churchwardens insane, and so excited the beadle as to make that quiet functionary a nuisance to the domestic hearth. Nor did Tomlinson regret this as a humane preacher ought to have done; on the contrary, he said that all this upset was the sure omen of "a gracious revival," and that if it could be kept up in active force for a month, a wonderful transformation would take place in the parish. This was no doubt true, but the parish declined to be transformed; indeed, the beadle went so far as to intimate to a brother officer that in knocking down a man like Tomlinson, any man worthy of the name might find a good deal of honest satisfaction. Tomlinson created quite a panic in the parish. Some were thunderstruck, some thought that judgment was nigh at hand, others considered it unlucky to see such a man prowling in the town, and one ardent soul called the attention of the Bishop to the havoc with which the parish was threatened. Thus Tomlinson was disappointed, and began to feel that even in the Church of England the most distinguished genius may basely go without recognition.

"Call this a national church!" said he; "then where am I?" That was a solemn poser, and, in fact, a poser that never was answered. The sexton was so "paralysed" by what he called this "bull of Bashan," that he would not follow Tomlinson into the vestry to do the customary offices, "for," as he admitted to a fellow boot-maker in the town, "I was so chawed up and blistered all over that I did not know what the deuce so passionate a little demon might do if he got me into a corner." The sexton was not the man to stand upon the purity of a metaphor, or to reject a forbidden word when it exactly expressed the feeling of the moment, and therefore I hope that this quotation will not be so narrowly or maliciously interpreted as to do the sexton any harm either in the family or in business. For want of outdoor exercise a boot-maker must often be driven out of the monotony of propriety into the confidential use of energetic terms, and I consider that in such a case large consideration should be given to extenuating circumstances. The simple fact is that the parish was afraid of Tomlinson ; he was so infinite in his own esteem, so hideously pompous in his rotundity and his feeble waddle, and so raving mad in the pulpit, that not a shopkeeper in the parish would open an account with him. And even at home poor Tomlinson's lot was hard, for his wife had not been reconverted to the Church, but remained an incorrigible and hardmouthed renegade.

"What has your fine church done for you ? " she said to Tomlinson in a tone whose aggravation was perfect.

" My dear," said he, " patience, patience."

" Fiddlesticks ! " his wife replied ; " patience has worn me to a bone."

" Talent will be recognised in the long run," Tomlinson added ; " the Church of England needs preaching-power ; rich in theology and brilliant in tradition, she yet needs——"

" It is quite clear she does not need *you*," Mrs. Tom-

linson interrupted, with bitter emphasis on the last
word.

." My turn will come, dear."

" Yes, on the day of judgment all our turns will
likely come."

" Before that, love," Tomlinson meekly added ; " any
post may bring me a letter from the Bishop ; think of
that, dear, not from a purse-proud deacon, but from
the Bishop ! "

"I am expecting a letter from the Bishop myself,"
said Mrs. Tomlinson, " a letter to tell you to pack up
and be off ! "

" My dear ! "

" Why not ? " Mrs. Tomlinson inquired.

Perhaps Mrs. Tomlinson was embittered by the
recollection of an interview with Mrs. Bell, the churchwarden's wife, a lady whose excellence of motive was
always pleaded in extenuation of a frankness which
was wont to take no account of human feeling.

" Can you not, dear, persuade Mr. Tomlinson to take
a little something just to tame him down before he goes
to church ? I think the chemist could do something
up for him that would hold him in, dear, and slightly
tame him down, for really it is intolerable, and Mr. Bell
says that no bull could make such a noise if all the
dogs in the town came upon him in a pack. Mr. Bell
is quite serious."

" Then you object to earnest preaching ? " Mrs. Tomlinson inquired.

" Gracious me ! " said Mrs. Bell; " earnest preaching !
What ever can you mean ? I object to earnest bray-

ing, dear, and earnest bellowing, and earnest roaring : you know, dear, the church is not a zoological gardens, or even a travelling menagerie ; now I daresay Mr. Tomlinson was quite a shining light amongst the Dissenters——"

Mrs. Tomlinson stood aghast at this allusion, for her reverend husband had done his best to conceal the fact that he had ever been associated with that partially disreputable body, and by cultivating a drawl and a haw-haw had supposed he might pass for an Oxford man, double first-class and Fellow of a college. But there is a spirit in man, and even country parishioners have not been excluded from the inspiration of the Almighty.

" How do you know what Mr. Tomlinson would be amongst the Dissenters ? "

" Only what my housemaid tells me, dear."

" Your housemaid ? "

" Yes, dear. She used to be in the service of Miss Beebee, of the Green Hollows, and she has told me what Miss Beebee thought of your husband's preaching, and how kind Miss Beebee was to you all, and of course we wish to be kind, and all we want is to tame him down a little, quiet his nerves a trifle, and soothe him somehow."

" My husband is a revivalist," said Mrs. Tomlinson, in a tone of indefinite pride.

" Possibly so, dear, and that is exactly what we do not require in this old-fashioned parish. Very few of us are deaf, it is astonishing how few. And if you will not think me rude, dear, I should like to say that if Mr. Tomlinson wishes to secure promotion in the Church, he must drop a good many of his Dissenting ways."

" And pray what may they be, Mrs. Bell ? "

" Well, dear, he drops in rather too often at lunch-time, or tea-time, or dinner-time, as the case may be, and Dissenters have wonderful appetites, and there's poor Mrs. Adamson, the widow on the hill, says that she has hardly time to begin her tea when, to her horror, she finds Mr. Tomlinson has gobbled all up, and looks at her quite reproach-fully."

" Then why does she ask him to tea ? "

" She does not, dear ; Mr. Tomlinson stops without asking. My housemaid tells me that Dissenters are very fond of tea ; they have been mostly brought up on tea ; they often have meetings for the purpose of shaking hands and drinking tea ; she says the ministers are the worst of all, and that Mr. Tomlinson has been known in his Dissenting days to drink, at a meeting, eighteen cups of tea ! "

" Do not believe all you hear, Mrs. Bell."

" Quite right, dear, but I don't care how much tea the good creature drinks—for Mr. Bell is the largest tea-dealer in the district—if we can only tame him down a little, and bring him within the limits of a Christian gentleman and clergyman."

A conversation of this kind might well account for the strong tincture of bitterness in the remarks which Mrs. Tomlinson addressed to her husband, a bitterness which Tomlinson hastened to counteract by an announcement which seemed to have in it the promise of money and comfort.

"I have a pleasant surprise for you, my dear. A young colonist, whose education has been wholly neglected, has advertised for board and lodging in the family of a clergyman; see? in the family of a clergyman, not in the family of a Dissenting minister; these are the *incidental* advantages of my new position; never overlook incidental advantages. Well, this young colonist is coming. For a time he will put up at the inn, and as soon as possible we must make a boarder of him. There is no lack of money, as well as no lack of ignorance."

Mr. Tomlinson having said this, stroked his chin, adjusted his spectacles, and in calling his wife by her Christian name he threw into the word "Fanny" an emotion only to be accounted for by the brightest prospects of success.

The young colonist was a strapper, considerably over six feet high, yellowy brown in complexion, and altogether about the most muscular lion's cub that has ever been seen out of a show. There was decided character about him at every point, but most of all in his deeply cavernous mouth, large enough not only to swallow Mrs. Adamson's tea and toast, but the widow and table and everything on it. His impossible clothing must be left to the imagination, for its amplitude, its independence of the human figure, and its impartial amalgamation of colours, cannot be adequately described in words.

" Is Nehemiah anywheres handy ? " said he, soon
after making Mr. Tomlinson's acquaintance.

"Still in the old place," said Tomlinson, entering
into the humour of the inquiry.

" Guessed as much.   The mother country ain't big,
so I thought Nehemiah might be round here snug
and handy.   Perhaps you can fetch him to-night
for a chew and a mug."

" Surely I must misunderstand you," said Tomlinson.   " I thought you were inquiring about an Old
Testament saint who bore the name of Nehemiah."

" A sorter clergyman, I guess you mean.   No.   I
mean Battison, whiskey slogger, a man who could
drink a mill-dam dry if it ran the real stingo.   But
I say, boss, you ain't a real clergyman, are you ?
I mean the genu*ine* sort, you know."

" Certainly I am," said Tomlinson ; " what makes
you think the contrary ? "

" Are you a downright gamecock with a pedigree ? "

Mr. Tomlinson did not like the inquiry, but could not
wisely resent it.   As he looked up to the ochre-
coloured giant he felt that in point of size he was
the smallest of bantams.   He never felt so small
before.

" You know," said the giant, " in the colony we should
be rather like eating you slap off at breakfast and
washing you down with some sort of muddled water,
you are so fat and comfortable.   You can't be much
short of two hundred and fifty, I reckon by the eye."

"Two hundred and fifty what ? " Tomlinson inquired.   " Not years, I hope."

" I guess you weigh two hundred and fifty; now own up; don't you ? "

" These are private matters," said Tomlinson, adopting a severe manner.

" But what was you about as a child not to grow yourself a pair of longer pins ? You don't show up well in inches. You cannot be much more than a yard and a half, eh ? "

" Such subjects are not discussed by gentlemen in our relation."

" But, boss, you ain't humbugging me about your being a genuine clergyman ? You ain't the man to put a paper collar on and make-believe it's linen ? You ain't the man to stuff yourself out with a pillow-case and make-believe it's real human nature ? I guess you won't try to play off on a genuine colonist ? "

" Certainly not," said Tomlinson. " I am as good as a bishop as far as I go."

" You don't look it, boss ; you have a fed-up look ; you seem to have been put together by a baker and butcher : boss, you muddle me."

Mr. Tomlinson could have returned the compliment, but hirelings must be silent.

" I guess I'll advertise through my agent again," said the giant. " I don't feel as you are genuine. A clergyman has no business to be so fat ; he ought to be more skin-and-bone like ; it don't seem to me as a genuine colonist that God Almighty wants outdoor servants quite so heavy as two hundred and fifty, or quite so short as a yard and a half. You don't look handy. You are a sorter squashy man. Something inside me tells me you are not genuine."

15

Mr. Tomlinson could have borne a good deal of insult in view of the terms which had been arranged in the course of correspondence, but it is due to him to say that on seeing the giant and hearing him, and especially feeling the iron grip of his comprehensive hand, he got quite a new view of the uncertainty of human life, and piously resigned himself to a new disappointment. Incidental advantages are sometimes illusory.

The next Sunday was an awful time in the parish church. Mrs. Bell fainted at the end of the first explosion, and was carried out exclaiming—" Do tame him down if you possibly can." The beadle, like a thirsty David, refreshed himself with a draught of communion wine, and both the churchwardens went straight home without saying one word. Tomlinson swelled and raged, and hammered the pulpit with malicious fury, and altogether acted with violent effect the part of a pious maniac. Parish churches were not built for noise. They do not respond to declamation. They will bear any amount of massive eloquence, delivered with harmonious dignity and well-handled passion, but they coldly disown all rant and din and wildness.

"Well," said Mrs. Tomlinson to her exhausted pastor and husband, " you have succeeded admirably in making a fool of yourself."

" In what way, Fanny ? "

" In mouthing and bellowing, in shouting as if you meant your old congregation at Green Hollows to hear you, in every way."

" You don't understand me, Fanny ; you really don't. The Church of England needs first-class preaching, impassioned oratory, and vivid dramatism. What

would you have me do? Would you have me go
back to the Dissenters?"

"I would, but they wouldn't," said Mrs. Tomlinson
very tartly.

Then Tomlinson had not found heaven in finding
the Church? No. He had found nothing of the kind.
Few such changes are happy in their consequences
either on one side or the other. Clergymen are born,
and Dissenting ministers descend from generation to
generation, and it would seem to be impossible for
them to unite to the extent at least of amalgamation.
It will be something when the ecclesiastical Rhine and
Moselle find a point at which they can roll in a common
channel, but to the end they will show to close observers
which is which. Tomlinson did the utmost in his
power to put off the Dissenting old man with his deeds,
but the Ethiopian could not change his skin. He
practised all sorts of voices in private, now like a
supposed bishop, now a dean, now a squirely arch-
deacon, and once—for truth must be stated at all
hazards—once Tomlinson tried to speak in the tones of
an imaginary archbishop. That experiment was very
memorable from a dramatic point of view; Tomlinson
had put on his surplice in the bedroom; one or two
black ribbons belonging to his wife had been cunningly
arranged over his bulky shoulders; a prayer-book was
open in his hands, and he himself, an unmitred but
expectant Grace, say His Grace of Canterbury, stood in
front of the looking-glass, and extended his forefinger
towards an imaginary cathedral crowded with eager

auditors, who, at infinite personal inconvenience, had assembled to hear the prince of orators. The crisis had reached the point of agony, when a voice keen with impatience and anger exclaimed——

"Mrs. Bell wants you; go down to her, you greasy imbecile !"

These were not proper words to address to an ordinary parish priest, and certainly not to an arch-bishop, and perhaps under no conceivable circumstances was it proper for a wife to use them to her husband.

"Oh, Mr. Tomlinson, if you cannot be tamed down a little, you really ought to go back to the Dissenters. Now the Methodists, say, would they not like to get hold of an open-air preacher ? "

"Do you suppose, Mrs. Bell, that I have the honour of being an open-air preacher ? "

"Certainly I do, and, in fact, it is too small a place for you. I think you ought to try the sea ; then there would be a pair of you. But I called to say that the chemist has made something up for you——"

"Madam ! what may your mysterious meaning be ?"

"To quiet the nerves, you know. No harm in it. A child might take it for that matter. The chemist says it is wonderful for taming——"

"Madam ! Do you suppose you are talking to a wild beast ? "

"Not in private, Mr. Tomlinson. The mixture is not made for you in your private capacity. I was very particular to explain that to the chemist. It is just to operate in the pulpit when the fit comes on——"

" And what fit is that, madam ? "

" I really don't know what the name of it is, Mr.
Tomlinson. There are so many fits. The chemist
said something about epileptic ; but I don't go so far
as that myself, for Mr. Bell has an uncle afflicted in
that way, and I must say he was worse than you are,
because he foamed at the mouth a good deal more,
though he did not stand out quite so much at the eyes ;
but you both clutch at the air about alike. I thought,
perhaps, that you would tame down a little——"

" Madam, I have no wish to be rude ; but I must
protest against the word 'tame.' It savours of a wild
beast ; it suggests tigers and leopards ; it disturbs the
imagination by visions of iron cages, and red-hot bars,
and chains——"

" Oh dear, Mr. Tomlinson, how can you think of
such awful things ? "

" How can you think of them, Mrs. Bell ? "

" I don't, Mr. Tomlinson. I am only going by what
my housemaid tells me. She says that when you were
the Independent minister at Green Hollows——"

Mr. Tomlinson started, for Mrs. Tomlinson had not
told him about the housemaid.

" She says you sometimes became black in the face,
and that many of the elderly people were quite glad
when you went away, you made them so nervous,
and even Miss Beebee often turned white and looked
uncomfortable."

Then Mr. Tomlinson had not found heaven in finding
the Church ? Human nature is much the same in all
ecclesiastical conditions, as Mr. Tomlinson found to his

great discomfort. Men cannot so easily bury their dead selves, whatever the poets may say. Some man, great or small, some mistress or maid, brings back the past and forces it, all the more sometimes that the act is unintentional, upon the reluctant attention of the self that was supposed to be dead. The most annoying circumstance connected with the unlamented secession of such men as Tomlinson is that they are supposed by ignorant persons to represent the better class of Nonconformist ministers! They are the good men who, having repented of their wickedness, have confirmed their penitence by self-sacrificing withdrawment from the schismatics ; and bishops rejoice over them, and account them as the first-fruits of harvest! Nor does the mischief end here. Tomlinson not only withdraws ; he presumes to report to the other side the vulgarity of the mob he has left. He could not stand it. He was being debased by it. It had a dwarfing effect upon his mind. Thus he makes the air dark with lies, yet fails to make himself a gentleman. But what about Mr. Tomlinson's " political wisdom" ? Did he enjoy Miss Beebee's property and so become a really, because a financially, independent minister ? When that benevolent lady departed this life events did not disclose themselves in Mr. Tomlinson's favour. Miss Beebee's mind was not marked by that peculiar kind of comprehensiveness which obliterates all distinctions and includes in a common benediction the left hand and the right. Miss Beebee loved some things and hated others, and amongst the things she honestly detested was the principle of the State establishment of religion.

How far she had mastered the philosophy of that principle it is now too late to inquire, but we may hope that our ignorance in no way impairs her happiness. It is almost certain that her narrowness was inspired by prejudice, and was in no degree amended by a liberal desire to know what could be said on the other side. Be that as it may, she visited Mr. Tomlinson's secession with penalties. The whole of her property she gave and bequeathed to Professor Stokoe, who, on learning his good fortune, gurgled something about an experiment which he was about to make by placing water drawn from the Great Geyser of Iceland in an evaporating basin. So much for bachelor philosophers coming into unexpected fortunes!

CHAPTER XIX.

THE Rev. Edwin Bonas, man of the automa-
ton coat, has undertaken to pacify Miss
Gray and show her the sinfulness of
having even once attended the ministry
of a Baptist heretic.   He was, indeed, so
interested in the case that he deferred his
intention for one week of going into the
Retreat for exercises of penance.   Mr. Bonas had
reduced all human repentance and obedience within a
circle of directions sold for the modest sum of one
penny; so all he had to do when any new case of
rebellion or schism arose was to put up his eye-glass
and scan the inexpensive pages.   When an incipient
schismatic ventured even to inquire what Nonconformity was, he was sacerdotally commanded to take
a glass of water when he was very thirsty and to put
it down again just as it touched his lips ; and if it was
feminine heresy, the offender was to dress herself for
walking, and as soon as she was quite ready to go out
to put off all her things, dust as many prayer books as
she could find, and pinch her arm until she could bear it
no longer.   Surely it is rather handy to have sin and
penalty so exactly balanced, and everything neatly
packed and labelled that is needful for chastisement

and edification ; at all events, it puts no strain upon ingenuity, and carries with it all the mystery and charm of anonymousness. In her then state of mind Miss Gray was more than willing to receive intelligent and healthy religious instruction ; she was absolutely eager and hungry for it. There is a time in spiritual experience when it would seem as if one word would bring light and order and peace, if we could only find the voice powerful enough to say it. Voices of criticism are always audible ; suggestions tending to the utter destruction of all faith are making tumult enough ; but the voice that can give shape to shapelessness and stability to indecision and helplessness is often felt to be wanting. So the soul has to live on controversy or to submit to be thrown from one dissatisfaction to another by any empiric who cannot fear God because he idolises himself. We have been thrown upon an age of analysis and definition, and have left far behind the quiet and sober days when we were content to work in the light without taking the sun to pieces to see where the splendour came from.

"I remember," said Bonas, "the person you went to—to—*see;* I once encountered him—that is, in a distant sort of way—forget his name—I—I—remember another person with him—a person with boots—ya-as—person of the name of Paterson——"

"The Rev. Mr. Paterson, of Mixford ? " Miss Gray inquired.

"No, no ; by no means ; not 'reverend,' I hope—not reverend—rawly !—the chief of a mob—not related to the Apostolical order."

"I believe he is a better man than many clergymen are," Miss Gray spiritedly if not argumentatively interposed.

"Oh, rawly! Very extraordinary! Our individual unworthiness—let me call your immediate attention to the twenty-sixth Article—special declaration——"

"A fig for Articles!"

"Rawly!"

"You seem to think I have done wrong in going to hear——"

"To *see*," Mr. Bonas interrupted.

"To see and hear, not the minister you mean, but the Rev. Mr. Whiteman; is that so?"

"Ya-as. Rawly! Not reverend."

"Then what do you advise me to do?" Miss Gray put this inquiry with a humour which she admirably disguised.

"To make full and unfeigned confession."

"Will a sort of general confession be considered enough, Mr. Bonas? Consider yourself my ghostly adviser, and tell me. I am all attention."

"Rawly!"

"Well, now, please to proceed."

"Are you in that state of mind which is proper and needful?"

"I don't know. I have a good deal to confess, if I choose to. Won't a general confession be enough?"

"Not a general confession, certainly. Oh, no. Whatever is said in confession, you must remember, is said under seal. If you mention anything against parents or against the dearest friend you have on

earth, I will, if you so desire it, celebrate for their conversion or their humbling and purifying of heart. We
must be united in confession. Let me give you an
example from the notes of a young woman, whose confession I received in church this morning; of course
the name is hidden with me : ' Since my last confession,
which was on the 10th of the present month, I have
been too hasty in my morning prayers ; once I did not
get up in time ; once I spent too much time in dressing,
and as this was on a Friday morning, I deeply feel
the sinfulness of the act. I once spoke sarcastically
of a priest who did not please my vain and foolish
taste in the way in which he preached his sermon.
Five times I have thought of worldly things in
church. I have twice answered my father disre-
spectfully. I have felt too much interest in a young
man who attends a Dissenting meeting-house and
keeps the post-office ; when I have gone to the post-
office for stamps he has spoken to me, and I have been
foolishly pleased. Once I told an untruth. Twice I
said yes when I ought to have said no ; and once, on a
Friday, I kept persons waiting because I was so long
in dressing, and on that same Friday I quite forgot to
make any difference in my meals.' That is the true
way to confess. The soul thus throws off its burden,
and receives absolution."

Miss Gray was silent, and there was a troubled expression on her pale face.

"We must not stumble at the word absolution. We
must accept it. The power of absolution was given to
us in our ordination, when we received the Holy Ghost.

And if you will read the history of godly and sainted men, who were the very glory of the Church of England, you will see that the most illustrious Anglican Catholics went to the penance of confession. In 1625 King James I. besought Bishop Williams to give him absolution. In 1710 Bishop Bull received absolution before his death. In 1650 Archbishop Williams showed what value he set upon confession and absolution; there was no regular presbyter to give him the sacrament, so the prelate purposely ordained an honest and pious servant of his own to administer to him in those holy offices. Amongst ladies who have observed this holy sacrament of confession and received the grace of absolution, I may mention Lady Rachel Russell, who confessed to Dr. Fitzwilliam every month; Elizabeth Lady Capel, who died in 1660; Sibylla Lady Anderson, who was absolved the day before her death in 1661; and the wife of Bishop Wilson, who died in 1705; the Bishop, in enumerating God's mercies to her, specially mentions the ministry of absolution. So, you see, Miss Gray, I am asking you to unite yourself with a holy band who, notwithstanding the disturbances of the Reformation, have maintained the true faith and practice of the Catholic Church of England."

Miss Gray made no attempt to conceal her amazement at the wonderful change which had come over Mr. Bonas as to his way of expressing himself. On other subjects, and in mixed company, he spoke briefly, with considerable hesitation, and in a mincing way. But now he was quite fluent, almost energetic, and never at a loss for an argument which from his point of view was convincing and final. Miss Gray now saw the real priest in his true character, and probably he considered her interest in his remarks as creating an opportunity for the display of still intenser earnestness, for with great solemnity he whispered a *Gloria*, and sighed—" Jesu, mercy !"

" You need have no difficulty," he presently continued, " on the ground of confidence, for the hundred and thirteenth Canon binds every priest receiving confession to absolute secrecy. I have transcribed the very words of the Canon : 'If any man confess his secret and hidden sins to the minister, for the unburdening of his conscience, and to receive spiritual consolation and ease of mind from him, we do straitly warn and admonish the said minister that he do not at any time reveal and make known to any person whatsoever any crime or offence so committed to his trust and secrecy (except they be such crimes as by the laws of this realm his own life may be called into question for receiving the same), under pain of irregularity.' This is one of the canons of the Church, and we are solemnly bound by it." As Mr. Bonas dwelt upon these points the tears came into Miss Gray's eyes, but whether from bodily pain or spiritual excitement is not explained. The eager priest put his own construction upon the fact, and proceeded in a well-modulated voice accordingly : " Even Latimer and Ridley expressly approved confession, and Cranmer distinctly taught the doctrine and urged the practice in these words : ' God hath given the keys of the kingdom of heaven, and the authority to forgive sins, to the ministers of the Church. Wherefore let him that is a sinner go to one of them. Let him acknowledge and confess his sin, and pray him that, according to God's commandments, he will give him absolution, and comfort him with the word of grace and forgiveness of his sins. And when the minister doth so, then I ought steadfastly to believe that my sins are truly forgiven me in heaven.' Who, then, Miss Gray, are we that we should set aside the counsel of the most saintly and venerable elders of the Church ?"

Miss Gray had no answer immediately ready. She could but sigh in a kind of troubled wonder, and add how difficult it was sometimes to know exactly what to do. "There are so many good people on all sides of a question," she said, "that one cannot tell which is right and which is wrong. Now, I daresay if Mr. Whiteman——"

"Oh, rawly !" Mr. Bonas interposed in his old tone.

"Was here, he could give another view of the subject, and papa does not approve it; but I do not wish to argue."

"Argument is useless, Miss Gray; I will not argue, it is presumptuous."

"I only wish to do what is right."

"Then follow my advice, Miss Gray. Immediately proceed to the blessed sacrament of confession, and the relief of mind which will follow will be unspeakably great ; all fear of death will be taken away; the dark clouds will be dispelled, and you will be happy in God : happy if you live ; happier still if you die."

"You have received confession from other ladies, I understand?"

"Only this morning, as I have told you. The notes I have read were received by me this very morning. Several ladies confess. The joy they experience is incredibly great."

"But I really don't know how to begin. I don't know what papa would say."

"No one can die for you, Miss Gray, so no one ought to stand in the way of holy duty."

"I do not know what to say."

"Many persons come to us in precisely that state of mind, and we feel it to be our duty to assist them by questions."

"Well, if you can help me in that way, it may overcome my difficulty."

Mr. Bonas here stood up, clasped his hands, closed his eyes, and reverentially said a *Gloria;* and having followed this by the *Veni Creator*, he proceeded—

"Have you neglected public worship on Sundays?"

"No."

"As you will appear before the Judge on the great day, I beseech you to reconsider your answer."

"I have not done so."

"Have you regularly, faithfully, and invariably, when at home, attended your own parish church?"

"With one exception."

"And that one exception you now confess and lament and contritely denounce?"

" Oh no.   Quite the contrary."

Mr. Bonas was taken back by this refusal, but suddenly diverged to another line :

" Have you read novels at home on Sundays when you could have gone to church ? "

" I have read novels on Sundays, but I am not aware that they ever kept me from going to church."

" Do you remember any special sins done by you on Sundays ? "

" No ; not at this moment."

" Have you gone to church on Ascension Day, Ash Wednesday, and Good Friday always, or have you used those days, or any other Fasts or Festivals, as mere gay holidays ? "

" I have not paid much attention to these days."

" Do you mourn your neglect of such seasons with much self-condemnation ? "

" No."

" Then I exhort you so to do, or else on the great day of account your soul will stand in jeopardy.   Have you ever spoken sarcastically of a priest of the true Church ? "

" I am afraid I have."

" This you do now hereby solemnly and penitentially confess ? "

" I acknowledge it."

" Try and remember the first falsehood you ever told, and inform me of the same in the sight of God."

" That is impossible."

" Can you remember your last wilful untruth ? '

" I am not aware that I was ever guilty of the meanness of telling a wilful untruth."

" Have you ever pretended to be ill for any unworthy
reason ? "

" Mr. Bonas, how can you be so cruel ? "

" Have you ever betrayed a secret or broken a
promise ? "

" I cannot remember having done so ; certainly not
wilfully."

" Have you ever said or acted an untruth to obtain
applause or produce merriment ? "

" That question I really cannot answer offhand."

" In what way does your pride chiefly show
itself ? "

" I do not know of any particular way."

" Do you always try and get before others impatiently
in crowds ? "

" Never."

" Do you often lie in bed longer than you need, and
especially on Friday ? "

" I have often done so."

" Did you study so hard as you should have done
remembering that your education was paid for by
your parents ? "

" I did not."

" Are you very long dressing and undressing ? "

" No."

" If a dinner is badly cooked, are you needlessly
annoyed and needlessly angry with the servants ? "

" Not needlessly angry."

" Are you annoyed because others are helped, and

16

there is none left of any particular dish for yourself?"

"Don't you think these questions are rather frivolous,
Mr. Bonas?"

"Oh no; they search the heart; they prove the
conscience; they allow no escape."

"They seem to me to be silly."

"But they are not. They are specially needful for
the children of the Church, who cannot be expected to
have committed any great crimes. Your sins are
almost sure to be minute, and even spiritual. Now,
there is one subject upon which I must interrogate you
in my official capacity—are you conscious that your
desires are going forth in the direction of any
heresy?"

"Not at all."

"Are you conscious that any heretical person is
getting an undue influence over you?"

"Not for a moment."

"Have you been in secret confidential communication
with any heretical person?"

"Never."

"Would it give you distress of mind if any calamity
befell a heretical person?"

"Certainly it would."

"Ought we not to rejoice when Providence sends
distress upon heretics?"

"No, no; that would be wrong."

"Can the Most Holy One do that which is wrong?
Pause, I beseech you."

"But the argument tells both ways."

"There is no argument, Miss Gray; argument is vain, and irreligious, and useless."

Mr. Bonas, having apparently finished his interrogatories, every one of which he put without referring to a note, as if fully master of the process of examination, inquired whether Miss Gray now wished for the ministry and blessing of absolution?

"Certainly not, Mr. Bonas; I hope you do not suppose I have made confession?"

"Most undoubtedly I consider you have."

"Then let me undeceive you at once. I understood that you were only going to show me how a penitent is assisted by having questions put. I did not suppose you were putting the inquiries directly and seriously to myself. I was merely taking part in an explanation, after which I had to consider whether I would personally confess."

"This is a very serious error, Miss Gray. I fear you have trifled with holy things."

"Nothing of the kind, Mr. Bonas. *You* have trifled with them. You profess to be a minister of the Protestant Church, but if you have not been playing at Popery in all this questioning and cross-questioning, then I do not know what Popery is. Please to understand me clearly. Perhaps I was wrong in drawing you on to make a fool of yourself, but I did want to see just how far you would go. I began in a mischievous humour, but I must end in a serious one. I cannot regard you as an honest man. In relation to you, I am as much a Dissenter

as Mr. Whiteman is, and I glory in my Dissent.
Your proper place is in the Romish Church.   Go
to it.   Good-bye."

The Rev. Edwin Bonas thereafter left the Vicarage.
The old gardener looked up as he thought he heard
an unusual noise from a rook, but it was only the
Rev. Edwin deeply uttering the favourite and expressive word — " Rawly ! " as he passed into the
shadows.

CHAPTER XX.

"GOOD-MORNING, Mr. Robson," said I, as the good Baptist deacon unexpectedly appeared at my study door. "I have just been wondering how it is that 'Church people' regard Dissenters as vulgar and unintelligent, and look upon us generally as a kind of social refuse. Can you account for it?"

"Not worth accounting for, my dear sir. Yet the subject is rather timely, after all, for I have just had a visit from Mr. Runch, the churchwarden, who seems to have got himself into a good deal of trouble by the visit he paid to our chapel. By the way, is Runch the kind of 'gentleman' they admire so much? Is he the pattern they want us to copy?"

"I suppose so," said I.

"Then I for one must decline," Mr. Robson continued, "for a more deplorable case of ignorance I do not remember to have noticed for many years."

"But, my dear Mr. Robson," I interrupted, "he is a Churchman, and I understand that to be a Churchman is to be a gentleman; information goes for nothing, refinement of feeling goes for nothing, benevolent interest in the welfare of others goes for nothing;

Churchmanship is everything ; Dissent alone is the un-
pardonable sin."

Mr. Robson was amused at my change of tone, for I
had always been looked upon as a somewhat tepid
Dissenter, quietly going on with my own pastoral work
and leaving the Church of England alone.   I acknowledge that my Dissent was not of the Paterson type,
that, indeed, I was rather afraid of Patersonism, and
that if anything my Dissent erred on the side of indifference. At the same time, I could not have patience
with the spirit or policy of such a man as Tomlinson
—a man without convictions, and utterly without
nobleness or unselfishness of impulse.   But recent
events had thrown a new light upon things, and had
constrained me to obey the instincts of self-respect.
I found that throughout the town it was felt that a
wonderful favour had been conferred upon the Baptist
chapel by the visit of Miss Gray and Mr. Runch!
Think of anybody in Midtown being able to patronise
the glorious Whiteman !   Yet this was the undoubted
feeling on the part of many.   I heard, too, that other
distinguished tradesmen were thinking of venturing
into the Baptist chapel now that Mr. Runch had led
the way and made it in some degree respectable, and
even the bellman had said he " would not much mind
giving the Baptists a turn some night now that Mr.
Runch had taken them by the hand " !   This was
more than I could stand.   Now and again I had been
touched to the quick by a sudden remembrance of the
heroic side of historic Dissent, but the emotion would
subside with equal suddenness, and once more I would

easily glide into the level of good fellowship and non-controversial relations with the Vicar. Now all was changed. The depressing truth forced itself upon my attention that Dissent always involves social penalties in one form or another, and that every Dissenter must either attemper his convictions by his circumstances or counterbalance the penalty by the approval of a good conscience. It is quite true that the sense of penalty may not be so acute in large towns as in rural districts, but that is only the result of social complexity, and in no degree due to an alteration of central faith. Some compromising Dissenters have mildly attempted to bridge the gulf ecclesiastical by deferential tailoring, the invention of toy-liturgies, and resolutions in favour of building chapels with steeples, but the expensiveness of the candle has ruined the profit of the game, and so it must ever be to the weary end. Compromise is impossible, because the contradiction is in things eternal, and not merely in the accidents of an hour.

"I have called to tell you," Mr. Robson continued, "that a very singular circumstance has occurred, arising out of the matter you have referred to. Miss Gray has had an interview with Mr. Whiteman, and Mr. Whiteman wants to see you at four o'clock about it. The matter is altogether very delicate, yet it is most deeply interesting. See Mr. Whiteman as soon after four as you can, and let him have the benefit of your opinion."

What was Hecuba to me, or I to Hecuba? Nothing. Plainly, simply, absolutely nothing. Yet I wondered, with no small excitement, why the interview had been sought, and what course it had taken, and what issues it had affected. In the metropolis the incident would have come and gone without commotion, but in Midtown it created an epoch, and needed consummate handling in order to prevent it creating a disaster. The rain makes more noise in a bucket than it makes on the sea. That day I could do next to nothing in the study, though I had planned to write full sixteen pages of solid quarto before retiring to rest. Four o'clock would never come. I was convinced that my watch had stopped. So I shook its creaking machinery, but without finding that I had any power over the sun. I took a look at my " Daniel in the lions' den," not without a thought that my trial was in some respects the greater of the two. There are no lions' dens now-a-days, else life would be worth living, and a man would have something to get up for in the morning. But these little troubles, little pinchings, little teasings, who can bear them ? They are too small for prayer, and too minute for sympathy. Yet there they are, contemptible enough singly, but quite a cloud when they come together. I quite feel that I underwent an unappreciated martyrdom that day as I wearily waited for four o'clock. At length patience had its perfect work, for Whiteman withheld nothing from me of all the unexpected but not unhappy interview. It appeared that Miss Gray had made a call upon Mrs. Whiteman, frankly avowing that her purpose was to ask Mr. Whiteman some questions about the sermon she had heard and about the chapel she had been to, and Mrs. Whiteman gladly encouraged the simple desire.

Mrs. Whiteman was well aware that her brilliant
husband often said things which she herself could not
distinctly follow, so she did not wonder that strangers
should be at a loss to take in his whole meaning at one
hearing. Mrs. Whiteman was quite right. Mr. Whiteman probably never preached a sermon that was complete in itself; there was at least an atmosphere of
reference to other and inexpressible things, and a
breathing as from eternal mysteries pervading the
entire service. Mr. Whiteman himself was but part of
a larger personality. What wonder, then, if a young
stranger had been almost dazed by the new glory which
had fallen upon her spiritual vision? Happily I was
able so to collect the particulars, and understand the
spirit of the interview, as to qualify myself to give a
full note of what transpired.

Nellie was, of course, with her father, as usual,
having, in fact, become quite indispensable to him.
Nellie was one of those children so soft in manner,
so boldly timid, so healthily sensitive, as never to be
in the way, yet never out of it. No one felt that she
was a third party in an interview; she was simply
part of her father—the part which completed his life
and gave the charm of grace to the strength of his
dignity. Miss Gray was soon made to feel that if the
minister was blind, his daughter could see. How
Nellie looked at her! How tenderly! How wistfully!
Why? The simplicity of Miss Gray's dress could not
have long detained her attention, for what is there in a
plain stuff dress and a bonnet without a feather? Nor

could personal beauty have explained the lingering and
contented look, for Miss Gray was as one of a thousand,
simple, pleasant, unpretending, and quite wanting in
conspicuousness.   Why, then, Nellie's undisguised
but unobtrusive interest ?   All the time she was saying to herself—"The Vicar's a sweet old thing, so his
daughter is sure to be good."   It will thus be seen
that though Nellie was wanting in variety of expression,
she was by no means inconstant in feeling.   Miss Gray
was able by sympathy to understand the look, and to
endure it without annoyance, and, indeed, to feel that
Nellie was a necessary link between her and the blind
man whose serene face was even nobler in private than
she had admitted it to be in public.   Preliminaries
were soon over, and earnest talk was unrestrained.

"I found, do you know, Mr. Whiteman, that when I
left your chapel, I had been quite in a new world,
where everything was strange, and where I could not
altogether make out what was going on."

"Then you had never been in a Nonconformist chapel
before ?"

"Never! Oh dear no.   It was perhaps very silly
of me, but I did not know exactly what you are, and I
expected to be amused, and I thought you would be
pulling the Church of England to pieces, and I had all
sorts of queer ideas."

"You have changed your opinion, then ?"

"I have indeed. Oh, Mr. Whiteman, how is it
possible for you to pray as you prayed that evening ?"

"Nonconformists pray as they are moved by the Holy

Spirit. They do not compose their prayers, or commit them to memory, or repeat the prayers of others ; they solemnly consider the sacred character of the exercise, and then use the language of the moment."

" Well, I cannot understand it. Do all Noncon-formists pray like you ? ".

" Yes, in substance. Every man, of course, has his own manner and scope of expression. Some are more fervent than others. Some of the most fervent and pathetic prayers I have ever heard have been offered by Methodist ministers. Many of the Methodists are truly mighty in prayer."

" I have heard of the Methodists," said Miss Gray. " They are very droll people, I understand ; don't they wear poke bonnets and call one another ' thee ' and ' thou ' ? "

" No. You are thinking of the Quakers,—a very fine body of sturdy Nonconformists, who have suffered for their principles, and borne a noble testimony in England and America and elsewhere, for two centuries."

" Now about preaching," said Miss Gray, suddenly changing the line of inquiry. " How is it possible to preach as you do ? "

" Do you mean without notes ? "

" I mean altogether, Mr. Whiteman. You seemed to have no difficulty, and to see everything so clearly, and really, if I may say so, you seemed to be more in heaven than on earth."

" Some clergymen of the Church of England preach quite as freely."

" Oh no, Mr. Whiteman ; I am quite sure you are

mistaken there. All the clergymen I know read their
sermons, and one sermon is so like another that I am
positive I could often hardly tell which is which."

"Possibly so. No doubt there are cases of that
kind. At the same time, not a few of the world's
greatest preachers have belonged to the Church of
England. I have their sermons on my bookshelves,
and I have perused them with the greatest intellectual
and spiritual profit."

"How very kind of you to say so."

"Why, Miss Gray ? "

" Because I have always supposed Dissenters hated
the Church of England, and spent their time in trying
to pull it down."

"Absolutely false ! We dissent from the Church of
England on conscientious grounds. Our position is
perfectly defensible, and our history is simply heroic.
But we preach Christ crucified ; we are sent to do our
part in making known the kingdom of God ; the more
clearly men discern its nature and its purpose, the less
will they look for external aid, and the more they will
decline ceremonial patronage."

"Christ crucified," were words which Miss Gray
repeated with a tender sigh.

"Yes, Miss Gray, that is the theme. That is life.
The whole mystery of God comes nearer to us in that
expression than in any other. Without that I could
never preach again. That must indicate the point of
harmony between heaven and earth, and the point of
harmony between all good men, to whatever communion
they may belong. To attempt to settle religious con-

troversies elsewhere than at the cross of Christ is to attempt to dispel darkness without the sun. Christ first, Christ midst, Christ last, is my motto. I feel, Miss Gray, that you love the Christ of God."

The warm tears came into her young eyes, and she was silent.

After a few moments' pause, Miss Gray, following an unexplained mental process, exclaimed—"How can Mr. Runch say that Dissenters are not gentlemen?"

Mr. Whiteman quietly smiled. "We are quite willing," said he, "not to aspire to the class which Mr. Runch adorns. You will find, Miss Gray, as your life enlarges, that there is a contemptible cant of gentility, a species of jackdawism too imbecile for exposure. Never be afraid of it. Some men rely upon snobbery as their only mitigation of obscurity. Whether Mr. Runch is one of them I do not know, nor do I inquire, nor is it needful to concern one's self about it. I do not suppose that the sermon you cared for was cared for equally by Mr. Runch."

"Not at all, Mr. Whiteman. I believe he thought you slightly mad."

Nellie moved nearer her father.

"Very possibly. Very possibly. I do not feel annoyed by the remark; indeed, if another quality of man had made it, I should have received it as a compliment. Great subjects do excite and even overwhelm and exhaust me."

"I am sorry," said Miss Gray, "that I named Mr. Runch. I did not mean to do so."

"No harm in doing it, Miss Gray; it brings up one

side of our case as Dissenters.   It reminds us that theie
are little penalties as well as large ones connected with
honest Nonconformity.   It is after all a very little
penalty to be snubbed by a man whom I would not
have reckoned with the dogs of my father's flock, and
I am sorry even if in my tone I have betrayed any
warmth in remarking upon his impertinence."

When Mr. Whiteman uttered a sentence of this
kind, his face kindled with a new expressiveness. I
think I see him as the scorn made his lips writhe for
a moment. I think, too, I see those eloquent lips as
the scorn passed away and allowed their natural
sweetness to return. Well for Whiteman that he had
given himself to prayer, and well for his opponents
too ! From this point the interview took a new turn.
Miss Gray would know something of the history of
Nonconformity, the sufferings of its followers, the secret
of their inspiration, and their methods of progress.
Then she would suddenly revert to religious mysteries
as they had, from her point of view, been peculiarly
apprehended by the Nonconformist mind.   Had not
the Nonconformists been very bold, almost irreverent,
in venturing to make prayers for themselves, and was
it not a dangerous thing to leave every man to make
his own sermons and speak them right off to all sorts
of people ?

"And, Mr. Whiteman, does every Dissenting minister preach as well as you do ? "

Whiteman could not but be amused by the *naïveté* of
the inquiry. "You make me blush, Miss Gray," said
he. "The fact probably is that some preach better and

some preach worse. But we do not set up one standard for all. Every man in his own order is our motto. Our concern is more about *what* is preached than *how* it is preached."

Then Miss Gray would look at the books, and wonder if they were too deep for her to read and if papa would be willing for her to read them. She said she hated Mr. Runch, and was not at all surprised that such people should have persecuted the Nonconformists, and were only too glad to get what respectability they could from going to church and mumbling words they had not sense to understand. Mr. Whiteman, whilst amused at these running comments, did not encourage them, viewing them simply as a method of compensating for Mr. Runch's rudeness, for which rudeness Mr. Whiteman cared about as much as he cared for the wind that blew a thousand years ago. Nellie, however, was more of a partisan. Mentally she cast in her lot with Miss Gray, and hated poor Runch with most deadly animosity, and in spirit she kicked all his ancestors and jumped upon them. Nellie's was not a strictly judicial mind, Nellie being, in truth, more an executioner than a judge.

When the recital of the whole occurrence had been concluded, I exclaimed with undue feeling—" Oh, Whiteman, I envy you ; what do you think will come of it all ? Can you see the end of it ? "

" No," said he. " Probably there will be no end. Why should there be either tragedy or comedy in such a simple tale ? I was as much struck by Miss Gray's earnestness as by her common-sense. Her mind is thoroughly alive. Had her lot been cast in other circumstances, she would have been very energetic in the propagation of her opinions; but now, in all probability, her course will be simply one of quiet usefulness."

"Oh dear!" said I, without knowing why.

"A new set of ideas has been started in my mind. I will have my thoughts committed to writing as soon as I can, and you and Paterson must come and hear my views. I think I see light upon a great question. I think I see the outline of such a church as the age requires."

CHAPTER XXI.

ANET SNOW was seldom without a casual opportunity of relieving her mind respecting the treatment which Mr. Paterson endured at the hands of his congregation, but it was when William Jacobs called upon her that she most eagerly took advantage of her privileges. William Jacobs presented a very strong temptation to the tongue of an exasperated woman, being a beaming brother with a double chin, expressive of a degree of complacency and satisfaction wholly incompatible with the common terms of human existence, and suggestive of a style of life altogether unknown to her reverend but much-enduring pastor and master. William Jacobs was too stout and sleek to be able to lay any credible claim to the practice of self-denial, but those who knew him best were ready to assert that Jacobs was neither a glutton nor a sluggard, but was naturally so conditioned that he could have grown fat even upon the manna which was rained in the wilderness. Be this as it may, William Jacobs, under-foreman in a flourishing brewery, was genial in spirit, domestic in habit, and not disinclined to the society of Janet Snow. The only thing known against Jacobs was a certain flippancy of manner, which cost

17

him his place in the chapel choir.   As a member of
that respectable but disputatious body, William played
a fiddle, along with two other scrapers on that expressive instrument.   On one occasion Mr. Paterson gave
out a hymn beginning, "And are we yet alive?"
whereupon Jacobs whispered, "Pass the rosin, Jack,
and we'll let him know who's alive."   That remark,
known by its author to be inconsistent with decorum and
a good conscience, cost William his position in the
choir, and doomed him to the obscurity of a mere seat-
holder.   This was certainly a trifle mortifying, as
William loved just a little publicity, and never concealed his opinion that chapel music was good in proportion as it provided for special action upon the fiddle.

" Not as I want the fiddle to do everything," he would
benignly say ; " at the same time, where would the choir
be without one ? " a remark which offended the leading tenor, who, through his partiality for the young
lady who presided at the harmonium, had acquired
undue and ill-regulated influence in the musical department of Mixford Chapel.

William Jacobs had for one evil moment thought
of offering his services to another meeting, whose
orthodoxy was not altogether indisputable, but his
good-nature prevailed, and consequently he remained
faithful to the chapel where he had fiddled so long and
so loudly.   This faithfulness might in some subtle way
be traceable to the influence of Janet Snow, but it is
unreasonable to impair its integrity by going in quest
of second causes and grovelling explanations.   One
thing is certain amid all speculation and mutability,

and that one thing is the settled detestation felt by Janet
Snow in the case of a church which did not respond to
the merits of Mr. Paterson.

"And how is the minister to-night?" said William,
drawing his chair to the kitchen fire; "you know,
Janet, I am not one of those who doesn't swear by
parson."

"Then why don't you do more for him?" said Janet;
"what's the use of blowing the bellows into an empty
grate?"

"That's a good 'un," William remarked, "but I didn't
know as parson was a grate."

"And many other things you don't know," Janet
quickly retorted; "likely you don't know that parson,
as you call him, brought in a wandering kind o' preaching body to share his ha'penny herring last night and
the last spoonful o' coffee I had in the house. You
may not know it, but I know who does know it." Janet
shut the window with a bang, and placed a candlestick
on the table.

"Is the minister at home to-night, Janet?"

"No, he's not."

"Is he off again to have another go at the bishops?
Eh, Janet, but parson does hate bishops."

"Parson hates nobody," said Janet.

"I tell you what, Janet," said William, softly: "I
often wish parson would treat himself to a drop o' beer.
Now *there* I could do something for him, even if it was
only out o' my own allowance. Now, what's your
opinion, private opinion, Janet, of a pint o' beer nicely
heated and a sprinkling o' nutmeg, and, if you like,

just a thin wedge of cheese, I don't mind how thin ? "

" There wouldn't be much left of it," said Janet, " if you got the first chance."

Jacobs laughed. He liked to be where Janet was, and to laugh at her sharp sayings, even though they cut himself. Do we not all prefer the frowns of some women to the smiles of others ? Jacobs found summer where other men would have bitterly complained of winter, so let him enjoy himself according to his own quality and fashion, knowing that his double chin will suffer no serious loss.

" Eh, Janet, but you've got lips like a pair of scissors, but I know ye mean no harm. Now there's another thing, Janet, I want your opinion upon, and that is a nice little bit o' Welsh rabbit, with just a thought of white vinegar and a turn or two o' buttered toast. Now what say ye ? " Jacobs beamed, and sidled up to Janet, and expected " confirmation strong."

" Away with you and your suppers," said Janet; " you are a guzzling good-for-nothing ; if you only had pudding enough for yourself, not a button would you care if the minister had nothing to eat but your story of how you enjoyed yourself. You seem to think that when you have mentioned a supper you have given one. If you would do more and talk less, you wouldn't be so like those people who are keen enough to tell you it's raining, but not half so keen to lend you an umbrella. I don't like donkeys that can do nothing but bray."

" Janet, Janet," said William, " come now, come

now. You don't see no ill-will i' my face, I reckon. And that's because I ha' none, Janet. To prove my words, I tell you what we'll do. I'll just nip out and fetch in half a pound o' cheese, two pints of ale, a quartern loaf, and a three-cornered bit o' butter, and we'll warm the kitchen up a bit. Eh, Janet? Come, let's be what I call human."

" This kitchen's not going to be made into a public, I can tell you," said Janet. " So you know. Why don't you fiddle in chapel now ? "

" Eh, Janet, there you step on all my toes at once. It was all nothing but the rosin and that sour old tenor Chettle ; he might ha' known I was but gaming, and was only going to make the fiddle do its best. Parson says, 'And are we yet alive ?' and I says, ' What a question to ask !' says I. ' Why, in course,' says I, ' we are alive, or how could we be sitting in Mixford Chapel ?' 'It were all old Chettle, Janet, but no ill-will do I bear him." Jacobs was silent a while, and added, " I have the fiddle i' my topcoat inside pocket, Janet, so if you would like to hear it, you can without paying much."

Janet said no fiddle had ever been played in that kitchen, and if she knew night from day, no fiddle ever should be played in it. But if Jacobs was so anxious to do something, she wished he would do something useful by " telling that chubby-faced Robinson, the painter and glazier, to put a new pane into the study window, for the minister was very like to die of influenza because of the horrid draught, and him sitting there without a fire when the cold was like to bite your nose off." Jacobs said that, in his private opinion,

Robinson, though not a bad painter, had no more real religion than a shoe-sole, and asked Janet if he was not about right in saying so.

"Shoe-sole!" said Janet, with blighting contempt, but with deeply hidden meaning.

"That's how I put it," said Jacobs, "and if a man's got no more religion than a shoe-sole, he may paint his head off if he likes, but when he comes to be added up and settled down he'll be blue enough," a sentiment which Janet endorsed without clearly comprehending.

"And where will you find any real religion in Mixford Chapel?" she added.

"Now, Janet, I don't hold wi' that altogether," Jacobs replied; "I'm bound to say that there's a sprinkling on't in Mixford Chapel. Take such people as the Maxwells and Ryders, and there's even old Neddy the baker; what say ye to him? And that old Butterworth, ye know, Janet?"

"Ay," said Janet, "he's dead and gone, and I'm not going to say a word agin him, nor agin old Neddy, for I've a spice loaf i' the cupboard now he sent in last night, but as for the rest on 'em, I wouldn't give a penny a quart for the soup they would boil down to, stingy, pecky, dressy creatures. So you know my mind."

"Well, Janet, you're partly right and partly wrong, I reckon. Fair's fair, you know. Mind you, I believe some o' the folks are downright good, and they do a lot o' good, too; so we better not make out that they are all like Robinson. Mrs. Ryder does a lot o' good. So does Mrs. Maxwell. And so does Mr. Wilson, the ironmonger. They all said they were uncommon sorry when I left the singing pew, and old Mrs. Simpson says she misses the fiddle awfully when they sing the tune of *Tynedale*, where the chorus comes in after every verse."

But Janet was implacable. She had but one standard of judgment. Whoever treated the minister well was sure of heaven, and whoever failed in this point disobeyed and dishonoured the whole law. It was not a broad view ; it was not a view for which the merit of magnanimity could be justly claimed ; it was, indeed, a view which might be charged with some measure of partiality and incompleteness ; yet my heart warms towards the faithful creature, and my imagination creates for her a heaven worthy of her simple and pure love.

CHAPTER XXII.

ISS GRAY'S visit had evidently made a deep impression upon Whiteman's mind, and had started the thought whether some enlargement could not be effected by which many who are now outsiders might be brought within the pale of the true Church. Upon this subject Whiteman had dictated a paper to his son George, and Paterson and I were invited to hear it and give our opinion upon it. It fell to my lot to read the paper aloud, which, notwithstanding its length, I now venture to give in full. The first title of the paper was simply—" The Open Church."

" Perhaps the *Larger* Church would quite as clearly express my thought, and save it from the suspicion of such minds as are too active to be either logical or just; yet the word *open* better represents the generous freedom and the independent dignity which ought, in my opinion, to mark the boundary and the function of Christ's body the Church. On a controverted question disputants may do wisely to keep strictly within the lines of individual conviction, but this very limitation should entitle them to the use of an emphasis too poignant and definite for collective service. For no one, therefore, but myself will I venture to speak, and for that very reason I will speak with a boldness which is not deterred by collateral responsibility.

"The chronic difficulty relates, of course, to what is known as agreement upon theological dogmas. 'How can two walk together except they be agreed?' I answer, they cannot; and yet that answer, perfectly appreciated so as to lose nothing of frankness, does not injuriously affect the contention to which I am pledged. What is agreement? To what does it apply? These are the vital questions. Hitherto agreement has been limited to the narrowest and shiftiest of all ground, viz., the ground of opinion. What if it should turn out that agreement upon opinion is of necessity superficial, and at best a mere gossamer of words? Possibly so, for words are changeable, and so arbitrary, when used merely as tools of grammar, as hardly to fit the same living thought two days together. On the other hand, my contention enables me to hold that feeling is infinitely deeper and surer than opinion, and that when opinion is divided, feeling may be unanimous, and consequently that the agreement which is essential to a common walk is an agreement based upon a common feeling. The danger is that the term 'feeling' may be so narrowly and wantonly interpreted as to exclude everything but emotion and rhapsody. Here the mocker finds a small field for the exercise of frivolous talents; but I shall not interrupt my interview with serious men to shorten his vain amusement. To give concrete vividness to the argument, take the different views which are prevalent with regard to the Divinity of Jesus Christ; the one view makes Him God, the other view makes Him man; how can men holding those respective views walk together, or realise the trust and succour of Christian fellowship? It is evident that the very terms of the inquiry need the most careful settlement, and that therefore an abrupt or categorical reply is impossible. What is meant by 'God,' and what is meant by 'man,' in this inquiry? To my own mind, Jesus Christ is at once the Son of God and God the Son. About this I have no mental uncertainty. With my whole mind and heart I believe in the Deity of the Lord Jesus Christ. The inquiry, therefore, bears upon a case like mine with special interest and definiteness, and calls for an explicit reply. Suppose, then, that a person who inclines to the opposite view should seek to cultivate Christian fellowship with me, what should be my response? First of all it is clear that the man who seeks such fellowship, knowing what my theology is (for such knowledge must be assumed on both sides), must be a man of reverent mind. No flippant mind could seek fellowship under such conditions, or if it did, its flippancy would defeat the object. Flippancy must be regarded as blasphemy. The very first and the very deepest assumption must be *reverence*. I have, therefore, to respond to an approach made by a reverential mind, and having to do this, I must do it with spiritual solicitude and tenderness. I begin, therefore, by asking what relation the inquirer sustains to the Lord Jesus Christ; and I may find that the inquirer steadfastly looks to the Son of man for example, guidance, inspiration, and sympathy; he loyally

endeavours to imitate the spirit and action of Jesus
Christ; things are right or wrong in the inquirer's
judgment according to the view which Jesus Christ
would take of them; this answer, expressed with
reverence and love, excites in my mind the thought
that after all this man is practically owning a Godhead
which he theoretically denies; Jesus Christ is the
sovereign of his life and the arbiter of such destiny
as may be involved in moral action. At which point,
then, shall my response begin to take shape? If at the
theoretical point, our correspondence must be instantly
foreclosed; if at the practical point, my interest in the
man will invite further confidence, and may lead the
man to express himself thus: Jesus Christ is the
highest expression of Himself which the eternal God
has yet given; He is the perfect Humanity; He unites
and explains the whole human race; not a speck can
be found upon the snow of His purity; in a word, He
is the very image and spirit of the invisible and holy
God. From such an answer it is perfectly clear that
the man who seeks to enter into Christian fellowship
with me is thoughtful, reverent, and deeply pious in
feeling, and that to brand him as a heretic or keep him
at bay as an alien would on my part be an act of profound injustice. On the ground, therefore, that I hold
what I believe to be the larger truth, that is to say,
the Deity of Jesus Christ, I cannot withhold Christian
fellowship from such an inquirer. My reply to him is:
I hold all that you hold; most undoubtedly Jesus
Christ is the Son of Mary, the Son of man, the Ideal
Humanity, the very image and symbol of Divine purity;

so far we are one, and so far we may hold fellowship;
but I hold infinitely more, and to that complete Faith I
must endeavour to win you ; it is happily not in your
power to drag me down, any more than a child can
bring back a man to infancy, but it may be in my power
to assist your growth in grace and knowledge.   I hold
that in returning such a response under such circumstances I am serving the cause of Christ infinitely more
than if I declined communication, and pointed the inquirer to a community supposed to be organised for the
propagation of his views.   Understand this clearly, for
I am not dealing with a case in which theological dogmas
have been formally and ostentatiously adopted.   The
fact that the inquirer is for some reason approaching
the evangelical side must be considered as part of the
argument, and not as a mere incident in the story ; this
motion of the heart has a meaning ; a beginning so
hopeful may lead to the happiest issues, and is therefore not to be repelled by such discouragements as
are opposed to the very spirit of evangelical solicitude.
Where the inquiry is put in a different spirit, a different
answer must of course be returned; as, for example,
where the inquirer wishes to become a disputant, or a
proselytiser, fellowship is simply impossible ; but the
impossibility must not be laid at my door, as if the
evangelical faith were narrow and uncharitable.   Individual instances must determine individual action, my
one point being that the evangelical Church is bound by
the very greatness of its faith to encourage all who seek
the fellowship of its believers, although they have nearly
everything of a doctrinal nature yet to learn.   This is

what I mean by an Open Church, and this is what I mean by the possibility of religious feeling seeking fellowship where speculative opinion might beget distrust.

" So far, then, it is clear that, if my contention is to be upheld, the Christian Church must not be regarded as a theological academy, but rather as a school and home of the heart. Once turn the Church into a hall of divinity and theological controversy, and alienation cannot be prevented. But to do this is to profane the Church, by narrowing and dehumanizing it. What is now understood by systematic theology is not only not to be found in the teaching of Christ, but is utterly opposed to some of the noblest conceptions of the spirit and purpose of the Saviour of the world. By turning the Church into a divinity hall it becomes the athenæum of scholars, the special possession of men of leisure, clever men, men of speculative mind, or men of more or less intellectual genius ; but where are the broken-hearted and the contrite, the men who can but say, 'Lord, I believe ; help Thou mine unbelief,' the souls that cannot argue, but fain would pray ? It was always to such that Jesus Christ addressed His tender Gospel, whilst to the wise and prudent, the self-idolatrous, the scribe and the pedant, He had no message to deliver that was not charged with reproach and judgment and overwhelming condemnation. Where, then, is the warrant for a theological Church, in the sense of theology assuming a scientific form and demanding assent to a standard of words ? I find no such warrant in Scripture, but I can distinctly trace its origin to the rise of priestism, or, in bolder terms, to the rise of popery. That broken-hearted and contrite souls are allowed a place in Christian communion is not denied, but is it not always with a sense of patronage, or with qualifications that reduce the fellowship to an expression of pity, rather than recognise it as a claim of right? The clever theologians practically assume that by virtue of scholarship or ability they are the Church; consequently, they speak of others in condescending terms suggested by a consciousness of theological inferiority. Now the exact converse of this would seem to me more closely to represent Christ's view of His own Church. I cannot but feel that were Christ to reappear as in the days of His flesh, His first work would be to banish scientific theology and pedantic theologians from the courts of His temple. The most of our institutionalism He would burn as with fire; our endowments and funds, and investments and securities, our parchments, creeds, and chancery protections, He would consume as stubble; and again would wend His way to the Cross, followed by woman's pity and deserted by the pride of men. Is there, then, to be no theology in the Open Church? The inquiry is almost frivolous, because it overlooks a necessity of intellectual responsibility. A deeper and truer inquiry is, What, then, is to be the place of theology in the Open Church? That is the vital question. Everything affecting fellowship and co-operation turns upon the answer that is given. It is supposed by many that theology and truth are co-ordinate terms; hence it is logically assumed that to fight for theological propositions is to fight for truth. This is a partial view of a complex case, and is, indeed, a view as inferior as it is incomplete. What proposition originating in the invention and bounded by the language of man can express the truth rising in the Eternal Mind and transcending all time and space ? Where is the tabernacle of words which can hold Him whom heaven and the heaven of heavens cannot contain ? What is impossible in words begins to be possible in feeling—that is, in contrition, in reverence, in desire after holiness, in speechless communion with God, and in the aspiration which prays best when it rises above the troubled region of words. Propositions are individual, feeling is universal ; in the profoundest and amplest sense, ' one touch of nature makes the whole world kin.' How, then, it may be asked, are contending theologians to be treated ? Assuming always their reverence and their humility, they must be made to feel that they will be listened to not merely in a spirit of toleration, but with the eagerness which impassions all love of larger knowledge. Instead of being discredited, hooted, and exiled, they will be trusted and welcomed and adopted because of their holiness, docility, and incorruptible candour. But can they all be right ? Yes, they can all be right in heart. But may they not be mistaken in judgment ? Yes ; they will themselves say so ; but there is no human infallibility by which heinous mistakes upon infinite subjects can be corrected. The nearest approach which man can make to infallibility is in purity and grace of heart.

" In view of inquiries which a testimony of this kind must excite, let me enlarge the exposition by changing

the point of observation. In my judgment it is infinitely more important to believe in a Divine revelation,
than in any particular theory of inspiration; in the
possibility of the forgiveness of sins, than in any metaphysical or forensic explanation of the process; in the
immortality of the soul, than in any controverted view
of that mystery. But at once the narrow question will
arise, *How* do you believe ? *What* do you believe ? In
what form of words would you *express* your belief ?
That is the beginning of sin, (1) because it involves a
limitation of the Holy One of Israel, and (2) presup-
poses that there is some human standard or priestly
canon by which theological orthodoxy can be determined. The true questions are, What spirit are ye of ?
Have you the spirit of Christ ? Are you meek and
lowly in heart ? Have ye received the Holy Ghost ?
These are questions which a man must put to himself,
and to which his life will be the only permissible public
reply.

" It has been said, with the thoughtless approval of
many, that established churchism and political conserva-
tism have scepticism at the heart of them, the idea
being that in both instances human nature is distrusted.
As well say that organised society has scepticism at
the heart of it. If not, why all the laws, penalties,
restrictions, and responsibilities, which invest the
commonwealth with security ? Nor is the pungent
generalisation sustained by the example of the very
men who endorse it, for they, too, have their standards
and creeds, their trust-deeds and touchstones of

orthodoxy. Where, then, is their consistency in charging upon others the very scepticism which taints their own theological and ecclesiastical policy ? There is no such consistency ; so the taunt may be returned without vindictiveness. We come, however, upon very delicate ground in referring to trust-deeds which have hard-and-fast theological lines. If I undertake to show how an open church and a close trust-deed can coexist, I must be allowed to take my own argumentative way in working towards a conclusion. First of all, I deplore the existence of conservative theological trust-deeds, and I affirm that in very deed they have scepticism at the heart of them—the worst kind of scepticism, too, not merely a distrust of man, but a distrust of the living Paraclete. But have not men who subscribe for the building of what may be called religious property a right to determine the creed which shall be for ever associated with the use of that property ? No. Most emphatically, No. They have no right to usurp the dignity and function of the Holy Ghost, and therefore they have no right to limit the progress of the ages, and continue a legal domination which, were they themselves living, they might be the most eager to readjust or modify. I, therefore, encounter the first inquiry with a deter- mined negative. That inquiry conceals the most vicious of sophisms under the most innocent of forms. In every sense 'there is an appointed time for man upon the earth,' and he can only extend his posthumous influence legitimately and with public edification by right of reason, foresight, sympathy, and moral

18

sublimity—never by unchangeable legal enactment respecting verities which by their very nature can never come within the region of civil or criminal law. Better legislate about the shining of the sun, or the flowing of the tides. Speaking, as at first, and all through, in my own name alone, my position is this: As an evangelical believer I desire all men to accept the persuasions which lead in the direction of evangelical theology ; it has made me what I am, in so far as I desire to be right and to help the noblest progress of the world ; it fills me with joy, it quiets me with holy peace, it enriches me with ineffable hope. Why not, then, write it in a trust-deed and consecrate certain buildings to its propagation for ever ? For the very reason that I believe it to be of God. If I distrusted its Divinity, I would endeavour to give it legal immortality. In what attitude, then, in relation to society, would I leave what is called religious or ecclesiastical property ? I would simply protect it (or its money value, should it be for any sufficient reason brought to market) from secularisation, and provide that it should be used for Christian worship and study, according as God might reveal Himself in the perusal of the Scriptures, and in the providence of the ages. I have, of course, heard all that can be said about designing men, and wolves in sheep's clothing, and possible apostasies, and yet, in full remembrance of all that I have heard, I am prepared to trust the Living Spirit of God and the Christian honour of His Church. Any other position would seem to me to have scepticism at the heart of it, and to necessitate greater perils than it escapes. When the evangelical faith is preached because the law has provided for the preaching of it, all that is distinctively evangelical is lost; but when it is preached because of the inspiration of trust and love, any other security is incongruous and impotent. As to the matter of right, I have contended that, by the nature of the case, no such right is tenable, because it assumes finality, infallibility, and papal domination. No man has a right to shut up a plant in darkness, and starve it for want of light. No man has a right to place himself under penal covenants to another man not to read or think. No man has a right to exclude the fresh air from any house he may have erected even at his own expense. There are no such rights. Every man has a Divinely-given right to live and grow, but not to take away his life, or limit the area of its expansion. Wise men will not follow their money too far in the construction of testamentary instruments; then why attempt to stereotype the form of theology, and foreclose the action of the Divine Spirit?

" But certain theological or doctrinal trust-deeds are already in existence. What is to be done with such documents? The question is both difficult and easy: difficult if treated literally; easy if treated spiritually. Which is the greater, the dead stones or the living men? Which is really the more *permanent* quantity, the masonry or the humanity? It is often supposed that the building is for ever and the community is for a time. This is a mistake. Let the community abandon the building, and where is the guarantee of

its permanence ?   A few months of neglect will bring
it to dilapidation and ruin.   I hold that the living
Church is the eternal quantity, and that, by the right
of its being such, its judgment and will must from
time to time determine everything.   There is an
order of law as well as of everything else ; that is to
say, a relation of primary and secondary, and an
understood subordination of every human statute to
higher and unwritten law.   Human statutes cannot
live against strong public opinion.   Statesmen and
jurists tell us that legislation is always determined by
the unwritten judgment and feeling of the country, and
that many a statute has become a dead letter because
public opinion has outgrown its claim or necessity.
This is the view which I should take of theological
trust-deeds.   So long as the living Church upholds
them they must be of virtue, not simply because they
are written, but because they are livingly accepted
and approved by the Church, and are consequently
invested with the force of immediate conviction and
sympathy.   Thus the whole question becomes one
of priority ; which is to be first, the stones or the
men ?   The dead men or the living men ?   The
form or the power ?   The mistakes of the letter must
be corrected by the growing wisdom of the spirit ;
the narrow morality must be enlarged by the infinite
righteousness ; the sceptical trust-deed must be subordinate to the living God.   If there is peril, by so
much should earnest men be on the alert ; if designing
men will plot, honest men should pray ; if the heretic
is so resolute as to attempt spoliation, the true believer

should encounter him, not with a dead trust-deed, but with a living and vehement faith.

"The gravity of the subject lies in the fact that for some reason or other there is a great turning away from old and once sacred paths. It is idle to deny or under-rate the apostasy. Looking here and there, at instances in many respects unique, a contrary picture may dis-close itself, but under a broad and unbiassed survey the fascinations of the outlook are few enough. On every hand the new wine is bursting the old bottles. The Church changes under the baleful spirit of fear, and through foolish suspicions rather than through niggardliness, it does not enlarge its hospitality as the guests increase in number and vary in necessity. Hardly a man need have been lost. Another leaf might have been put in the table. Other lines might have been added to the bill of fare. The discipline of the house could have been varied without being im-paired. It is not enough to be in the Father's house ; we must have access to the ' many mansions.' Open the Church to *all* truth—to Science, to Music, to Philosophy, to Art, to Philanthropy, to Prayer, and to the mighty Preaching which bows all things as by an infinite majesty ; and then there will be few who will go astray for lack of bounty or want of love."

CHAPTER XXIII.

PATERSON, being in one of his least discriminating tempers, pronounced the paper
a tissue of nonsense from beginning to
end, and declared that charity so wild and
monstrous had never been known in the
history of the world.   Whiteman benignly
smiled, and then quietly appealed to me for
a calmer opinion.

"You simply knocked me over," said I, " so I want
time to recover.   Can you put the whole argument
more concisely ? "

" Yes.   All I want to say is that an open Bible
means an open Church."

" In what sense ? "

" In the sense that every man must be left to form
his own opinion, after availing himself of the best
assistance within his reach."

"And is not that done every day ? " Paterson inquired.

" It is."

" Then what more do you want ? "

" I want that fact to be recognised in our church
life, so that diversity may not destroy union, and so

that Protestantism may show that it is even more vitally consolidated than Popery."

"Right enough," said Paterson ; "but hold communion with Unitarians I never will."

" I don't want you to do so."

" But, my dear Whiteman," Paterson continued, " your words cannot admit of any other meaning. That is the point of your whole argument."

" Not at all," said Whiteman. " I distinguished my purpose more carefully. I supposed a case ; if the case does not occur, the argument cannot be applied. If I assume a fine day as the basis of an illustration, you must not consider the illustration as applying to a snowy night. Where the man is a pronounced Unitarian, he will never care for communion with our side, and never seek it. I am thinking of inquirers, not of dogmatists."

" I observed your careful distinction upon that point," said I, turning to Paterson, and using somewhat of a tone of rebuke in making the remark.

" Why," said Paterson, with a sneer unworthy of him, "there are not a thousand Unitarians in England."

" How many Christians are there in England ? " Whiteman inquired.

" Say two millions," Paterson instantly replied.

" Very well," Whiteman continued, " taking two millions as the figure, I make bold to say there are more than a million and a half of Unitarians in England."

Paterson rose from his seat, and with strong emotion

declared that Whiteman must surely be going out of
his mind.   Whiteman, noticing in Paterson's tone an
unusual excitement, begged him to sit down and be
calm.

"I do not mean," said he, "that there are a million
and a half of avowed Unitarians in the country; but I
do mean very solemnly to say that many a man does
not know he is a Unitarian, and might be even shocked
by having the term Unitarian applied to him; yet in
all his thinking and feeling he gets no further in reality
than the simple manhood of Jesus Christ."

"You do not mean, I hope, to insinuate that so
many professors of Christianity are playing the
hypocrite?"

"Nothing of the kind, my dear friend," Whiteman
replied.   "I am speaking of men who are not theologians, who do not know the very first principles of
scientific theology, but who are really sound at heart
in their love of Christ and their wish to serve Him;
and I mean to say that the very most of them
are practically nothing more than believers in the manhood of Jesus Christ.   They do not go into metaphysics
at all, and I am heartily glad of it.   When, however,
the question of Christian communion arises in their
mind they will probably be vexed by evangelical
examiners as to their metaphysical conceptions of the
Godhead, and in particular of the nature of Jesus
Christ.   To all inquiries upon such a matter they will
have no answer; or if they do answer at all, they
will fix attention almost exclusively on the humanity
and not the Divinity of the Son of man.   I mean that I

would not exclude such people from Christian communion; I should make them heartily welcome to membership in my own church; if they said that their minds were fully made up upon the subject of the Deity of Jesus Christ, and that they rejected it, no case involving the consideration of doctrine on my part would come up, simply because the people on the other side would not approach me, but look upon me rather in the light of a fanatic or an idolater. I seem to have given you both the impression that in some way I was thinking of the case of advanced or pronounced Unitarians, whereas you will see in a moment that such people never could approach evangelical preachers or churches; the only approach could be made by persons who are in an inquiring or uncertain state of mind, and who, on the whole, lean towards the society of persons who are known to entertain evangelical sentiments."

" I am glad you have made that matter so clear," said I, " because it must not go forth that we are in any way anxious to obliterate the distinctions between Unitarianism and Trinitarianism."

" There is a sense," Whiteman continued, " in which the Trinitarian is a Unitarian, but there is no sense in which a Unitarian can be a Trinitarian. The Trinitarian has the larger doctrine, and therefore he is in a position to recognise men who are making some approach at least towards his own conclusions. That recognition should not be niggardly, or impaired in moral dignity by some suspicion of heterodoxy; it should be broad and generous, and calculated to encourage approach and confidence on the part of all friendly inquirers."

Paterson was not to be soothed by these generalisations. He insisted that for his part he would have nothing to do with Unitarianism in any form whatsoever, and in saying this he thought he reaffirmed and glorified his principles as an evangelical Dissenter. Paterson was thoroughly honest in all his thought and speech, but it is impossible for his most ardent friend to deny that his thinking was furious rather than reflective and philosophical. Paterson delighted to describe himself as an out-and-out man upon any side which he adopted. He hated the Established Church as such; he hated Unitarianism still more; he hated everybody who did not begin where he began and end where he ended: in this respect he was probably typical of a considerable number of Nonconformists; but it must never be forgotten that whilst Paterson's speech was often rough and determined, in his heart of hearts no gentler man ever engaged himself in Christian service.

Suddenly breaking the continuity of the discussion, Paterson exclaimed—

"A pretty mess Tomlinson has made of it! You may remember how he and I came to sharp words about his proposal to leave Nonconformity, and go into the Church. Well, he went into the Church, and a nice time he has had of it in that lovely institution. You will be amazed when I tell you that Tomlinson wrote to me the other day asking if I thought it possible that he could return to the Dissenters and find a pulpit amongst them, and the miserable little soul added that he had never felt at home since he had left the brethren

amongst whom he had been brought up. I thought by
this time that Tomlinson might have been a dean at
least, if not an archbishop; and, behold, he is looking
back to forsaken friends, and asking if they will be kind
enough to open for him a door of re-entry!"

"Then you have no thought yourself, Paterson," said
Whiteman, in carefully modulated tones, "of seeking
admission into the Established Church?"

Paterson laughed outright, and regained all his good-
humour in view of this portentous suggestion. "On
that point," said he, "you may make up your minds
at once and for ever. There is no flaw or crack in my
Dissent. I go on all fours, and I go straight on, no
matter who or what is in my way. My opinion is
that the Church will be disestablished in about five
years."

Whiteman smiled. "Not in fifty years," said he.
"You make a grievous mistake about Disestablishment.
If the archbishops themselves were to say to you,
'Paterson, draw up a scheme for Disestablishment, that
shall be honest and right in all directions,' I should, on
hearing their proposal, instantly defy you to carry out
their wishes."

"Why not?"

"Simply because the question is the most complex
one in the whole political sphere. It is not a question
of Disestablishment only, but of Disendowment, and that
means the equitable distribution of an infinite amount
of property. I wish to tell you, Paterson, that there are
Dissenters who are not of your temper; there are men
who are unwilling that St. Paul's Cathedral should be

turned into a cattle market, or that Westminster Abbey
should be made into a railway terminus."

"Is there anything wrong then in a cattle market
or in a railway terminus?" Paterson bluntly inquired.

"Not at all," Whiteman replied. "They are both
right in their own places. After all, you cannot take
out of life the subtle influence of sentiment; you may
laugh at it, you may underrate it, you may call those
who are subject more largely than others to its influence superstitious and fanatical; but as a matter
of fact there is in this nation a sentiment which will
not allow the cathedrals of England, its great minsters
and its noble churches, to be secularised and de-
graded."

"That is a very strong point in my own argument,"
said I; "and I see no way of satisfactorily meeting it.
I certainly agree with you more distinctly than with
Paterson. I will go further, and say that I shrink from
the idea of selling these great buildings to any sect or
party that can give the most for them. I do not know
that this position of mine could be very completely
maintained by mere words; it is not a matter of simple
commercial argument; it is, as you say, a question of
feeling and sentiment, and a question not distantly
related to our deepest religious emotions."

"Well," said Paterson, "you may sentimentalise as
you please, but for my part I consider that the freedom
of the Church is greater than the allotment or use of
any particular ecclesiastical building, and in order to
gain the greater I would sacrifice the lesser. I know
I am a violent Dissenter. You may call me a red-hot

Radical in these matters, if you please; but I am quite willing that every church that can establish a good title to its property should hold that property; and I am equally willing that all property that unquestionably belongs to the nation should be bought by any religious sect that can pay for it, or be turned into national institutions for the good of the people, or even be secularised, and made railway-stations of, or picture galleries of, if you like. That's my creed, and I have no mind at present to change it for a more superfine namby-pamby belief."

We both protested that Paterson was too rough in his judgment, and would be better for the softening influences of more educated and genial society than that which he met in his own town.

"You live in too small a town, Paterson," said I. "Why, there is only one street in it! so what can we expect from a mind which exists under such narrowing conditions? You want enlargement and refinement; you are altogether wanting in critical discriminativeness; you have only two colours, black and white; there is nothing mystic about you, Paterson—you haven't got the poet's power of dreaming——"

Paterson broke in upon me, and said that of all things in this world the last he would think of claiming to be would be a dreamer or a poet. "I go by facts and realities," said he; "and the one object I have in view as a Dissenter is to disestablish the Church, and to make all men free and equal in the sight of the law, and to purge everything of the nature of ecclesiastical stigma, so that, let a man be what he may, he may be accounted as good as any other man so far as church relations are concerned."

"But you will not allow that with regard to the Unitarians," said I.

"Ah!" Paterson replied, "that is a matter purely theological, and I am speaking about questions that are exclusively ecclesiastical."

"But," said Whiteman, "some men are just as particular about ecclesiastical as you are about theological distinctions. You must not think that the Church of England holds its ecclesiastical creed lightly. That church believes in its own form, and does not look upon it as a mere matter of mechanical arrangement, but as expressing a critical interpretation of Christian history, and therefore it is not likely that an easy surrender will be made of its long-established faith."

"Well," said I, "to return to the subject of your paper, may I ask you what you are aiming at in the establishment of what you call an Open Church? Is not the Church open already? May not a man adopt any sect or communion that he pleases without any legal penalty or stigma following his election?"

"Of course he may," Whiteman replied; "but there are boundaries which separate one sect from another, and I want those boundaries to be regarded as of the least possible consequence, and to make it felt on every hand that such boundaries may be thrown down upon occasions when a manifestation of Christian communion might amount to a solemn Christian argument and appeal. We have to deal not only with ourselves who are inside those communions, but with the teeming thousands and tens of thousands who are outside them, and who roughly take it that nearly every sect represents in some way or other a different religion. It is Christiánity itself that suffers by this misunderstanding of the position and action of parties. If we had to discuss the question within our own boundariès, we could easily settle the matter; we are prepared to accord perfect liberty of action in the matter of ecclesiastical forms; but we have to explain ourselves to millions of men who know nothing about our interior relations, and I cannot but feel, therefore, that it would be of infinite advantage if something could be done to manifest more clearly to the religious public that our differences are, to a large extent, in name and form only, and that in all vital matters we are profoundly and inseparably united."

Background.

THE time of Vision returns, and all I have just passed through falls into perspective. Time and space are at the command of a mind which is under the mysterious influence of some sweet but nameless opiate; and even what we call Life and Death await its will and proffer unreserved obedience.

What an outlook, backward and forward!

What is my life—ay, what? I want to know what my life is. In the light it is comely sometimes, in the darkness hideous; now it is a valiant soldier, mighty in the fray, and now a mean coward, skulking in the darkness, if mayhap it may steal and not be seen, and look as if in prayer it had lost its worldliness and were clear set for heaven. My life says, I will, and I will not; and how it says either I cannot tell; sometimes it is a tender mercy, beautiful as the morning dew, and sometimes a great cruelty, having no law but its own thirst. Like a pendulum, it swings from prayer to blasphemy, and back again to prayer ; and if it would die at prayer, I might go to heaven, but if it stop at blasphemy, I must go to hell, and blaspheme there through the ages, and grow worse, and still worse, until God Himself cannot know me as the child baptized in His own name, and held up in public prayer in the old village church a million years before. My life ! what is it ? Is it eternity begun ? Is it God set in miniature ? Is it Divinity gone mad ? I fight, and win, and die. I plant the green vineyard and gather purple grapes, and as the wine foams in the full flagon, I fall down and cannot taste the inviting cheer. I build a high house, with roof that wind can never stir nor storm blow through, and when the blazing fire roars from the gleaming hearth, and Comfort, rosy-faced, beams upon me from the pictured walls, I'm sent for and thrust into the grave and prayed over as a failure here,—perhaps a failure there ; handed over to the resurrection, to the Great Unknown, to ghost-land, and a cold stone with lies on it keeps my breast well down in the cold earth.

What is my life ? A youthhood bright with cloud-less hope ; a passion ; an eye at a telescope ; a picture nearly living, 'with quivering joy throbbing through its colours and making them palpitate with life. A

hand upon a lock easily turned, and the door opening
upon green fields and vineyards, and orchards blush-
ing with the loveliness of May.　No pain or ache, no
twist in the long string of pearls ; a face at every
corner beckoning me with sweet smiles ; a wind
southerly, and rich with promises and blessings ; a
wild strength ; a scornful laugh at difficulty ; a
challenge to presumptuous rivalry ; a victory ere the
fight began. O youthhood ! It was then that destiny
whispered to me ; then the face came like a revelation,
and the voice came from a cloud, and the other life
came which made mine immortal.　And childhood
was forgotten, the white mice, the busy squirrel, the
drawer full of childhood's treasure,—all gone, all
laughed at, as I stood at the top of the high ladder
that overlooks the noble paths of manhood.　I could
not die.　Where could death strike me ?　A breast
clad in the armour of perfect health ; a head that
never throbbed with pain ; a heart sound as forest
oak,—these laughed at death, and bade the monster
throw his weapons down and be a conquered ally.
The doctor was for old women and misborn men,
with leeches, pills, blisters, mixtures as before : a
slope into the grave, the paid servant of Mortality
and Ruin.　Life was then a wild ha ! ha ! a summer
picnic ; a casket full of glittering jests and quips and
cranks ; a stealthy look at beauty ; a long evening
talk ; a moonlight stroll ; a row on a stream of molten

silver. It was all sweet nonsense ; words with double
meanings ; seriousness spoken as irony ; a pleading
Will you ? an answering If you will. Such bond-
making, such oaths of fealty, such troth-plighting.
Oh, my soul, half blind with tearful memories, the long
green lane is passed, and what remains is stony,
bleak,—a rough road down into old age and helplessness.

But can such summers die ? Can the colouring
fade out—the may, the lilac, the chestnut bloom, the
laburnum gold ? Will the summer birds cease their
song—the blackbird, the thrush, the nightingale ? I
have seen all, heard all, and they are just going.
Why will they go ? Why not always here ? Does it
become too cold for them ? Do they feel the warning
chill, and think of flight ? Why not think of me ?
"What will he do ? " they might say—"do when we
have gone, when the flowers die, and the green
leaves wither, and the winged singers flee away ? "
And the friends that started with me, where are
they ? The brown-haired lad, all smiles, and songs,
and jokes ; the mother whose embrace was heaven ;
the kind ones ; the hearts that loved me ; the tongues
that never spoke one word of bitterness,—where are
they all ? It is so cold now that they are not here !
Are they waiting for me ? Do they ever look for me
from the sunny gate of heaven ? Are they near me ?

Do they expect me? Shall we talk old things over again, and be happy with immortal joy? O strange life! so wild, so calm; short as a span, long as infinitude; a low wail of grief, a psalm triumphant, a victory supreme.

What is my life? A sullied robe; a crime concealed; a treason against God. I "know the right, and yet the wrong pursue." I have sinned. I have grieved my Maker. I have played the mean trick; kept back the price; spoken the false word; said Yes, meant No; thought of self first, others last and least. The prayer has been upon my tongue, the loved sin under it. The hymn religious has not cleansed the mouth that sang it. I have bent my knee in prayer, and straightened it again to fight. I have wept over sin, and done again the sin that made me weep. I have stopped half-way home, and gone back to have one more day with the devil. I see oaths, vows, promises, lying behind me like tender blossoms shaken from the branches by rough winds in spring-time. If I live, I shall get worse; if I die, I'm lost. The circle round me is fire; I cannot force my way through the burning cordon. My heart aches with the question, What shall I do? If I fight the great flame with straw, how great a fool I make myself! Would I quench it with my tears? It is but a dewdrop shed on Etna—an attempt preposterous and wild. Back again, and still again, and once more, and daily and incessantly the question comes, " What shall I do ? "

My life ? A ship that started well. All canvas set. A fair wind. A sea all sun. Then a cloud ; then a lurid glare ; then a lightning-bolt ; and the ship staggered in pain and fright. A great north wind, harsh, mighty, tempestuous, and then a sickening fear that I might never reach the shore. Perhaps go down in mid-sea ; perhaps perish in sight of land ; perhaps go in more lost than found, a wreck to cry over.

My life ? A bright bird, tuneful, brilliant exceed-ingly ; seeking the sun ; singing as I soar ; cleaving the wind and getting higher, and singing more blithely and more still ; when an arrow strikes me, and I fall bleeding to the earth. Music gone ; heart going ; nothing but my own blood about me.

At this moment I am standing by a woodside in the deep darkness of midnight, where I hear, as it were, the rustling of innumerable people as they speechlessly hasten through the forest. Not a figure can I see, not a tone can I hear, yet I seem to know who comes and who goes by the sound of the hurrying feet. That is a woman's soft tread, and that the run of a little child, and now the sound is as of one who has been lurking in guilty concealment, and goes forth with a stealthy crouch, and again is the slow and ponderous thud as of men who would drive away fear by forced composure, and now is the noise of some who have fallen, but cannot cry for help.   This mystery of movement pains me.   I, too, am dumb, or I would call to the hastening spectres to stop and tell me what they hope to find in the entangled wood.   Are they visitors from another world, come to see what they may of human ways, and flying back lest sudden light should reveal their plan?   Now I hear a sound as of scuffling, men striving for mastery, and the air is troubled as if charged with the sighing of weak wrestlers.   Now a bird flutters uneasily in its nest.   Now a shattered branch is wrenched from some sturdy trunk by the leverage of its own weight.   Now the soft plash as of a plentiful rain.   I am bewildered.   Would that some one would make plain what I cannot understand.

Sea-shore.—I never saw such water, such heavenly blue, such snowy foam, such golden sand.   Surely that fair sea has never been lashed by angry winds, or strewn with wreckage and cruel death.   It lives as Music lives; it talks in the cipher of Love.   Not a white sail is to be seen on all the gentle undulation. It grows more and more solitary.   At first I was pleased with the peaceful scene, but it begins to oppress me. The monotony is intolerable. Oh that a child would laugh, or a bird sing, or one white sail would flap against the horizon ! This is very weird. Am I looked at by spectators who have hidden themselves in those black overhanging rocks ? Are they secretly laughing at me ? Are they meditating mischief against me ? But look ! The foam brings messages ! It throws written words upon the yellow sand, and throws them purposely for me ! I will read them,—they will dissolve the spell of solitude. Ha, ha ! How familiar the words are in some aspects !—Jemima arrived safely, and the morning of Daleham's wedding was the brightest even in a year memorable for sunniness. The church bells clashed merrily, and half the little town put on some sign of holiday. Nehemiah Battison gave the toast of the morning, and gave it with that solidity of joy which comes of remembered sorrow and sin for ever buried. At one moment his voice faltered, but he plucked up courage and spoke of reunion and home and heaven. A troop of little children passed through the room of the wedding breakfast, and each gave a flower to the bride in gratitude for the bridegroom's service in the humble Sunday-school.—These words were thrown by the blue waves on the amber shore, and I knew all their meaning, and blessed God for the good news from a land far off.

The Churchyard.—I know it in my dream, and walk through it as of right. A holy quietness pervades this garden of God. The broad summer day is kind to it, filling it with light, and giving birds heart to sing even upon branches of yew and cypress. We speak of consecrating the burial ground, but the burial ground consecrates the whole town. Men lower their voices as they pass the sod which hides their dead, or gaze upon it as upon a twice-consecrated sanctuary. The town would be poor but for its churchyard. Here the child plants a flower ; here the mother softly calls to children who cannot answer ; here the broken heart sighs for restoration ; here the Christian is assured that his tears do not impair his victory over death. Still in my dream my heart is heavy as I read the storied stones, so elliptical yet so pregnant in their records :—

"NEHEMIAH BATTISON
AGED SEVENTY-FOUR.
Like as a shock of corn fully ripe."

"REV. LAMBERT GRAY,
FOR MANY YEARS THE HIGHLY RESPECTED VICAR OF
THIS PARISH.
Though there be darkness, it shall be as the morning."

"WEAVER STEPHEN.
FELL ASLEEP AGED SIXTY-NINE
In whom there was no guile."

Oh, sad, sad, is the story of death! Oh the heart-
ache! Oh the silence! Yet the silence is broken as
with gracious violence. I hear a voice—" I am the
Resurrection and the Life. . . . Thy dead men
shall live. . . . And death shall be no more, neither
shall there be mourning, nor crying, nor pain, any
more." To this Voice all nature makes glad choral
response. And heaven joins the grand enthusiasm,
saying, " Blessed are the dead which die in the Lord
from henceforth; . . . they shall hunger no more,
neither thirst any more, neither shall the sun strike
upon them, nor any heat." Oh to be with them!
sighs the heart burdened with many a care. Even
so, Lord Jesus, come quickly.

Midnight again.—But full of stars! Not at all a
time of fear or restlessness of mind. Curiously, I
see everything that is going on. I see a man who
must, from his uncertainty of progress, have lost his
way; yet his cautious foot strikes no obstacle: his
hands are put out as if he were blind. He looks up,
and his fine face beams with religious amazement, as
if he saw friends bending over him or beckoning him
to celestial glory. I' thought he was alone, and practically he is, but I observe a sweet girl looking after
him as if ready to rush forth and save him from
unseen danger. *She* sees! Her eyes burn with
eagerness. Her whole figure is itself a kind of

vigilance. On, but slowly, moves the man. He halts. He puts out his hands upwards, as if he would lay hold of the stars he cannot see. By some sense, if not of vision, he must hold them, and hold them as men hold things which are their own. Why does not the child run after him, and tell him the poetry of the night, or lead him safely home? She knows he likes to be here, and she knows that in his heart there is no real loneliness. I can trust any child who looks as Nellie looks ; that observation is as holy prayer. She needs no suggestion from without. Her heart will tell her what to do. Look! The wanderer halts again, and leans against a rock ; he speaks ;—he prays ;—his words are clear :—

"LORD, THAT I MIGHT RECEIVE MY SIGHT."

Printed by Hazell, Watson, & Viney, Ld., London and Aylesbury.

WORKS BY THE SAME AUTHOR.

THE INNER LIFE OF CHRIST. Discourses on the Gospel of Matthew. 3 Vols. Eight Shillings each.

APOSTOLIC LIFE : As Revealed in the Acts of the Apostles. Three Vols. Eight Shillings each.

THE PEOPLE'S BIBLE. To be completed in Twenty-five Vols. Three Vols. now ready. Eight Shillings each.

TYNE CHYLDE : My Life of Ministry, partly in the Daylight of Fact, partly in the Limelight of Fancy. Uniform with the above. One Vol. Eight Shillings.

SUCCESSFUL BUSINESS : How to Get It, Keep It, and Make the Most of It. Cloth. One Shilling.

Opinions.

DEAN ALFORD *says :*—" The author (Dr. Parker) has a clear eye, a fluent style, and a marked capacity for a kind of dramatic interpretation which is not very common. . . . The dialogue is direct, trenchant, now and then even resonant in its forcefulness."

C. H. SPURGEON :—" Dr. Parker is no repeater of old remarks, nor is he a superfluous commentator. His track is his own, and the jewels which he lets fall in his progress are from his own caskets ; this will give a permanent value to his works, when the productions of copyists will be forgotten."

DR. MARCUS DODS :—" He knows not only human nature, but men. He is therefore as fertile as life itself, and never wearies us by monotonously reproducing favourite types. Had he handled brush and palette instead of using spoken discourse, he would have been found thumb-nailing in the streets, the theatres, the political gatherings, and all the resorts of men. He illustrates the principles he enforces not by figures, but by instances, and in two or three firmly drawn lines gives you his idea. He makes his point and passes on, never spoiling by over-elaboration. He knows the difference between one straight, hard blow and a succession of fumbling undecided pats. A good swordsman, he is alert, rapid, and thrusts home to the hilt."

PROFESSOR TYNDALL :—" About six months ago I was staying with some friends at Heathfield Park, when ' Job and his Comforters ' " (published in *Tyne Chylde*) " reached my hands. Despite the serious ground-tone of the little book, I could not help joining my friends in their outbursts of laughter over its dramatic drollery."

PROFESSOR WILLIAM GRAHAM, D.D. :—" The outlines of each character are measured, distinct, unmistakable, in their graving, while the colouring comes and goes, faithful to the changing phases of the scene. What remains with one after the book is read—and in parts read again and again—is the masterly, unstrained strength, the easy spontaneous abundance, the exact wording, that comes out of the exact seeing what is to be said. This appears not in one part only, but in all. A Cain, a Lot, a Reuben is struck off in a sentence or two and dismissed ; but we shall know them again, and at once, when we meet them in London streets ; while an Abraham and a Joseph get their five lines—better than any fifty—that define the whole inner man, and demonstrate the artist. There is no aim at going into every particular of the life ; enough is given to mark its essence and growth. All is strong, genial, sufficient. The old mummies are unswathed ; the breath of warm, ruddy, old life comes back into the dusty, withered cheeks. They rise up like Samuel, in the garb they wore in Padanaram and in Egypt, and with the accent and tones that gave their words a power to last through all generations. This implies a rare gift in any man ; but Dr. Parker proves once more that the witchcraft of genius, lifted up into a higher divination, and a sacred aim, is still among us."

LONDON : HAZELL, WATSON, & VINEY, LD.. 52, LONG ACRE, W.C.

SOLD ALSO BY HODDER & STOUGHTON, 27, PATERNOSTER ROW, E.C.

COMPLETE IN TWENTY-FIVE VOLUMES.

Price Eight Shillings each.

THE PEOPLE'S BIBLE:

DISCOURSES ON HOLY SCRIPTURE.

———◆———

" Since Matthew Henry, no one has arisen with the same qualifications for the work, and if he is spared to complete it, Joseph Parker will, in the centuries to come, have the same place as Matthew Henry has had in all English-speaking lands. We rejoice that he begins this great task in the prime of his life, with the fire of his eye and spirit in no wise quenched or overborne."—THE CHRISTIAN LEADER.

———◆———

Vol. I.

THE BOOK OF GENESIS:

A book of *Beginnings* : the beginning of Creation ; the beginning of Humanity ; the beginning of Family life ; the beginning of disobedience ; a kind of day-break-book ; a wondrous dawn ; an hour of revelation and vision.

———

Vol. II.

THE BOOK OF EXODUS:

Phases of *Providence* : in leadership, in national deliverances, in organisation, in codified human life, in all the mystery of human training and discipline, showing how the tabernacle of God is with men upon earth ; a refuge, a judgment, a symbol.

———

Vol. III.

LEVITICUS—NUMBERS.

Religious *Mechanics* : the Mechanics of sin-reckoning ; the Mechanics of Sacrifice ; the Mechanics of Intercession ; the Mechanics of Purification ; the higher meaning of all these intricate and costly formalities ; the unprofitableness of bodily exercise ; the revelation and development of true Sacrifice.

OPINIONS OF THE PRESS.

THE CONGREGATIONALIST.

There is a freshness in the whole conception, and it is almost needless to add that everywhere we find vigour in the thought, felicity in the illustration, often remarkable power in expression, and, the highest quality of all, spiritual insight which is rich in suggestion and in profit. Dr. Parker has unquestionably great expository power. He takes a comprehensive view of a book of the Bible, fixes upon its leading ideas, groups them with extraordinary skill, and presents us, as the result, with a very striking outline of the whole. . . . It is in this spirit that this book is undertaken, and under such treatment the Book of Genesis—to which the first volume is confined—is invested with a new and, even to those who are most familiar with its contents, a surprising interest. It is, to say the least, a book which shows extraordinary power both of analysis and generalisation. Behind it must have been most careful and minute study of the sacred record, by a mind which, alike in its sympathies and its special qualities, is peculiarly fitted for the work.

THE CHRISTIAN LEADER.

Dr. Parker comes forward single-handed to comment on the whole Bible. A giant's task ; but it is a giant who has undertaken it. And he has undertaken it in no spirit of levity, rashness, or haste. Day and night these many years he has meditated in the law of the Lord. All he writes is saturated with the spirit of the Bible. Dr. Parker has called no man father of the earth ; even those writers he has most warmly commended have left no trace on his style. He has brought great and commanding gifts to bear on the study of the Bible, and has found no need to covet another field. It is a whole man in the maturity of his strength who is here face to face with the Book of Genesis and expounds its essential truth.

THE EXPOSITOR.

Dr. Parker's genius is too well understood to call for remark. When the debt to refinement has been paid by frowning on the absence of the scholar's self-suppression and on the too realistic descriptions, and on the amorphous character of Dr. Parker's work, we may give ourselves up to the enjoyment of his pithy and profound comments on men and manners. Here is nothing tawdry, nothing commonplace. Open the book where you will, you read on and on. Not only the racy, vigorous language, but the fertility of ideas and the penetrating observation of inner and outward life engage the attention. Dr. Parker looks at life in the concrete and in the individual. He knows not only human nature but men. He is therefore as fertile as life itself, and never wearies us by monotonously reproducing favourite types. Had he handled brush and palette instead of using spoken discourse, he would have been found thumb-nailing in the streets, the theatres, the political gatherings, and all the resorts of men. He illustrates the principles he enforces not by figures but by instances, and in two or three firmly drawn lines gives you his idea. He makes his point and passes on, never spoiling by over-elaboration. He knows the difference between one straight, hard blow and a succession of fumbling undecided pats. A good swordsman, he is alert, rapid, and thrusts home to the hilt. We cordially wish him health to complete what promises to be a most useful undertaking.

THE CHRISTIAN WORLD.

That "The People's Bible" will, with its bright, vigorous, fresh, and almost racy, treatment of Scripture, be immensely popular, may be regarded as certain, and we doubt not that it will lead many to an earnest, genuine, independent study of the Bible, upon lines which, although they may widely depart from the old ruts of theological investigation, will not be less reverent, or less promotive of true spiritual life.

THE ROCK.

The plan adopted differs considerably from that upon which most commentaries are arranged, as, indeed, might have been expected, coming from such a source. Dr Parker makes no attempt to increase the number of critical works, and as there is no lack of commentaries planned on the familiar lines, the latest worker in this department of Biblical literature may well be congratulated on having ventured into less familiar and well-worn paths. The discourses are marked by considerable freshness and vigour of style, combined with unusual skill in the illustration of the various points adduced by similes and incidents drawn from daily life.

SUNDAY SCHOOL CHRONICLE.

The book bears the stamp of its author's genius on almost every page; we say genius advisedly, for Dr. Parker's insight, grasp, and power of expression are of the nature of the poetic gift. Though in many respects a man *sui generis*—more so, perhaps, than any other preacher we could name—he has, nevertheless, something in common with men so different from him as Beecher, Raleigh, Magee, and Spurgeon, which gives him the key to multitudes of hearts.

THE METHODIST TIMES.

This is a worthy commencement of what Dr. Parker intends to be the literary and devotional masterpiece of his life. A pastoral commentary on the Bible will be the best memorial of one of the most striking and successful ministries of our time. In this work the force, the originality, the effective style, the intensely practical teaching of the famous pastor of the City Temple, are exhibited at their best. We devoutly pray that Dr. Parker may be spared in full mental and physical strength to complete the colossal task he has undertaken.

UNIFORM WITH "THE PEOPLE'S BIBLE."

In Three Volumes, price Eight Shillings each.

THE

INNER LIFE OF CHRIST

As revealed in the Gospel of Matthew.

VOL. I. "THESE SAYINGS OF MINE." VOL. II. "SERVANT OF ALL."
VOL. III. "THINGS CONCERNING HIMSELF."

OPINIONS OF THE PRESS.

THE CHRISTIAN WORLD.

We have no hesitation in describing these "expositions," for such they really are, as most luminous in their highest interpretation of the Divine sayings. They glow with holy fire, and they are inspirational alike to intellect, conscience, and heart. At times Dr. Parker seems to flood a familiar scene or saying with a light that surprises us, and withal it is such genuine truth that you know it is no fancy illumination, but a true light, although an unperceived one before. Intellectual genius does unquestionably belong to Dr. Parker, and the first sermon on the Genealogical Tree is quick with it. . . . Doctors Farrar and Geikie have done much in illustration of the life of Christ; and "These Sayings of Mine," by Dr. Parker, should accompany these volumes on the library shelves, for he is here doing the divinest and most difficult work of all ; he is not the historian or the painter, but he is the spiritual philosopher, removing difficulties here and there in the way of faith, never hesitant or apologetic, but so full of a living theology of the mind and the heart, that we are borne along, not only convinced, but grateful, for the Divine life thus vivified in the soul. This book is what we call the thinking of a living man, not of a mere book-making defender of the faith who wants a library of reference in his company always. The volume has interested us beyond measure at times ; it has thrilled us with vital convictions of truth, and . . . . is destined, we think, to take a foremost place amongst the books of this era, written in relation to the Christ of History, and will give a new illustration to the wonderful fact that, in this nineteenth century, the one subject which occupies the highest minds and awakens interest in the great world's heart is "JESUS CHRIST, THE SON OF GOD."

THE EXPOSITOR.

Very powerful and able the exposition often is ; one of its chief excellences being that all the truths suggested to Dr. Parker's mind by the Scripture in hand, are duly related to the thought and experience of to-day, and often interpreted by them. . . . But no man can bring an unprejudiced mind to these expository discourses without being healthily impressed with them, and at times even charmed by unexpected glimpses of truth, and by equally unexpected delicacies of insight and touch.

THE REVEREND DR. DEEMS,

Editor of American Edition.

" The first knowledge we had of him in America was, I think, the publication of his work styled 'Ecce Deus.' It exhibited a freshness and a power which would have secured its place, on the ground of its other higher merits, even if it had not had the additional virtue of antagonising certain errors of 'Ecce Homo.' Whoso read it, felt that its author must be a man of much more than ordinary ability. When it was announced that Dr. Parker was the author, thousands on this side of the Atlantic became interested in him. It prepared the warm reception which he met when he came to the Evangelical Alliance in 1873. It is well remembered that no representative from Great Britain produced such a marked impression as Dr. Parker did, by the magnificent address which he delivered in the Madison Avenue Presbyterian Church. His book, 'The Paraclete,' maintained his reputation, and enlarged the circle of his readers.

" But nothing that he has published so shows the man, I think, as the following sermons. I heard three of them."

UNIFORM WITH "THE INNER LIFE OF CHRIST."

In Three Volumes, price Eight Shillings each.

APOSTOLIC LIFE,

Being a Pulpit Study of the Acts of the Apostles.

(At the end of these volumes the author has added the greater portion of his work "THE PARACLETE," *long since out of print.)*

OPINIONS OF THE PRESS.

THE FREEMAN.

Dr. Parker is emphatically a preacher to the nineteenth century. He deals only .with "live questions," with the thoughts, aims, and needs of the men around him. His style is varied according to the demands of his aim. He uses every available method, and though we cannot always accept his solution of the great problems which everywhere confront us, we are generally helped by his wise, sympathetic, and manly speech. No man can read these volumes without gaining a clearer view of the personality and work of our Lord ; of his relation to, and revelation of, the Father ; of the nature of eternal life and the indispensable condition of its attainment. Many who have been perplexed by the sophistries of doubt will find here a resolution of their doubts, and amid the darkness which surrounds them will see at least the dawning of light. For of Dr. Parker's ministry this may be safely affirmed ; Christ is its motive, its inspiration and end, and to bring men into intelligent, trustful, and active fellowship with Christ is his manifest aim. Of the mental stimulus supplied by his expositions, of the numberless seed-thoughts, their presentation of new aspects of truth, we have left ourselves no space to .write. These qualities, however, are here, and are among the most conspicuous features of the work.

THE EXPOSITOR.

Persistently resisting the temptation to scene-painting, and refraining from once again diluting Conybeare and Howson, Dr. Parker goes direct to those aspects of his subject which have spiritual significance. His knowledge of city life and his penetrating insight into the character and motives of men, lead him to recognise the determining features of each situation in the narrative, and to present it with unerring skill as a mirror to the nineteenth century. Not for one moment does he lose sight of his audience, and if on one or two exceptional occasions he offends against taste, he is

never dull, never maundering, never commonplace. He never spoils the Scripture narrative by telling the story over again ; he does not fatigue his audience by explaining what is self-evident ; but beginning where the ordinary commentator leaves off, he uses each passage of the book as the medium through which he may throw light upon conduct, or awaken conscience, or stir some elevating aspiration, or pillory some common vice. These volumes are indispensable to the preacher.

THE SWORD AND TROWEL.

These three goodly volumes exhibit the minister of the City Temple at his best. He is a man of genius, and whenever he speaks he has something to say, and says it in his own striking manner. Of fresh thought upon "The Acts of the Apostles" we have here a vast treasury. Though that most interesting part of Holy Writ has had more than its due proportion of expositors, yet Dr. Parker is no repeater of old remarks, nor is he a superfluous commentator. His track is his own, and the jewels which he lets fall in his progress are from his own caskets : this will give a permanent value to his works, when the productions of copyists will be forgotten.

CHRISTIAN COMMONWEALTH.

Dr. Parker's great work is not always a safe guide as regards some particulars of the Apostolic programme, but in the main we can say with entire confidence that no other work has been produced upon the Book of Acts of so much value as this one. These volumes will live. The general scope of thought is correct, and this flows on like a mighty river through all of the three volumes. We should be glad to know that they were in every preacher's library.

THE PREACHER'S ANALYST.

Apart from all else it is a marvellous collection of concentrated suggestive thought.

" The author (Dr. Parker) has a clear eye, a fluent style, and a marked capacity for a kind of dramatic interpretation which is not very common. . . . The dialogue is direct, trenchant, now and then even resonant in its forcefulness."—DEAN ALFORD'S review of "Springdale Abbey."

In One Volume, price Eight Shillings.

TYNE CHYLDE,

𝔐𝔶 𝔏𝔦𝔣𝔢 𝔞𝔫𝔡 𝔐𝔦𝔫𝔦𝔰𝔱𝔯𝔶,

Partly in the Daylight of Fact, partly in the Limelight of Fancy.

Tyne Chylde is a book of Parables, Visions, Colloquies, and other varied matter published at different times, but now out of print. It contains AN OUTLINE OF THE AUTHOR'S EARLY LIFE; HUZ AND BUZ, OR BROTHERS NOT AKIN ; RIGHTEOUS AARON AND CHARITABLE AMOS; A PARABLE ON FAITH ; A PARABLE ON REVELATION ; A PARABLE ON PRAYER ; THE TURK IN ENGLAND ; THE NEW PROVIDENCE ; AKRABBIM THE JEW; A CHRISTIAN ARGUMENT ; A SPIRITUAL BIOGRAPHY ; as well as

JOB'S COMFORTERS;

𝔄 𝔕𝔢𝔩𝔦𝔤𝔦𝔬𝔲𝔰 𝔖𝔞𝔱𝔦𝔯𝔢,

In which Huxley the Moleculite, John Stuart the Millite, and Tyndall the Sadducee, attempt to comfort Job out of their scientific books.

FROM THE LATE ARCHBISHOP OF CANTERBURY (DR. TAIT).

" My dear Dr. Parker,—I have just been reading your 'Job,' and beg leave to thank you for it, as likely to do much good.—Yours very truly, A. C. CANTUAR."

FROM THE RIGHT HON. W. E. GLADSTONE.

" I shall endeavour to make it known in quarters where it will be appreciated. The task was delicate as well as difficult, and I sincerely congratulate you on the manner in which you have approached it in both aspects."

FROM PROFESSOR TYNDALL.

" About six months ago I was staying with some friends at Heathfield Park, when 'Job and his Comforters' reached my hands. Despite the serious ground-tone of the little book, I could not help joining my friends in their outbursts of laughter over its dramatic drollery."

LONDON : HAZELL, WATSON, & VINEY, LD., 52, LONG ACRE, W.C
SOLD ALSO BY HODDER & STOUGHTON, 27, PATERNOSTER ROW, E.C.

www.ingramcontent.com/pod-product-compliance
Lightning Source LLC
Chambersburg PA
CBHW020321140726
47905CB00013B/1941